# Empowering Education

Educating for Community
Development: A Critical Study
of Methods, Theories and Values

# Empowering Education

### Educating for Community Development: A Critical Study of Methods, Theories and Values

## Roger Hopkins

BOOKS

Winchester, UK
Washington, USA

First published by O-Books, 2013
O-Books is an imprint of John Hunt Publishing Ltd., Laurel House, Station Approach,
Alresford, Hants, SO24 9JH, UK
office1@jhpbooks.net
www.johnhuntpublishing.com

For distributor details and how to order please visit the 'Ordering' section on our website.

ISBN: 978 1 84694 517 5

A CIP catalogue record for this book is available from the British Library.

Design: Stuart Davies

Printed and bound by CPI Group (UK) Ltd, Croydon, CR0 4YY

We operate a distinctive and ethical publishing philosophy in all
areas of our business, from our global network of authors to
production and worldwide distribution.

To my wife, Ruth, my children, Nia and Owain
and my brother and sister, James and Elizabeth

# CONTENTS

*"Community development is basically an educational process. It is concerned not just with the achievement of certain concrete tasks, but with the development of the community's capacity to function in an organized rational manner. It depends on inter-personal skills and social skills, abilities to assimilate and assess information, reflection and action".*
(Irish community group, quoted in Scott, 1985)

*"It is not our business", he said, "to help students to think for themselves. Surely this is the very last thing which one who wishes them well should encourage them to do. Our duty is to ensure that they shall think as we do, or at any rate, as we hold it expedient to say we do"*
(The Professor of Worldly Wisdom in *Erewhon* by Samuel Butler)

*"Where I grew up learning was a collective activity. But when I got to school and tried to share learning with other students that was called cheating. The curriculum sent the clear message to me that learning was a highly individualistic, almost secretive, endeavor. My working-class experience didn't count. Not only did it not count, it was disparaged"*
(*Border Crossings* Henry Giroux 1993)

*"Education is the ability to perceive the hidden connections between phenomena"*
(Vaclav Havel)

*"We believe that education leads to action"*
(Myles Horton Founder of the Highlander Folk School (1932)

*"If situations cannot be created that enable the young to deal with feelings of being manipulated by outside forces, there will be far too little sense of agency among them. Without a sense of agency, young people are unlikely to pose significant questions, the existentially rooted questions in which learning begins"*
(Maxine Greene, *The Dialectics of Freedom, 1988*)

*"Don't pay attention to "authorities", think for yourself"*
(Richard Feynman, Letter April 23rd 1976)

*"A person with one theory is lost. We need several of them - or lots. We should stuff them in our pockets like newspapers"*
(after Bertolt Brecht [c. 1945] in Maryk 1993: vii)

*"The educator who formulates pedagogical theory without regard to the political, economic and social setting of the educational process courts triviality and merits being ignored in the community and in the classroom".*
(Jerome S Bruner *The Relevance of Education* 1974)

*"Years pass. The Soviet Union falls. The dance of commodities resumes. And the wind in the trees of Akademgorodok says: can it be otherwise? Can it be, can it be, can it ever be otherwise?"*
(Francis Spufford *Red Plenty* 2010)

# Preface

This book describes the contents, and the teaching methods used in their delivery, of a course in community development that I created and taught for the outreach department of a local higher education institution. The book was written in the hopes that it would be useful to those individuals currently teaching, or who intend to teach, community action or community development in the future. It is also aimed at those individuals who are currently implementing community development projects as paid workers or volunteers.

The book is aimed at developing not just the action skills of its readers but their knowledge levels too. I believed that while introducing my students to community development methods and techniques I was also introducing them to ideas and views about society of which they were often unaware. The course was therefore not just about a basic understanding of the concepts and processes associated with community development, but contained a wider purpose linking community development work with critical thinking, teamwork, citizenship, ethical values, the creation of new ideas, a connection with different perspectives and disciplines, as well as making a contribution to the well-being of others in society. By the end of the course that I will examine, I believe I had gone a long way towards achieving my aim.

This book was conceived and written during the years 2006 to 2008 when the triumph of global capitalism was almost universally taken for granted. The policies initiated by Ronald Reagan in the USA and Margaret Thatcher in Britain seemed to be providing the western world with an ever rising standard of living, while the old ideologies centered around the efforts of socialist and social democratic political entities seemed to have run out of ideas about generating societies that were at once both prosperous and inclusive. My course was established in order to combat the communal apathy generated by this individually-orientated society and, by so doing, it was my intention to keep alive collective action and critical skills - so generating ideas for the creation of an alternative, extended democratic system.

Events in the autumn of 2008 showed beyond dispute that the global capitalist system that had dominated society for the previous thirty years was far from perfect and that neoliberal capitalism was not the final word in how society could best be organized for the benefit of all its members. As this transformation was taking place, and the obvious distress of the system became increasingly clear, one of my students confidently informed me: "your course is now redundant. There is no longer any need for it. The politicians will make sure that the old system will never reappear in its former state and a more consensual and collective approach to economic and political matters is bound to take its place". I replied that if past experience was any guide to present actions politicians would seek a restored - if slightly modified - status quo rather than any radical reformation of the economic order. In this process the politicians would be heavily supported by businessmen, financiers and press owners, and it was my belief that capitalism would reform itself, and again attempt to dominate the economy and society in its free market form. An on-going critique of the capitalist system was therefore still necessary and, I pointed out, whatever happened in the business and financial spheres, I believed that the alarming increase in government powers of surveillance and control, which British society in particular had experienced in the last ten years, meant that the need for my course and its ideas about collective thought and activity - and democracy - would remain pertinent for a long time into the future.

# Introduction

For the last twenty years I have spent a large proportion of my working life in the often overlapping fields of adult education and community development. My work has been focused on helping individuals and communities identify their social action training needs - and delivering relevant education courses once this identification has taken place. Social action, in my view, includes community development activity, local activism and the advocacy of social (including political and economic) change. In the process of this needs identification and educational delivery, I have gleaned insights into group and individual experiences of community-based adult learning and gathered simultaneously oral examples from these players of the impact this learning has had on them. Additionally, I have extensively researched my work by reference to authoritative writers in the radical adult education/community action tradition, including Saul Alinsky (1989), Paulo Freire (1972 1990), Michael Newman (1994, 2006) and Myles Horton (1990): a group of authors whose concern for the disadvantaged and marginalized - people whose views have only rarely, if at all, been heard in the past by the tutors in the organisation in which I taught - is made abundantly clear in their work.

The research I have utilized to sustain my work consists of my experiences of working, since the early 1980s, in many socially excluded communities in south east Wales. In particular, I drew on my experiences as a community worker who was placed by my voluntary sector employer in a specific neighborhood, of which I had no previous knowledge, and told to generate social and economic initiatives "with the help of the local populace". I had received no formal education or training in community development methods and had, to a large extent, learn as I went along. During this process I discovered, through a process of trial and error, some basic methods of effective development, and these, together with a subsequent study of development theories, and networking with colleagues, has led to the information on development found in this book, which I hope will be useful for all who read it.

I have also utilized the knowledge and experience of my colleagues who have been concerned with the practical delivery and design of community curricula, and the ideas, views and values of a range of community organizations in the south Wales Valleys - and in the states of Tennessee, North Carolina, Arizona and Pennsylvania with whom I consulted in the USA while travelling there as a German Marshall Employment Fellow in 1990.

I began writing with an interest in two areas of work – community-based adult education and community development – and through talking with community groups, tutors and students, as well as reading around the subjects of adult education and community development, I created an education course that I thought could effectively cater for the day to day action needs of community workers and social activists. All the ideas that my course and this paper contains have been developed in community classes and in reflective assessments with colleagues and students both during and after programme completion. The sources used to reinforce the findings of my work are listed in the text, but in order to put my course in a wider social and political context, and to supplement educational ideas and theories with the theories of significant social philosophers, I drew frequently on the ideas of Herbert Marcuse, Jurgen Habermas, C Wright Mills and Raymond Williams.

The inclusion of Raymond Williams in particular may seem surprising because though he was an advocate of the benefits of culture, he did not write directly or extensively about education. However, he was a tutor in the Extra-Mural Delegacy of Oxford University for many years, and scattered throughout his work are illuminating reflections on informal education and its symbiotic links with ordinary people and everyday culture. His concept of education stood in opposition to traditional education which focused on the perpetuation of academic culture, and he thus saw adult education as offering a unique opportunity to combine community learning with pedagogy - thereby expanding the democratic influence of educational practice and using teaching as an instrument for social improvement.

I first came into contact with Williams' work in 1963 when I read his book *Culture and Society*. This caught my imagination with its description of how well known writers, including George Eliot, Coleridge, Arnold, Ruskin, Lawrence and Orwell, explored the changing relationship between "industry, democracy, class, art and culture" during the brutal laissez-faire period of the late 19th century and early 20th century in a revelatory manner I had not previously encountered. What particularly excited me was Williams' message that the path to empowerment is embedded within culture, and that from everyday working class experiences and actions can emerge real alternative institutions and ideas. His next book, *The Long Revolution* (1961), explored the concept of culture itself. In this work, he stressed that culture should be seen as a "whole way of life", including the growth of education and democracy, and not as the "civilizing arts" or even "the best that has been thought and said". Such an approach appealed to me very much indeed, as did Williams' use in novels such as *Border Country* (1960) and *Second Generation* (1964), of the idea of community, political and social solidarity, his detailed attention to the negative influence of political and commercial power - and his optimism in keeping alive a commitment to socialism as "an imagined community" that can be realized by utilizing ordinary people's generosity, and by encouraging their ability to organize and to co-ordinate social and political action. Indeed, it is by using education to heighten awareness of the strength of community values, and the need to organize and act, that Williams believes participatory democracy and economic justice will be sustained. This is the process that Williams (1975: 241) aptly labeled the "long revolution" and of which he wrote:

*"I believe in the necessary economic struggle of the organized working class. I believe that this is still the most creative activity in our society. But I know that there is a profoundly necessary job to do in relation to the processes of cultural hegemony itself. I believe that the system of meanings and values which a capitalist society has generated has to be defeated in general and in detail by the most sustained kinds of intellectual and educational work".*

It should not be a surprise therefore that a central theme of this work is the belief that a community education programme can be an effective vehicle for adult learning in the spheres of critical thinking, personal development and community action, and that I hoped that my community courses for adult learners would, in their own small way, make a positive contribution to the long range struggle of a political and cultural "war of position" so cogently highlighted in Raymond Williams' writings.

# PART ONE:

## COLLECTIVE BELIEFS

## AND INDIVIDUALISTIC ATTITUDES

# Chapter One

## Four beliefs

My work in community-based adult education has been based on four beliefs. Firstly, that non-formal education - teaching and learning delivered via group participation in a variety of social settings - a type of education that draws on ideas and ways of working well known to the ancient Greeks, and to twentieth century students of Dewey and Freire – is very relevant today as it attends to the everyday, to people's sense of themselves in time and, particularly, place. As *Yeaxlee (1929)* argued, we must attend to such elementary and informal forces of education because though:

> *"Insignificant and troublesome to the expert, these have a charm for the common man: he can appreciate them just because they are not elaborate and advanced: they meet him where he is, and do not demand that he shall make a long journey, or make a violent and unnatural effort, to reach them. They are the only recruiting ground for higher educational adventures on anything beyond the present small scale. But also they are the only ground wherein a very large number of people will ever find themselves at home at all".*

This is the realm of community education and the focus for adult education tutors. They must seek to "meet people where they are", and to address the familiar and the taken-for-granted, as well as work with them to come to terms with the strange or new.

Secondly, I believe that learning and reflecting on local collective action is part of a process by which ordinary people are attempting to maintain and extend control over their lives by acting together in groups, and that this should be supported and developed, while recognizing that such a process, and the resulting learning, is often complex, ambiguous and contradictory.

8

In this setting, education is concerned with community as well as with the individual person, with participants who are not always interested in possessing knowledge as one might own objects. Rather they often regard it as a tool to help alter local conditions. Such education is therefore unpredictable, risky and sometimes emancipatory. As Lindeman put it in 1951, it is education:

*"which is not formal, not conventional, not designed merely for the purpose of cultivating skills, but...something which relates (people) definitely to their community. It is an educational venture that is localized, has its roots in the local community. It has for one of its purposes the improvement of methods of social action...These are methods which everyone can understand. No conspiracy. No manipulation about this. We are people who want change but we want it to be rational, understood."*

Thirdly, that the traditional philosophy that has guided group and community action development programmes in the past is no longer relevant for dealing with the complex problems inherent in communities and community organizations today. This philosophy implicitly assumed that action rested on specific individuals who could generate and direct community initiatives, and that they were motivated by what Searle (1990) has called "I-intentions". Such motivations and actions often generated a sense of powerlessness in less ego-centric activists: they wanted more involvement as part of a collective effort in which each individual involved has in his or her mind a "we-intention" - a requirement supported by the analytic philosopher Margaret Gilbert (2006) who argues that true collective action rests on a special kind of commitment – joint commitment – which is not generated by a set of personal commitments independently created by each member of the community group, but is, rather, a single commitment to whose creation each member makes a contribution. One great advantage of such a joint commitment, in Gilbert's view, is that it allows those who are part of a community group to demand corrective action of all the other members if they act in ways that negatively affect the workings of the whole group.

Such a joint commitment approach also stresses the need for trust, open communication, shared vision and shared values, and my third belief envisions the learning group as the setting in which such durable, collective attitudes can be developed. I believe that it is here, at a core site of adult learning and knowing, that our powers for forming human consciousness are to be found. I believe that it is here, in a discussion-based learning environment, that we can shape individuals through the content and quality of the knowledge we generate. It is here, that the idea of community must take root if it is to reshape the implementation of social learning and social relationships via the rejuvenation of the concept of a "community of scholars", the opposing of the academic shibboleth of objectivity, and the acceptance of subjectivity that can influence students' philosophies and their practice of living.

I was particularly concerned with this collective aspect of learning because my own experience of school and university had been dominated by a compartmentalization, and individualization, of learning. The subjects I had studied were generally treated as self-contained entities - psychology was separated from economics, physics from history, art from geography. Knowledge was accumulated through an individual effort to collect compartmentalized and fragmented pieces of information that had very little connection with a social, holistic view of society and how people exist, and how they can act, in their local and global worlds.

This individual orientated learning process generated a fragmented mental paradigm in me, and it tacitly stimulated a competitive attitude towards both education and life in general. Although competition can generate enterprise and innovation (and it certainly gave me the motivation to reach university), I felt that the balance between competition and collective effort was being skewed too far. I found myself responding unthinkingly to academic authority, solving problems generated by others, and reading and writing in response to only pre-set, impersonal curricula. As a result, my originality was discouraged. I found it was unacceptable to create one's own work: I had to study the works of others while my own writings were ignored and disregarded. I also had to focus on my tutor's questions while my own questions and views were discouraged - a process which pushed me to merely reiterate received information and undermined my desire to learn, but which also made me more determined than ever to base my own teaching on a more collective, less directive approach to learning.

Fourthly, I believe that adult learning is a complex human activity that must be judged by the context within which it takes place. In the valleys of south east Wales it often occurs in marginalized communities – areas left stranded beyond the high-water mark of industrial development – where local people are struggling to put in place collective alternatives to traditional "top-down" social and economic development strategies created and driven by local authorities and the Welsh Assembly Government. I thus saw learning as an integral element of opposition to conventional local power structures; and by closely analyzing this oppositional process via group discussion of micro and macro politics, ideology, social theory and economic trends, I discovered that the relationships between these factors provided more material for collective reflection on the educational implications of community action – and suggested even more questions for the group to consider, including:

- *What global forces are influencing the decline of public activity, and how do these shape education and learning?*
- *What are the local politics of the situation?*
- *What are the ideological values and actions of community activists and their teachers? To what extent do these values and*

*actions help or hinder learning and action?*
- *What does all this mean for education? What interventions are possible and helpful?*
- *What is the role of group teaching and learning in non formal education within the current market-driven, higher education context?*
- *What skills and attitudes do teachers have to possess to counter the current situation?*

## The Neoliberal Context

Consideration of the question concerning the global environment within which the programme operates formed a core element of the programme. Just as my teaching programme was fixed in a context that connected its learning to the local economic environment, I constantly made it plain that it also operated within the context of the global capitalist system. At the start of the course I therefore quoted from the findings of the US economic historian Robert Brenner (1998) who has analyzed the downturn in the global economy that started in the early 1970s, continued throughout the 1990s and continues into the new century. According to Brenner, this long decline has been characterized by low rates of productivity, profitability, investment and real wages, together with accelerating social inequality and rising rates of deprivation and poverty. Furthermore, Brenner is of the opinion that this significant decline is not caused by supply-side factors – the cost of maintaining a welfare state or high labor wages – but rather by "the unplanned, uncoordinated and competitive nature of capitalist production" which generates overproduction and a declining rate of profit (1998, 24-26).

How has the capitalist system tackled this crisis? Primarily by reducing the cost of labor and increasing its flexibility. Businesses and governments have achieved this through a raft of measures, including reducing the full-time workforce and expanding the part-time and casual workforce, by reducing expenditure on social

welfare, outsourcing work to international suppliers, linking
education more closely to production and generally reorganizing
work - processes that, in the words of Fernand Braudel (1982: 239)
emphasize "that capitalism is always adapting, insinuating itself
here, retreating there, always seeking for opportunities and legit-
imizing itself in new ways. It stamps and moulds, in turn, all those
areas and levels that it touches". I made it clear therefore that as
local people with local concerns we could not ignore the impact of
capitalistic neo-liberal policies which seemed to be increasingly
popular, not just with the business sector, but also with national
governments, (including the UK government), around the world.
In other words, running as a leitmotif throughout the programme
was a consideration of the impact of capitalism and what Naomi
Klein (2007), has labeled the "holy trinity" of neoliberalism –
privatization, deregulation and social spending cuts - part of a
conscious agenda that aims to re-establish the conditions for
capital accumulation and to restore the power of economic elites.
As David Harvey has pointed out in *A Brief History of Neoliberalism*
(2005), neo-liberal policies are not about the new, but about a
return to class power and privilege. In an era popularly described
as "post-political", Harvey believes that class war has continued to
be fought, but only by one side, the rich, to the significant
detriment of post industrial communities.

The neo-liberal project has also contributed to the emergence of
the modern market state. What exactly are the characteristics of
this market state? In his book *The Shield of Achilles* (2002: 229), in
which he analyses cycles of conflict in the past, and their likely
shape in the future, Philip Bobbitt answers this question by
comparing its elements with those of the traditional nation state:

*"Such a state, (the market-state) depends on the international capital*
*markets and, to a lesser degree, on the modern multinational business*
*network to create stability in the world economy, in preference to*
*management by national or transitional political bodies...Like the*

*nation-state, the market-state assesses its economic success or failure by its society's ability to secure more and better goods and services, but in contrast to the nation-state it does not see the State as more than a minimal provider or redistributor. Whereas the nation-state justified itself as an instrument to serve the welfare of the people, the market-state exists to maximize the opportunities enjoyed by all members of society. For the nation-state, a national currency is a medium of exchange; for the market-state it is only one more commodity. Much the same may be said of jobs: for the nation-state, full employment is an important and often paramount goal, whereas for the market-state, the actual number of persons employed is but one more variable in the production of economic opportunity and has no overriding intrinsic significance".*

All these characteristics, plus the fact that the market-state "is largely indifferent to the norms of justice, or for that matter to any particular set of moral values so long as the law does not act as an impediment to economic competition" (Bobbitt: 230) - together with its tendency to redistribute wealth to the already rich at the expense of the economic solvency of existing disadvantaged communities - have helped to significantly undermine the quality of life in many UK communities. Indeed, such attitudes and trends, linked to the global spread of capitalism, have fostered rootlessness, transitoriness and dispossession in an increasing number of communities. With people moving to find better jobs, corporations moving to find cheaper labor, and neighborhoods reconstituting themselves within a generation, peoples' sense of belonging to a stable community, and the resulting security it offered, has been lost in the chaos of accelerated change and mobility. The result of all this change is a loss of connection to where people live and between people themselves. These develop-ments, I believe, make it imperative that committed activists in such communities take the measure of the strengths and weaknesses of this system, understand the challenges it poses and, simultaneously, help their communities prepare for tomorrow's battles against it.

I highlighted too that it was not just geographical communities that had to prepare for battle against the neoliberal agenda. The higher education sector - which was supporting the programme my students were taking and which I was teaching - had increasingly to justify its activity as a promoter of non-business orientated courses to marketeers who saw them as irrelevant and far too impractical. A university system that allowed people to indulge in "academic entertainment", and then awarded them a degree, was not, in the view of Adrian Monck, Professor of Journalism at the City University, London, worthy of public funding. The professor was also of the opinion that "by all means let people study history, the classics, novels, the media. But let them do it in their spare time – not as a state-sponsored, loan-financed languor". Instead, Monck believes, "we should give graduates the ability to excel in the subjects we know will feed an information-based, technology-driven global economy. We may not know exactly what those are, but we can be damn sure they are not liberal arts and humanities subjects" - a view enthusiastically endorsed by Netscape founder Marc Andreessen who believes that: "graduating with a technical degree is like heading out into the real world armed with an assault rifle instead of a dull knife. Don't miss that opportunity because of some fuzzy romanticized view of liberal arts broadening your horizons". (The Guardian, 8 April 2008).

These views, which are representative of a growing opinion among many academic managers, suggest that academics should not bother themselves with subjects that promote a liberal education and critical thinking over job training and the needs of the global economy. Ironically, I pointed out, it was a locally-born academic, Raymond Williams, who had anticipated this scenario, and the resulting crisis in university education courses, over 30 years ago. I recalled reading in his 1966 book *Communications*

Williams' view that capitalism posed an on-going threat because it had the dynamism and capacity to develop what he labeled "permanent education" for its own, profit-generating purposes:

> "The need for permanent education, in our changing society, will be met in one way or another. It is now on the whole being met, though with many valuable exceptions and efforts against the tide, by an integration of this teaching with the priorities and interests of a capitalist society, and of a capitalist society, moreover, which necessarily retains as its central principle (though against powerful pressures, of a democratic kind, from the rest of our social experience) the idea of a few governing, communicating with and teaching the many... Organized economically, in its largest part, around advertising, it is increasingly organized culturally around the values and habits of that version of human personality, human need and human capacity. This strong and integrated world is capable, I believe, in the coming decades of adapting to its own purposes both politics and education". (pages 15-16)

What Williams was saying, in effect, was that the current crisis would be one not only of economic life, but of society as a whole – and he has largely been proved right in his diagnosis. I realized that my course did not meet the criteria of the neoliberal agenda, had only, as a result, a finite timespan, and could not, on its own, tackle the new consumer focused values of society: but I thought it could play a small part in the struggle against the McDonaldisation of higher education (and the threat to its own continuation) by opening up my classroom to dialogue, debate and the questioning of current trends. I was under no illusions though that the struggle would be an uphill one, as the move towards the integration of higher education into the values of the market economy was far advanced, and I reminded my class that this movement had been boosted in the years since 1997 by the influence of the Dearing Report into higher education which explicitly stated that universities had four functions: a) they should "be a significant force in the regional economy, b) support research and consultancy and attract inward investment, c) provide new employment and meet labor market needs and d) foster entrepreneurship among students and staff".

On the BBC news on 31 January 2002 the British Secretary of State for Education, Charles Clarke, voiced his view that education for its own sake "was a bit dodgy", and a recent announcement from the UK universities minister makes it clear how far the universities have moved away from delivering education for its own sake to inculcating market and economic values, and how much they will have to change again in the near future. The announcement states that more change will be necessary because their students "will be studying for something that is directly relevant to their job or to their next career move", and that 30,000 new university places will be co-funded by business employers. It has also announced that the government department overseeing the reorganization of UK universities has excluded the word "education" from its title - another trend which reinforces my opinion that universities are increasingly becoming institutions that serve the rational bureaucratic state and capitalist economy, a view backed up by Frank Furedi, professor of sociology at the University of Kent, who recently wrote in The Guardian that, "the title Department for Innovation, Universities and Skills clearly expresses the mission of an organization that is in the business of cobbling together training programmes for selling furniture and paper credentials". (22 April 2008).

I made it clear to my class that I was not against equipping young people for productive work or universities proving alternative courses to my own. But I stressed that I saw a society that contained unjustified inequalities, shattered communities and unfulfilled people and, perhaps even more sadly, a vast swath of silence and inertia that seemed to preclude any alternative vision or any active stratagem to generate an awakening. I had asked myself the question "how can I get my work to stimulate social and economic action, to get people to question and break with* the current status quo?" My community-based development course was my response, and I decided to implement it as quickly as possible in order to contribute a small input into helping communities help themselves in surviving in, and offering an alternative to, a global, competitive economy.

# PART TWO:

# PLANNING FOR LEARNING

# Chapter Two

## A course for change masters

During the early 1990s, I set up a short course in community development where all the students were part timers. In the course, the students and I pooled our experience of community work in a joint attempt to think about the educational needs of community workers. We agreed on the problems we thought a good, accredited community-based course should tackle, and we then examined and analyzed our experiences of them in order to diagnose the sources of our difficulties. Next, in the light of the diagnoses, we tried to find better ways of dealing with the problems educationally. The course described in this book is the fruit of our considerations, and was aimed at adult students who were working in local communities as either paid workers or unpaid volunteers in community development. The course focused on developing the workers' skills, in particular their community work skills, and their ability to apply these skills to their work practice, thereby helping them generate effective social action responses within their communities.

This programme implicitly recognized that the South Wales Valleys required educational assistance in helping their inhabitants combat their current depressed state. But by approving such a course the institution was saying, too, that despite some social commentators announcing that people were lethargic and apathetic, that they no longer identified with the communities within which they lived, that they were the prey of forces beyond their control which had removed their local industry, taken away their leaders, and forced them to travel away for work - leaving them with less time and less energy for community affairs - it had explicitly recognized that some inhabitants of the Valleys had observed this social "disintegration" and were concerned about it - and that these community activists could be the catalysts for positive change. I, too, had realized that in times when conventional social strategies were faltering, few tasks became more central to a community's survival than the ability to identify concerned people and develop their potential for action, alongside that which lies within the professionals, and other staff, who provide public and private services within it. In short, I had seen the need to promote the capacity within communities of what the Harvard professor, Rosabeth Moss Kanter (1987), had labeled "change masters".

In her book of the same title, Kanter reiterates the theme that the key to surviving widespread uncertainty and instability is the ability to develop, spread, implement and sustain innovation: to increase steadily the number of new ideas, test them, and build the capacity of individuals and communities to take what works for others and make it their own. Routine responses are appropriate to routine times, but survival in times of change, notes Kanter, requires creativity and the skill to apply it. And the key ingredients in successful application are the "change masters", people with the capability and vision to size up a problem, design solutions, marshal resources and motivate people to take collective action.

So, as communities in South East Wales sought to redesign their approach to social development, they had to be educated and encouraged to expand the pool of their own "change masters" by tapping the energy and experience of community activists and spreading these attributes to other groups in their localities. My intention was to move beyond the traditional curricula, and offer classes for groups (no more than fifteen people) of new community workers and volunteers, the aim of which was to educate these workers and volunteers in the community development skills that, as well as using themselves, they could also pass on to existing change masters and to those activists who possessed the potential to become future change masters. Wendy Godfrey has summed up my overall i philosophy extremely well when she wrote in her book *Down To Earth* (1985):

> *"Community development is working with people, not doing things for people...it seeks to avoid creating dependency, the dangers of imposing views and solutions, the arrogance of reducing others to objects of charity or even self-satisfaction in doing others good...Community development is about encouraging people to discover their resources and possibilities in order to work for positive change in their community...People have the right to participate in the decisions affecting them but they also grow through taking responsibility for their own success or failure. Community is founded on a sense of belonging and of worth...People are diminished if they are excluded from decision-making. They are enhanced by recognition and responsibility. The means and the ends of community development are not merely to provide people with services or resources, but to make possible the process of discovering and learning together by which communal life is created".*

In my eyes therefore the objective of the community development worker is to build people rather than things, confident that those whose uniquely human capacities have been fostered will themselves build the physical things they require. To make community-based social and economic development happen, local people need an education that enables and empowers citizens to analyze their own social and economic problems, to develop solutions to joblessness and poverty, and to gain the tangible mental and practical skills they require to generate development for themselves.

I recognized that this approach to community development was demanding, and that it took a worker with a particular type of personality – a person who must not preach but who is willing to meet people at their own level and create a desire to learn; who is able to stimulate desires; engender a spirit of willingness; hope for the future; a concern for the welfare of her fellow citizens; and a missionary zeal to do something about it through harnessing local collective effort. I was deliberately choosing a collective approach to development because I believed that once individuals participate in collective efforts to improve community conditions they begin to challenge the unseen influences of ideology and power which they have unconsciously absorbed since birth. To paraphrase C. Wright Mills (1959), they start to transform personal problems into issues of public concern. They start posing questions about their own world and then link them to a wider world: Why am I so poor? Why is my community so poor? Why are my wants and wishes ignored? Why are we and our wants and wishes ignored? Why have I been unemployed for so long? Why does this place have such high unemployment levels? By this identification of the self with general social problems, a cognitive process of personal empowerment is created which attempts to look beyond, and transcend, the existing status quo, and often forms a significant step in individuals transforming themselves into change masters.

**Going against the grain**
This belief in the efficacy of collective effort ran counter to the prevailing neoliberal ethos which stressed the benefits of individual effort and private resources. But so pervasive had the influence of neoliberal practice become that I believed the need for a collective counter movement to combat this trend was now essential. To illustrate my apprehension, I pointed out that in the past the concept of community contained such elements as: a sense of place, identification of the inhabitants with the place, a social system consisting of patterns of behavior focused on common issues such as making a living, raising a family, and making decisions that affect most members of the community - and a common culture in which people share a large body of knowledge, beliefs, customs, morals and habits. These elements coalesced to encourage members of the community to depend on

each other and to work together to solve their problems. But these elements are now under threat from the onslaught of market forces and the philosophy of individualism. As a result, in an ever greater number of communities, wealthy people increasingly seek to insulate themselves from the rest of their fellow citizens, aspire to create their own separate communities, use their own money to purchase services exclusively for their own use, and vote against taxes that would extend these amenities, as public services, to everyone else. These private amenities include living inside gated, walled communities, relying on private security guards rather than on the police, sending one's children to well-funded private schools rather than to poorly-funded public ones, and purchasing private health insurance rather than using the publicly funded services of the National Health Service.

Underlying such privatization is the mistaken belief of the elitists that the problems of the communities around them are none of their business. Because of this, the concept of "we together" which characterized many communities in the past, was now under threat and had been, in many instances, replaced by the concept of "we separately". In my eyes, such neoliberal attitudes and actions were a sinister pathology sapping the vitality of communities and forming a significant threat to the health of democracy. They should therefore be countered - and the change masters were the people who could provide the leadership needed for the counter-attack. I believed that change masters operated in groups as well as operating as individuals, and that in south Wales such groups often needed educational support in order to work effectively in their communities - in particular support that contained a great deal of political and economic knowledge, skills in human relations and communication, as well as in practical, collective ways of improving local conditions.

By preparing and offering this support, I was consciously linking a critical, emancipatory education programme with social and economic development to counter the prevailing educational orthodoxy that stressed the need for neo-liberal philosophies and business-orientated attitudes even in teaching. I was more concerned with generating a form of learning that would prepare students for responsible roles as community workers, activists, critical intellectuals, and as participative, reflective citizens. During the compilation of the programme, and during the early days of its delivery, I often felt that I was working in isolation in a field that had little support or sympathy from my colleagues in neighboring academic departments. I was encouraged though to discover in my research that in other parts of the world alternative curricula were being offered to students, with one of the most impressive being the Citi Schools created by the Workers Party Municipal Government in Porto Alegre, Brazil. In these schools, which were created to attack the problem of poor students leaving education early, and which were run by councils of teachers, parents, staff and students, the goal was to stimulate a new attitude towards society and who should control it. Gandin and Apple (2003:196 quoted in Darder et al 2009:375-6), in their survey of the schools, report that they were part of a strategy to create a movement that "contains as a real social process, the origins of a new way of life". They then reinforce (p. 200) this point by writing:

*"...there is a constant struggle to legitimize the experience of the Citizen School, to make it socially visible, to pose the discussion over education in terms other than those of neoliberalism, to pull education from the technical economistic" realm favored by neoliberal assumptions and to push it to a more politicized one that has as its base concern the role of education in social emancipation"*

By reshaping the school curriculum to contain the aspirations and experiences of the community, and simultaneously encouraging the democratic leadership of its governing body, the Citizen School is attempting to transform the "separation between the ones who "know" and...ones who "don't know" (p. 211). "Know what exactly?" asked my class. "Know that choices are open to people" I replied. "That life is not "set" and that there really are choices to be made. The most important thing", I stressed, "is that people have to realize that their interests are vitally at stake in what they think, and what's also important is not just what opinions people hold but how they live those opinions". I thoroughly approved of the Citizen School philosophy, and recommended it to my class as an example of effective and imaginative community action to stimulate critical thinking, and as an illustration of what could be achieved through sustained collective endeavor.

## Encouraging reflective thinking

The programme was also designed to help community activists acquire the thinking skills needed to construct alternative community systems and devise methods and strategies for making those systems work. This meant that, in the words of Kanter again: "there must be a willingness to move beyond received wisdom, to combine ideas from unconnected sources". In addition to analyzing and acting upon their communities, my intention was to get my students to question their constant givens about the values they held, the attitudes and knowledge they utilized, and to focus on what people are and how they relate - and so become self-critical reflective thinkers and learners. In everyday matters, I was of the opinion that people tend to learn from their experiences in haphazard and random ways: there is little time for reflection in a structured, orderly way. The programme was formalized to provide learners with a structured and supportive environment within which they could reflect on, and explore, the personal and social implications of learning from their community activities. The more sheltered academic structure would, I believed, also provide an opportunity for learners to make the connections between their learning and their future actions as they engaged in the identification of the appropriate, on-going application of what they were currently learning on the programme (Boud et al 1985).

So, in addition to developing the instrumental skills of the workers, I realized that the course would have to develop the workers' intellectual understanding of their own work to enable them to reflect upon and improve their practice. Drawing on the ideas of Donald Schon in particular (1973, 1983 and 1984), I introduced the class to the notions of reflection-in-action and reflection-on-action. The former, I emphasized, has been described as "thinking on one's feet" and entails looking to our experiences, connecting with our feelings, and attending to the internalized theories we have generated to inform our actions in tackling problems as they arise. This process, I highlighted, could be linked with Schon's notion of reflection-on-action which is implemented after an action has taken place - often via talks with colleagues, the writing of a report or a group debriefing. By carrying out this process we formulate questions and ideas about our actions and the way we implemented them. I therefore encouraged the students to plan, act, observe and reflect on their work - and, again, plan, act, observe and reflect in a continuous mental spiral. I stressed that when working, students should constantly question, and make judgments about, the impact of their actions, ask what had come out of these actions – and devise on-going strategies for making such actions more effective in the future. In other words, by engaging with their experiences - and reflecting on them - I believed it was possible for the students to develop mental and practical strategies about working effectively with individuals, groups and even whole communities.

I felt this exposure to Schon's "reflection theories" was particularly important because of the educational and domestic backgrounds of the great majority of the students: most of them had undertaken vocationally-orientated curricula which failed to challenge deeply help beliefs or ways of life, and most had left secondary education before obtaining any formal academic qualifications. They were all literate, but had failed to acquire the reflective and conceptual competence which often comes as second nature to those who had received a middle-class education; their intellectual horizons were overwhelmingly limited by the television programmes they viewed, the computer games they played, and the newspapers they read; and they had also been denied the cultural infrastructure which made a sophisticated, reflective awareness possible - they no more read unusual books or watched television programmes that encouraged or stimulated reflective thought, than the average person attended royal garden parties or visited 10 Downing Street.

Additionally, many class members had had little exposure to culture at home. Most informed me that though they talked a lot in their families, they were basically unfamiliar with fluent, focused language and especially language which underpinned or encouraged access to the written word. Such access is essential for educational success, and not to have had entry to the concept of education in its wider, cultural sense, or exposure to the possibilities of words and their meanings, was yet another reason why I insisted that the group concentrate on community work topics, and explore how they linked to wider national and international events - and talk about them in focused language as often as possible - as opposed to listening to me and passively absorbing what I was saying.

## Intuitive versus analytical thinking

Because of their educational and cultural shortcomings, many students demonstrated an instinctive approach to problem solving. Instead of adopting a cognitive strategy that involved a logical, reflective process that arrived at a considered outcome, they reached a decision in a moment without apparently considering the available evidence surrounding the problem. I recognized that this intuitive, emotional way of thinking could sometimes produce relevant decisions, and very pertinent actions, about the problems being considered. Indeed, I had often thought that intuition was odd but sometimes useful. Generally though, I regarded the outcomes of this reflexive approach as too unfocused, superficial and arbitrary – in some instances, even damaging to the questions that I was considering.

The phrase used by Germans to describe the differences that still exist between those from the east and those from the west of their country after 20 years of reunification – "Mauer im Kopf" ("the wall in the head") – applied equally well, I reasoned, to the majority of my students' attitudes towards patterns of thinking and reasoning: they regarded reflective thinking as cold, arrogant and inhuman, the product of middle and upper class sensibilities, and definitely, in their words, "not for us". They greatly preferred an immediate, emotional response which came "from the heart" and which was, in their eyes, warm, humble, liberating and human, and therefore genuine. Furthermore, two of my students had recently read Malcolm Gladwell's book *Blink* (2005) which they believed reinforced their belief in spontaneity of thought. They pointed out that Gladwell argues that lightening judgments and first impressions may actually represent shortcuts rooted in slowly accumulated experience; so it is often better to trust our "gut" instinct because our emotional brain can process millions of bits of accumulated data simultaneously without interruption from lengthy, rational, reflective dissection which results in "paralysis by analysis".

What I favored, on the other hand, was a greater need for reflection, because though reflection in a mirror is, in the words of Biggs (1999): *"an exact replica of what is in front of it, reflection in professional practice gives us back not what is, but what might be, an improvement on the original".* My aim was to supplement the intuitive responses of my students with a more reflective and analytical sequence of reasoning because, as I pointed out to them, my whole education had been based on a belief in the effectiveness of rational thought as propagated by Enlightenment philosophers. These thinkers saw a division between a soul capable of reason and a body full of destructive passions and emotions. I argued that this tradition was still relevant, and that it had formed the basis of modern Western scientific thinking. Analytical thinking, I stressed, is focused, precise, logical, deals with one subject at a time, is brain orientated, and tends to the abstract. My group accepted the achievements of this way of thinking, but refused to jettison their belief in the efficacy of instinct and emotion. After much debate we all agreed to respect each other's point of view and further accept that perhaps both types of thinking had relevance - depending on the situation one found oneself in. I then summed up my point of view by saying that I thought that despite accepted tradition, it is often the everyday problems facing us (including those involved in community work) that are perhaps best suited to rationalist thought, while the more complex problems and their solutions sometimes require the processing powers of the sudden, instinctive brain (and I returned later in the course to a consideration of this point). After more discussion, we finally came to a consensus that analytical thinking is effective when there is sufficient time for reflection, stable conditions and a clear differentiation between the observer and the observed, whereas intuitive thinking comes into its own when conditions are dynamic, when there is pressure on time and where the differentiation between observer and observed is confused.

To illustrate how helpful analytical thinking could be in community work, I drew upon my experience as a new community development worker in a community that I had never been to before. I described how I was placed by my voluntary sector employer, on my own in the community, to develop community-based action responses to deprivation by encouraging local people to establish economic and social regeneration projects. At first, because I had not received any training in community development techniques, I reacted to my situation by acting on a hunch: I contacted some residents that I had met in a meeting, and attempted to work with them to create a local regeneration group. By doing this - and basing my actions on my vague impression that these people were, in the local parlance, "tidy people", who would attract similar individuals to their cause - I convinced myself that I was creating, quickly, a small base from which to launch new community initiatives.

I soon realized, after some reflection, that my initial, intuitive reaction was not the best way to proceed. I had forgotten that my link with a specific grouping of individuals meant that, in the eyes of other residents, I had allied myself with a specific faction while ignoring other interested, committed individuals. From the very start of my work therefore I had alienated some sections of the community without intending to do so, thus making my subsequent task very much harder. What I should have done was analyze my situation before acting instinctively. I should have adopted a rational, systematic approach and planned my action strategy before "jumping in with both feet". I should also have adopted an analytical planning process, because planning of this type clarifies the process of examining a community's current situation, sets goals for its future development, develops strategies to achieve these goals, and measures the results. Different strategic planning processes have different elements, but as regards community development, the most basic steps include:

- observing the community
- analyzing the community
- creating a collective vision for the future
- diagnosing the needs of the community
- developing consensual strategies to meet community needs
- stimulating collective action to implement the strategies

The great advantage of this type of rationally thought through planning is that it is not something that is done only once, but a process that can be regularly repeated. The important element is not a plan, but deliberate planning. By creating consensus around a vision of the future, a community builds a sense of where it is going among its inhabitants. This allows everyone - not just political leaders - to understand what direction they need to take. It helps them seize unexpected opportunities without waiting for permission from above. Strategic planning of this type does not of course promise that all decisions will be successful, but that they will be made with foresight - something that intuitive thought, and action cannot claim to do. Furthermore, it makes sense for workers and groups to analyze their own potential strategies, as well as reviewing the different strategies which other communities have utilized, and to assess which of these are suitable a) for their particular community, b) for the community worker, c) for the problems facing the community and d) for the worker's agency. The strategies that survive this scrutiny can then be blended together in a developmental sequence that will lead logically to the solution of the community's problems.

The logic of this approach is used frequently by the football coach who reviews his team's strengths and weaknesses, its opponent's characteristics, the playing conditions and other factors - and so develops his game plan accordingly. Paradoxically though, such analytical thinking and planning can often lead to intuitive thinking because, as many of the conversations I had had with community workers made clear, strategic planning implemented correctly can permeate the whole culture of a community, creating an almost intuitive sense of where it is, where it is going, and what is important - a view that reinforces John Bryson's (1988: 2) opinion that, "it is strategic thinking and acting that are significant, not strategic planning".

Although the students saw the logic of my example, and accepted that they needed some well thought out action template to follow in their work, they still advanced their view that in some everyday matters the instinctive approach was often relevant. They quoted the example of first impressions that had subsequently proved correct when meeting people at work in their communities, and in their social life generally. To reinforce the validity of their belief, they next used me as a successful example of the intuitive approach to assessing people. They informed me that at the start of the course, at registration, they had all swapped their impression about me as a teacher and a person - and that my subsequent behavior as a teacher and individual over their sixteen months of study had made no difference to what they had initially thought. Time, in their view, had only served to confirm their original, intuitive judgments.

## Analytical and reflective thinking - solving a problem

Despite the class's strong belief in the efficacy of intuitive thinking - and the warm glow that their judgment left me with - I continued to argue the case for analytical, reflective thinking in community development work. To demonstrate why this was needed, I set the class a problem to consider:

### The Problem

*A community development worker was faced with the thought-provoking question: "what do I need to know to help me understand this community and to work effectively in it?" I pointed out that in our discussions about what to do when entering a community for the first time, a majority of the students had replied that they should carry out a community profile – a comprehensive description of an area, its resources and its population that is defined, or defines itself, as a community - as quickly as possible. When I asked why such action took priority over other actions, the answer was that other workers in other communities had done this - and it was suggested in the guidelines laid out by the Welsh Assembly Government that was paying their wages - so it was obvious what they should do as a first step!*

### The Discussion

*I then split the class into three small groups to consider what steps a* community worker should take on entering a community, and I allocated a whole morning to our discussions. In these discussions, each group, independently of the others, decided that they should draw up a list of the information that any community worker would need to help her effectively develop programmes in her community. Drawing primarily on the experience of those students who had worked the longest in community-settings (but not rejecting the ideas of newcomers to community work), they discussed, argued, analyzed, listed and prioritized what they considered to be the relevant information. After lunch, the three groups reported back to the class, which in turn discussed, argued, analyzed and prioritized their collective findings to outline a logical method which a community development worker should use to help her understand the community she was working in.

## The Diagnosis

The class thought that the worker, by deciding that a community profile was the immediate priority on entering the community, was making a mistake. She should have remembered that in our previous discussion on strategic planning, the first, and most fundamental, role of the community worker is, on entering a community, to be a thoughtful observer - and to continue this role from the day of entry to the day she leaves. The process of observation must always contain two elements - "pure" observation and participant observation. The first element provides the worker with a great deal of information, and can be gained by being where local people are, looking and listening attentively. Since it is hard to learn while speaking, the worker must always remember that, in the words of Desmond Connor (1966) "she has two eyes, two ears and one tongue - and using them in that order can be very instructive indeed". Participant observation means getting to know people, joining in some of their activities and getting to know their ideas and views. Such a process gives the community worker the opportunity to acquire a view of local life from the inside and a chance to ask pertinent questions unobtrusively. Instead, the worker had been swayed by the timetable suggested in a policy paper of the Welsh Assembly Government which had been compiled by administrators (and academics) who had little or no experience of working at "grass-roots" levels in communities.

The class then agreed that after observing, the community worker should move through the social and cultural complexities of her community with some effective, logical template. In other words, the worker needed a tool for understanding the community, in particular a profile that contained information that was straightforward enough to remember quickly and easily; comprehensive enough to cover most aspects of the community; flexible enough to meet the different kinds of situations faced by different workers; soundly based in theory and practice; and capable of generating a number of development strategies from which she could choose according to her situation.

## The Action

Following her observations, the worker should compile a profile that gives her a holistic view of the community, which focuses on the major life patterns that can be identified within it, and on which plans for future development action can be based. Calling on their readings of community development methods that I had supplied them with, particularly the ideas of Christakopoulou and others (2001), the groups recommended that the profile compilation should focus on:

The community as a place to live – including the quality of the physical environment and people's attitudes to living there; ages and capacities of the inhabitants; the extent to which needs are matched with resources; and the extent to which local facilities meet people's goals and aspirations.

The community as a social entity – including residents' involvement in the social life of the community; the extent to which the community is supportive of itself; health and education levels; the viability of formal and informal networks; and participation in local voluntary and community organizations.

The community as an economic entity – including income levels and employment prospects of local inhabitants; human resource levels; technological skills; existence of entrepreneurial attitudes; prosperity and *viability of local businesses.*

*The community as a political entity – including systems and structures of political representation, leadership attitudes and local area governance; the extent to which local people can influence decisions that affect them; the degree of involvement in local decision making.*

*The community as a personal space – the degree of attachment that people have to the local area; folk memories and life experiences of local people.*

*The community as a moral entity – including the beliefs, values and sentiments of the inhabitants; and the sanctions which induce people to retain the norms of the community.*

*The community as part of its region – infrastructural, economic and social linkages between the local area and the region of which it is a part; the specific local identity based on its history that differentiates the community from the rest of the region.*

*The community worker must also consider other sources of information - key local players, local newspaper, diaries, surveys, maps, videos and photographs. When all the information is gathered, a display can be created of the community profile. The worker, together with local groups, may also want to use the materials to produce a handbook about the community.*

### Summary
*The exercise highlighted the effectiveness of community workers thinking reflectively before they attempted to act reflexively in communities. The process used by the tutor to get individuals to listen to the ideas of other people, analyze them, argue to accept or reject them and finally come to a concrete outcome, demonstrated just how valuable discussion which stimulates focused thought could be as a tool to effective information gathering and subsequent action in communities. I pointed out that this intellectual process can be utilized by individuals as well as groups, and that thought processes of this kind can be far more effective in generating ideas about the state of communities, and their future community-action strategies, than the haphazard, reflex thoughts that are based on no more*

*than unfocused hunches, spontaneous emotion-driven feelings and the*
*unthinking acceptance of what other workers are doing.*

*By asking the students to undertake this exercise I intended to*
*galvanize them into action - but only after they had thought things*
*through. I believed they must look at their community (and society as a*
*whole) from the viewpoint of a bleak, even dangerous, future, and then*
*make a firm commitment to intervene and tackle the problems that the*
*future contains.*

## Enjoyment and fear

After all the discussion and argument some students still begged
to differ about the merits of reflective versus "gut feeling"
thinking. Despite this, the whole process of cut and thrust, talk
and argument had generated a wonderful environment for
learning  - and teaching. What we had created was a "learning
space" where students and teacher could interact and connect
with each other because, as Robert Putnam has pointed out, "at
Harvard as well as in Harlem, social connectedness boosts educational attainment". Additionally, the "learning space" was a site
where the students were secure and able to enjoy their learning.
This was achieved not just by creating a sheltered physical space
in a community setting, but also by filling it with a collective sense
of trust and honesty by laying down acceptable inter-personal
behaviors and attitudes, and by clearly defining the verbal and
mental parameters that would be acceptable in class sessions.
Furthermore, I believed that the enjoyment of the students would
be reinforced by me allowing them to be the best judges of their
own interests, and that they should therefore be trusted to think
and decide for themselves without pressure, or the use of manip-
ulative techniques of any kind, by me. In short, just as Ivan Illich
championed conviviality (1975a), Parker J Palmer hospitality
(1993), and Nel Noddings happiness (2003) in education, I was
trying to create an educational environment where enjoyment was
a vital ingredient, where every student's views were met with

dignity and respect, and where fear of exposure, of appearing ignorant and of being ridiculed was totally negated.

To further generate friendly relationships between myself and the group, and between the group members themselves, I ensured that everyone, even the most apathetic member became progressively more confident and willing to participate openly by speaking whenever he felt he had something useful to contribute. This meant that I took everything that was said seriously, even those occasional inputs that often appeared incoherent. I did this because I knew that nothing was more inhibiting and prescribing of participation than the likelihood of having one's contribution mocked by other group members, and especially by the tutor. In my mind, even apparently inept contributions, if they were seriously made, could reveal genuine miscomprehensions and genuine educational needs. I never consciously therefore directly requested anyone to speak. I felt it vital that group members should be free to remain silent if they wanted to. Sometimes members remained silent for whole sessions because they preferred to listen to the views of other more experienced members. I saw this as a genuine reason for not participating - and provided members were mentally participating their temporary silence did not worry me.

But I was still concerned about the group's shy members. To try to alleviate their fears, I often suggested, in informal circumstances, that it was well worth the effort to speak if they really had something important to contribute to the discussion; that the other members genuinely wanted to hear their views; quoted cases of previous group members who had successfully overcome similar difficulties; and promised to help them get a chance to contribute whenever they were genuinely ready to make the attempt. Usually this approach was successful. However, if a student still remained diffident, I acted indirectly to make matters easier by suggesting that the class should divide into two or three sub-groups for exploratory discussions before tackling a problem in the main group. In these small environments, I knew that even the most retiring student found it far easier to speak. Also, I suggested quietly to the sub-group members that they should appoint their shy members to report their findings to the reassembled full group, because acting as spokesperson for the sub-groups generally helped to build up their confidence even more.

I was also concerned with combating a greater fear in my students - one that centered on their attitude towards the unknown, towards matters they were not used to, especially in the context of education and knowledge. I pointed out to them that nearly all my students had felt fear when asked to face subjects they regarded as foreign and threatening; and that such fear was common in all students (and teachers). In fact, by facing this fear, and recognizing it, we are all, as the French novelist and philosopher Albert Camus wrote in his *Notebooks (1991:13)*, *"seized by an instinctive desire to go back to the protection of old habits...At that moment, we are feverish but also porous, so that the slightest touch makes us quiver to the depths of our being. We come across a cascade of light, and there is eternity"*. In other words, according to Camus, what prevents individuals from learning is the fear of getting things wrong, of looking foolish in the eyes of one's contemporaries and so holding on to the illusion of dignity. I assured my class that many of my students had faced their fear, accepted their subsequent porosity and had, as a consequence, enlarged their thinking, modified their identity, and entered a new environment of unsuspected possibilities and unanticipated discoveries - and that they too could overcome this fear and so enter a stimulating world of learning and new ideas by embracing this learning process.

### "A collision of reflections"

I also used the course to discover whether certain aspects of my own teaching practice were not only effective in generating learning, but also whether my practice could be supported by the educational theories which I had researched while preparing it -

and whether the theories themselves could be justified from my classroom experience. As someone with lengthy experience of working with community and voluntary groups, I already believed in the mutual interplay of talking, sharing ideas and reflecting with my students, so the classes, and the education they offered, were clearly sited in the pragmatic constructivist tradition: a tradition that emphasized that learning was a search for meaning, and that people were constantly learning how to construct and deconstruct their own experiences and their meanings.

I was, therefore, of the opinion that learning must start with the issues which my students were currently trying to construct meaning from. To work effectively in this tradition, I realized that I would have to use a range of teaching skills and, simultaneously, possess strong beliefs, high self-confidence and self-awareness if I was to effectively engage a group of adults in learning processes where discussion outcomes could not always be guaranteed. The classes themselves gave the students in-depth opportunities in which they could reflect on their responses to their collective community building experiences. These experiences ensured that the students were already thinkers who possessed opinions, who had made their own connections between local social issues and their origins, implications and outcomes. In my view, the delivery of a modular curriculum within such an informal, non-academic setting, gave my students the opportunity to become reflective thinkers, not by introducing them to a new, academic method of reasoning, but by providing an educational space for a "collision of reflections" (Vygotsky 1987:107), and by adding a judgmental, questioning edge to their existing ways of reasoning about their work and their communities.

By delivering academic information beyond the experience of my students, I was confident I could help them evaluate their own experiences - which in turn influenced their personalized conceptual frameworks. It was by concurrently building up these

conceptual frameworks that the students related incoming information to what they already knew, thereby turning existing information into new thoughts and new ideas. In my view, therefore,
reflective thinking was not a new, advanced mental process but
the re-examination, re-evaluation and reformation of existing
individual cognitive processes.

One of my students then pointed out that what we were
discussing was becoming too pedantic - we were categorizing the
thinking process by dividing it up into different sections such as
critical, reflective and intuitive, and so on. Surely, he maintained,
this is complicating a straightforward issue, because though the
concept of thinking can be interpreted in many different ways, in
the final assessment, we are all still thinking. I saw his point, and
stated that I believed all teachers attempted to get their students to
think whether they labeled the process critical, reflective, creative
etc. To try to clarify the situation, I pointed out that whatever view
of thinking a tutor holds, it will constitute a form of application
learning - developing particular skills, learning how to manage
complex projects, and developing the ability to engage in various
kinds of thinking. I then cited the ideas of Robert Sternberg (1989:
quoted in Fink, 2003) who had developed what he labeled the
"triarchic" view of thinking, which he uses to help students learn
to think more effectively. Sternberg sees thinking as a general
concept (as did my student), but then identifies three distinct
subcategories: critical thinking, creative thinking and practical
thinking, and he describes them as follows:

*Critical thinking*, to Sternberg, refers to the process of analyzing
and evaluating something; literature tutors want their students to
analyze and evaluate when they ask students to interpret a novel.
They want students to analyze the novel in terms of various
concepts (plot development, character portrayal, the creation of
dramatic tension and so on) - class discussions are then often used
for students to learn how to assess different interpretations.

*Creative thinking* occurs when one imagines and creates a new idea, product or design; in these instances, novelty plays a central role. When tutors want their students to "think outside the box", to find new ways of answering questions, to develop new perspectives on the phenomena being studied, or to devise new solutions to old problems, they are urging their students to engage in creative thinking.

*Practical thinking* happens when a person is learning how to use and apply something as when trying to solve a problem or make a decision. The outcome of this type of thinking is a solution or a decision, and the effectiveness of the solution or decision is paramount. When tutors in business, education or engineering say to their students, "Here is a problem. How would you solve it?" they are asking students to engage in practical thinking.

To help tutors and teachers see the classroom meaning of these views of thinking, Sternberg created a list of questions that illustrated each of the three kinds of thinking for six different college courses, as shown below in Figure 1:

**Figure 1: Questions designed to prompt three kinds of thinking**

| Field | Critical Thinking | Creative Thinking | Practical Thinking |
|---|---|---|---|
| Psychology | Compare Freud's theory of dreaming to Crick's | Design an experiment to test a theory of dreaming | What are the implications of Freud's theory of dreaming for your own life? |
| Biology | Evaluate the validity of the bacterial of theory of ulcers | Design an experiment to test the bacterial theory of ulcers | How would the bacterial theory of ulcers change conventional treatments |

| Literature | In what ways were Catherine Earnshaw and Daisy Miller similar? | Write an alternative ending to Wuthering Heights, uniting Heathcliff and Catherine | Why are lovers sometimes cruel to each other and what can we do about it about it? |
|---|---|---|---|
| History | How did events in post WW1 Germany lead to the rise of Nazism? | How might Truman have encouraged the surrender of Japan without bombing Hiroshima? | What lessons does Nazism hold for events in Bosnia today? |
| Mathematics | How is this mathematical proof flawed? | Prove (a given proposition) | How is trigonometry applied to the construction of bridges? |
| Art | Compare and contrast how Rembrandt and Van Gogh used light in (specific paintings) | Draw a beam of light | How could we reproduce the lighting in this painting in an actual room? |

*Source*: Fink (2003)

I thought there was a great deal of merit in Sternberg's classification of thinking. Although I used critical thinking in a different way - I saw it, along with Brookfield, (1991) as a) identifying and challenging assumptions and b) exploring and imagining alternatives - I accepted that Sternberg's specific meaning was relevant to students' needs. Overall though, I believed that however the different categories of thinking were classified, what all teachers had ( I hoped ) in common was still the desire to get their pupils to think about "life, the universe and everything". In short, I was firmly of the opinion that we should be teaching our students how to think rather than teaching them what to think.

## Discussion and Learning

The course also represented my attempt to help students, who were predominantly drawn from working class backgrounds, challenge the predominantly middle class ethos in academia, particularly its "safety first", control - orientated attitude to the classroom that stressed that the classroom always remained the same even though the students were different. I hoped to achieve this by turning my classroom into an engaged, collective entity that was exciting, dynamic and fluid. To do this, I focused on getting my students to hear each other's voices and individual thoughts, thus making them and myself more acutely aware of each other, more respectful of the resulting conversation, and less reliant on the written word and on my position and power. I stressed the importance of discussion in which different views got a hearing, and in which the twists and turns of an argument, rather than any specific conclusion, helped the students expand their minds - an approach supported by Lipman (1991: 219) who believed "the tutor's main role is that of a cultivator of judgment who transcends rather than rejects right-wrong answers in the sense of caring more for the process of inquiry itself than the answer that might be right or wrong at a given time".

I realized, of course, that by adopting discussion methods of teaching I was operating outside the mainstream higher education tradition, but such a situation, I believed, offered me significant advantages. I could take advantage of the small size of my class, which contained a maximum of fifteen students; I was working in community centre venues where I could choose suitable rooms, arrange the seating for lessons in any manner I wanted to (as opposed to lecturing in a "fixed" lecture room where all the students sat in rows); I could arrange my teaching time to suit the learning pace of my class rather than allocate units of 60 minutes to set topics; and by teaching alone I could stress different aspects of the curriculum without offending the specialist, and compartmentalized, expertise of any colleagues and so focus particularly on those topics - real-life community problems - seen by the trainees to be closely relevant to the own needs and purposes. In other words, I recognized that I was dealing most of the time not merely with the instructional aspects of technical training, but with the provision of education to develop enthusiasm, understanding, and to generate new attitudes and new relationships. By adopting this discussion-based method I accepted that if the changing of attitudes was a prime purpose of my course, one of the first conditions of success was that everyone should be free, and feel free, to say exactly what he or she was really thinking.

Students who started the course could be initially skeptical about my use of the discussion method of teaching. This was because they were often doubtful of their own abilities, conscious of their differences, unaware of the mutual interests they had in common with other participants, and afraid that by becoming part of this method of learning they would be exposed as ignorant and naive to the other students. To counter this feeling of insecurity, I spent the first morning session of each new course explaining my teaching philosophy to the students, both in general and in relation to each of the course's separate activities. I stressed firstly that everyone had had experience of working with people; that educating for work with people was the central purpose of the course; and that very quickly they would all find they had a great deal in common. I then outlined the advantages of being in a group that contained so much first-hand experience of working with people in so many different communities, and stressed the opportunity this offered for the students to learn from one another during discussions. I next invited questions and tried to clear up any of the students' misconceptions.

Although my colleagues generally asked their new students to say a few introductory words about themselves at these first sessions, I found that this activity was generally counterproductive in my classes as it put those students who were unused to speaking in public at a disadvantage, especially if they had not prepared beforehand for such an exercise. I believed that attendance at the numerous tea and coffee breaks offered by the timetable was far more effective in breaking down social barriers and getting individuals to socialize together in preparation for my group-focused, discussion based, approach to teaching and learning.

The small class structure, and informal atmosphere, of the programme was therefore linked with a teaching method that stressed the benefits of discussion, not lecturing or control, as a learning tool. Discussion has been described by Newman (1994:84) as a "group communication that encourages people to collaborate in a critical encounter with themes and objects in their world". I had chosen this method because I believed, like Habermas (1992a:165), "that individuals can develop structures of consciousness which belong to a higher stage than those which are already embodied in the institutions of their society", and that the best way of achieving these structures was by generating talk which helped my students create more complex and compre-hensive understandings of their communities, their issues and problems - and of their own relationships to these issues and problems.

I knew too that a great deal of educational research stressed the effectiveness of discussion as a teaching method. For example, I remembered from my A level studies the words of John Milton in his *Areopagitica* (1664) that, "where there is much desire to learn, there, of necessity will be much argument, much writing, many opinions: for opinion is but knowledge in the making". Later, my research in Piagetian child psychology, while undertaking teacher training, had encouraged me to extend Piaget's theory of cognitive development into the environment of adult learning with encour-aging results. Greeson in 1998, I recalled reading in the book

*What's the Point in Discussion?* by Bligh (2000), reported students as asking more questions, sharing more information and generating many more ideas, after monitoring their discussions as group members; while Geerlings (1994) who interrupted students' discussions at regular intervals to sample their thoughts at that instant, found that their thoughts were related to the discussion topic 75 per cent of the time - a very high figure when compared with lectures where student thoughts were often connected with extraneous matters (see Bloom 1953). In 1995 Galloti set tasks to pairs of students and found that this collective approach made the students more critical and creative regarding their patterns of thinking. Subsequently, a number of comparisons of these discussion groups with other teaching methods - where the development of effective thinking skills was the criterion - showed that the number of experiments where discussion was more effective than conventional teaching methods was thirty seven; the number of experiments where there was no significant difference was only two; while the number where discussion had the same effect was three (again reported in Bligh 2000).

I was also aware that psychological evidence suggested that discussion could help people recall information when they needed it for such purposes as problem-solving and decision-making. The evidence here (McDaniel,1986) identified that a potential advantage of discussion was that it allowed a given item of information to be cross-related to many other items - so while there was a tendency in sequential presentations, such as lectures, for cognitive connections of ideas to be like a herringbone, in interrelated presentations these connections formed a network-like system which helped students come up with ideas that they would not normally think of when analyzing information provided in the traditional lineal manner. I believed, therefore, that discussion could be used to help my students think creatively, and so help them challenge and transform conventional ways of relating to their communities - and so subsequently engage in even more critical enquiry.

To further the impact of discussion and reinforce its influence, I used the following technique to create what I labeled "group self-instruction". That is:

- I focused attention on vital topics such as "What is a community?" or "Why is apathy so damaging?" or "Is community work an effective development tool?"
- The students were divided into groups of three or four in which they developed responses on the issue I had set, and later pooled their replies with the rest of the class
- I then "filled in" with knowledge and material not covered by the combined efforts of the students, and helped to reorganize their replies into a more concise form

This method, which encouraged openness to new perspectives, the willingness to temporarily suspend one's own convictions and make decisions in a rational, democratic manner was, in my eyes, far more effective in generating opinions and knowledge than the passive acceptance of lectures and detailed note-taking - and occasionally recycling this information via essays, tests or examination questions. I saw my class as a responsive, active and democratic entity: and while I encouraged discussion to help its members assess information and opinions, I did not attempt to guide them towards any specific, pre-ordained, tutor-influenced conclusions because I believed the only conclusions likely to affect the members' attitude and behavior permanently were those the students freely reached for themselves.

Another reason I placed great emphasis on discussion as a learning instrument for class members - and by implication for the community as a whole - was because I saw the community group as the prime catalyst of a community's response to its disadvantaged situation. How to generate group learning through discussion in class was therefore stressed, and used as a metaphor for community work: the development of the class was held up to the students as an example - a mirror image - of the real community and its own learning and development needs and processes. Class discussion about common problems thus brought significant educational value with it. Each class member carried with him certain assumptions about working with people, based on his experience in his own community organization, and until joining the class he may have never even questioned these. By becoming a class member, however, his assumptions were challenged by the different assumptions and experience of other class members. The student concerned now found he could take nothing for granted, and he had to rethink and test every assumption, every method and every way of tackling a problem, not only against his own experience but also against the experience of every other member of the class.

The class thus acted as a laboratory in which students could learn and practice thinking and communication techniques that could then be transferred into the community – a process supported and reinforced by Batten (1957: 81) who, I later discovered, had written:

> "The process of community development (or creation) is envisaged in two stages: the first, development within the groups themselves as the members become more knowledgeable people, more friendly and co-operative among themselves, and more able to conduct their business without outside help and guidance; and the second, development in the community at large as the characteristics developed within the groups influence the conduct of the members in their homes and their neighborhood".

I also used the group to help the students relate to people, form bonds with them and accept that other individuals had ideas, hopes, dreams and aspirations, and that this relationship building process must be transferred to the worker's actions in his community.

I pointed out that the first stage in relating to the members of a community is when a community worker makes contact with a local inhabitant, and that this stage involves creating a one to one encounter where an inter-personal relationship is transformed from – using the language of Martin Buber in his book *Between Man and Man* (1947) - an "I-It" mode to an "I-You" mode. In their intriguing and informative article "The sociability and geometry of community development practice", Westoby and Owen (2010) lay out lucidly Buber's ideas in this sphere. The "I-It" mode, according to Buber, is the mode of experience. In it, the worker collects data, analyses it, classifies it and theorizes about it. The purpose of the experience is to view it as "a thing", an instrument, to be used and put to some purpose. Such an experience is essential in the community development process as it allows the worker to dispassionately assess the community, analyze its strengths and weaknesses, and institute a plan for its improvement. But by adopting this mindset the worker creates a distance between the experiencing I and the experienced It: the experiencing I is an objective observer rather than an active participant engaging with a person, a community or society as a whole.

Westoby and Owen further point out that Buber believes that there is another mode which people must use if they are to form genuine human relationships which are vital to the sustainability of any group formation and the community development process generally. This is the encounter mode (the mode of I-You) where the worker enters into a relationship with the person encountered, where she participates in something with that person, and both the I and the You are transformed by the relationship. The transition out of the I-It mindset - from a calculating, cold, analytical one to a hospitable, reciprocal and purposeful one (I-You) - is a necessary precondition for building the inter-personal trust so vital in group creation and maintenance, because it stresses empathy with people and a belief in the qualities of trust, honesty and collective effort. If such a transition does occur it can be seen as a shift in thinking which can create a foundation for community action.

Discussion is vital in this process because dialogue between two individuals offers the process an on-going impetus in the transition from I-It to I-You mindset. Westoby and Owen stress that Buber identifies three connected "movements" in this dialogue together with a forward momentum within the movements. The first movement occurs when the worker introduces herself to another person: she says who she is and why she is where she is. Second movement dialogue occurs when there is a response from the other to the worker's first statements, while third movement dialogue is the worker's response to the person's response. This process requires the worker to listen closely to what is being said, and connect with what is being communicated. Genuine dialogue, according to Buber, progresses through all three movements, intertwining and moving forward. Buber describes this process of creating mutual relationships as a condition of moving from "I" (first movement) to "You" (second movement) to "We" (third movement).

The "We" stage of the development process must then be consolidated, because effective group formation now requires extending the opportunity to work together to more than two individuals in order to build a collective entity that can engage in constructive social action. This stage often takes the form of inviting another individual to join the worker and the concerned citizen. Kelly (2008: 71) has labeled this move from one person (zero relationships) to two people (one relationship) and finally to three people (three relationships) the 0-1-3 system, and believes that an application of this system would unfold as follows (quoted in Westoby and Owen: 2010):

- A worker encounters a community member (A) who expresses concerns about an issue – the lack of a community action group

- The same worker meets another community member (B) who expresses a similar concern
- The worker then prepares A to meet B to reach back to A
- All three get together to purposefully consider what they can do (hence 0-1-3; a movement from one person with zero relationships to two people characterized by one relationship and then finally three people with three relationships).

Andrews (2007: quoted in Westoby and Owen 2010) believes this movement is vital because the trio is the basic structural unit, not just for community group formation but for "community" itself. Andrews believes the trio generates objectivity, subjectivity and security, thereby making it a robust agent well protected from external threats. He therefore sees the trio as the cornerstone essential for building further progress towards group formation, and the expansion of the community development process generally - and not just as an end in itself.

So, through the work of my group, I aimed to produce socialized and community-spirited individuals as well as co-operatively minded and knowledgeable people. I anticipated that leaders developed in my group would later become leaders in their own communities, a process which could be seen as one of the processes which Welton (2003:198) has described as the "pedagogies of civil society...the optimal learning conditions that enable open, uncoerced and respectful communication amongst citizens who engage each other towards the creation of a common world able to attend to the needs of its citizens".

I therefore saw discussion as a process of imaginative expansion which helped establish class commitment to learning because, unlike written tests and formal examinations which are individualistic and static, talk is collective, fluid, often tentative and uncertain, but simultaneously exciting and continually in search of new ideas, insights and thoughts. I remembered that

Clifford Geertz (1973: 360) would have agreed when he said, "human thought is consummately social: social in its origins, social in its functions, social in its form, social in its applications". I therefore entered the classroom with the assumption that I should build a "conversation community" in order to create a climate of openness and intellectual enquiry. What I was aiming for was, in the words of Thomas (1997:75), "less orderliness, more fertility, more "ad hocery", more thought experiments, more diversity". I recognized that improvisation was a necessity and an inspiration, and that as long as I kept my mind open, listened to others, and tried to learn from everything I did, I could generate an exciting, if often unpredictable, learning environment. In doing this, I was working against the standard educational imagination which defined learning in terms of stimulus and response: if the system could manage the stimuli and inputs properly, it could secure regular and predictable outcomes. This was a systems thinking approach where the emphasis was on control, instruction, classroom management and performance outcomes - and it was not one that I was enthusiastic about.

## Group processes and learning

Neither, I reminisced, were many other academics. I recalled a bar in Phoenix, Arizona where I was attending a conference in 1990. Several delegates were relaxing with a few drinks and reflecting on how hierarchical many community development and education courses were in their respective parts of the USA and Canada. One, though, maintained that not all was lost, and that he had heard about a new approach to teaching medicine in Canada, initiated in the 1980s at McMaster University. Here, he had been told, some enlightened teachers had developed a small group approach to solving problems associated with prescribing treatment for the conditions of hospital patients - an approach the students generally encountered much later in their professional training. The McMaster method reverses the long tradition of having students study only content information during the first two years of their course, and waiting until their third year before starting work on the kinds of problems they will encounter in clinical practice. The medical students who made up the learning groups were not individually very knowledgeable initially about medicine, but they knew about their own illnesses and those of close friends and family, were not short of common sense and reasoning skills, and they empathized with their patients. They all possessed their own areas of knowledge that, when utilized in a group, created a pool of expertise which, after collective discussion and consideration, often lead to genuine insights about their patents' state of health and possible treatments.

In addition to its internal effectiveness, the Phoenix delegate believed that this small group approach to learning also generated wider benefits. The students involved were stimulated to research for themselves more information to answer the questions generated in, and reinforce the knowledge they had gained by, their group's activity. In addition, the exercise was premised on the belief that this way of generating ideas, knowledge and self confidence had an even wider application in that all the students involved would not just become fine students with first hand knowledge of their patients, but that they would put all this expertise and learning into effect in the wider community after graduating from the university.

On reflection, I thought there was a great deal in common between the Mc Master approach towards its medical students and my attitude towards community development workers, activists and volunteers. To make sure that my drinking partner was not embroidering the situation in his cups, I researched the McMaster situation, and looked deeper into my own group teaching, to see if there were any comparisons. I found the information provided by Fink in his book *Creating Significant Learning Experiences* (2003) particularly helpful as he highlighted that in McMaster, in place of the accumulation and memorization of medical facts via lectures, the educational emphasis had been transferred to clinical reasoning in small groups that stressed problem-solving, teamwork, integrative thinking, communication and self-directed learning - all generic skills previously ignored by a great many medical institutions. Once the students had been presented with increasingly complex problems, and sets of symptoms and case histories, they worked in groups to answer some key questions such as the following:

- What systems or topics seem to be involved in this problem?
- What do we already know about these systems or topics?
- What do we not know? (This is vital because it allows students to identify the learning issues they need to work on)
- How can I learn about that system (for example, the liver or the heart?)
- How can I use my understanding of the general system and of this particular situation to analyze and diagnose the problem?

Learning how to work through the correct questions in the right sequence is a very important part of the McMaster learning process - and these are all questions that professional practitioners confront in their work. The sequence of events in this process, as listed by Fink, is shown below in Figure 2:

## Figure 2
## Sequence of Activities in Problem-Based Learning

| In Class | Groups presented with a problem, decide what information and ideas are needed | Groups collect and apply new information and ideas to original problem | Groups present solutions to rest of class teacher and |
|---|---|---|---|
| **Out of class** | Individual students seek new information and ideas | Students review solutions | |

*Source:* Fink (2003)

Although this diagram simplifies the sequence, the basic idea in problem-based learning is to start the process in class by giving students a realistic problem. Each group then has to analyze the case and decide what the learning issues are and what ideas and information are required. Students, on their own and in subgroups, next proceed, outside the classroom and in their own time, to find information on, and consolidate their understanding of, the related learning issues. After this has occurred, the new knowledge is examined collectively in class to see if it adequately addresses the subjects being considered. The students then review solutions to the problem and, finally, each group presents its solution to the teacher and the rest of the class (Fink 2003).

After conducting my research into the McMaster method, I discovered another collective process at work in the field of community leadership, as described by Lela Vandenberg and Lorilee Sandmann in their paper *Community Action Leadership Development: A Conceptual Framework,* (1995). In this paper, the authors came to the conclusion that in the community groups they had studied, as well as in the McMaster groups (and I believed in my own group too), a process was taking place which interacted with, and weaved together, six concepts - visioning together, leading together, learning together, building community, developing energy and acting together - within a tutor supervised discussion or talk environment. When these concepts were acted upon they became operationalised and formed an interrelated process of group activity (see Figure 3) with each activity reinforcing and being reinforced by the others - all taking place within a context of free-flowing, but focused, discussion. Reading from the bottom up, Figure 3 shows a single phrase of the process. This is not a linear process but a system of multi-dimensional and fluid relationships: actions can happen simultaneously or repeatedly, and the whole process is one phase of a continuous cycle or spiral.

**Figure 3**

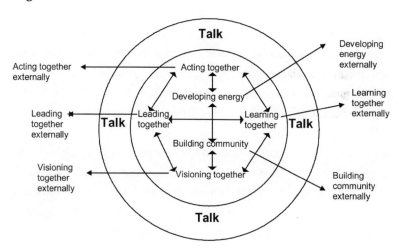

*Source:* Adapted from Vandenberg and Sandmann, 1995

In the figure, Vandenberg and Sandman stress that the actions highlighted with double headed arrows reinforce each other. For example, developing a vision or plan while involving all members in the task increases its relevance and group members' sense of responsibility for it. Also, developing a vision involves people learning together about relevant circumstances. In turn, the knowledge gained helps develop and refine the vision, and as people vision and plan together, they build a sense of community, generating feelings of identity, unity and commitment. As the sense of community gets stronger, the vision becomes more grounded in the reality of the community. In addition, the sense of community is directly related to power - as feelings of identity, unity and commitment bind a community together, so its power to act collectively, and coalesce the talents and abilities of all members, grows significantly. As they develop more power, group members' collective actions become even more effective; and as their actions achieve group goals, and move them closer to the group's vision, their power to continue the development process increases too.

Alternatively, the unidirectional arrows in Figure 3 indicate a one-way, external influence - in this instance the transfer of the group action process (and the knowledge associated with it) from the group of learners/students internally out into the specific geographical and organizational communities that the students will be working in on their return from the programme. In other words, Vandenberg and Sandmann believe that the processes that operate within a small community group, such as mine, take its members beyond the teaching methodology used, and propel them into a series of interactive relationships that go beyond individual learning to collective learning and collective actions: elements that are vital not only for the students but also for the communities in which they will work after completing the programme.

## A brief opinion of competency learning

Having collected and assessed all this evidence, it was not surprising that I favored a group approach to the teaching of collective action and community development rather than a linear, lecture-based approach. It was not too surprising either that I preferred the group focused method to the competency-based approach to learning. This I saw as being the basis on which much of the National Vocational Qualification programme was based. Several of my students had previously undertaken an NVQ level 2 qualification in community development, and had made it clear to me that they saw the programme as one in which they were trained to acquire specific competencies, and were forced to see themselves as mere clusters of work functions. I recognized that there was something very comforting about using a "skills" model of this type in community work: for those students needing to acquire accreditation it became merely a matter of getting the correct input from a recognized training provider - for whom the learning process became a relatively simple one of "skills transference". And the skills in question had always to match up to certain expectations. This is not surprising because, as Marilyn Strathern (1997: 315) has written:

*"The skills have already been defined...Nor is it any surprise that - in certain respects - the expectations mimic the skills of audit presentation..: clarity (rather than logic), itemization (rather than connection), bullet points (rather than paragraphs), and simplified organization (rather than involution or evolution in argument)".*

In this way, learning became viewed by NVQ students and providers as no more complicated than inserting information into a computer. In my eyes, this is learning that is appropriate for individuals working in an environment where there is a predictable relationship between cause and effect: between what the worker should do and the result he should achieve. "Do this in this way", the teacher can say, "and when you have acquired the necessary skills you will get the result you want". In short, it was a system in which creative thinking was inhibited by its predictive, ritualized, outcome-based course design which set out what the students were expected to learn - with no room for unanticipated, spontaneous collective debate or student-determined outcomes. In my eyes, such an education was concerned purely with the recycling of pre-packaged formats and information, and did nothing at all to encourage and stimulate the critical thinking and reflection that would be required of students in their dealings with people in communities whose behavior, in an infinite variety of future situations, will often be complex, irregular and unpredictable as they attempt to change people's outlook on life and their attitudes to each other. In other words, as has been pointed out by Nicholas Royle in his book *The Uncanny* (2003):

*"Teaching is becoming mechanised in a way that makes caricature seem improbably realistic: Dickens's Mr Gradgrind would have found it difficult to believe. It is not only the teacher who becomes an automaton, but also the student, for he or she too is obliged to live up to the "learning outcomes" set down in advance, in other words in a sense not to live at all, merely to "receive deliver"* - a view reinforced by Leonora Klein, a former barrister who started a new career as a teacher in 2008 but who resigned disillusioned, and returned to law work a year later because, as she wrote in The Guardian: *"Those who are responsible for education policy...have created a system where nothing can be taught unless it can be measured. They are making life absurdly difficult for the teachers who are battling, against the odds, to inspire their students. Worse than that, they are suffocating that most precious talent that every child possesses; a wild and strange imagination. They have forgotten that there are some things which cannot be measured". (April 14, 2009)* - a view very close to that of Myles Horton, the legendary American adult education activist, who forcibly expressed his contempt for the way in which modern education "has got to be something that

can be tested or controlled" resulting in the learner "being handled like a machine with predictable results" (Horton 2003: 225).

What we have here is pre-packaged education which students can tailor their (distributed) notes to in order to gain a good degree - and which will enforce the belief that the college or university concerned has "added value" to its work. In my view, this is a retrograde model of learning which might be suitable for the large numbers of students now entering higher education, but which is more concerned with the reproduction of passive acceptance of the status quo and entrepreneurial attitudes than it is with the teaching of liberal values and stimulating a process of critical intellectual inquiry.

# Chapter Three

## An alternative vision – chaos and questions

I had an alternative vision - one based on Socratic and facilitative modes of teaching (Jarvis, 1983), and drawn from Chaos Theory, which recognized that what happens at different levels of a system is connected but not mutually determined (Gleick, 1998). I believed that this model had practical implications for my teaching methods: a belief reinforced by my reading of Tsoukas (1998) who contrasts the old, Newtonian style which has informed a mechanical, controlling approach to education, with a Chaotic style. Tsoukas argues (1998:297) that "the world envisioned by chaos theory differs significantly from the Newtonian view", primarily because it conceives of organizations and groupings as developed through mutual influence and interaction, rather than through command and control. Systems-thinking is part of the modern or positive approach of transferring deterministic scientific approaches to the understanding of educational situations. In contrast, a Chaos Theory approach emphasizes that there are interactive feedback loops, with teachers influencing students, students influencing students, and students influencing teachers, but none of them absolutely determining the responses of the others.

I also drew on Chaos Theory's associated disciplines for inspiration and justification for my teaching methodology. I had studied the principles of Complexity Theory which referred to a system of thinking concerned with the behavior of natural systems such as (along with Chaos Theory) Dissipative Structure Theory (Prigogine and Stengers, 1984) and quantum physics (Hey and Walters, 2003). Prigogine emphasized that the mechanistic and deterministic world-view - emphasizing stability, order, uniformity, equilibrium and linear relationships between or within closed systems - was being replaced by a new paradigm. This new paradigm was more in line with today's accelerated social change and stressed disorder, instability, diversity, disequilibrium, non-linear relationships between open systems and temporality. Additionally, Tsoukas (1998:305 quoted in Turner 2004:164)) had underlined these key concepts in relation to organizational systems:

> *"Chaos and complexity theory draw our attention to certain features of organizations about which organization theorists were, on the whole, only subliminally aware. Notions like non-linearity, sensitivity to initial conditions, iteration, feedback loops, novelty, unpredictability, process and emergence make up a new vocabulary in terms of which we may attempt to redescribe organizations".*

Basically, complexity offered a way of thinking about human systems that, in my mind, proposed a potentially radical and innovative framework for educators, providing an alternative to the traditional belief that teachers are in control. It treated human systems as directly analogous to nature, which is often unpredictable and non-linear, and human systems appear to display many of the characteristics of complex adaptive systems. In particular, coherent patterns of behavior can arise from the apparently idiosyncratic interactions of random individuals. This property of complex systems, a phenomenon known as emergence, is highly significant, because it implies that the less the appearance of random variations, the lower the adaptive capacity of the system.

A simple model developed by Stacey (2000), aims to encapsulate the idea. To give a simplified explanation of this: an organization that generates increasing agreement and certainty among its members moves towards a state of stasis. This is suitable in stable, known circumstances. Decreasing agreement and certainty, on the other hand, creates movement towards a state of chaos. At the extreme of this state there is too little commonality to hold a group or organization together. Stacey's argument is that groups must obtain the capacity to operate just at the margin of that chaotic state, far from agreement and certainty, but without falling into total chaos. This margin is referred to in complexity thinking as "the edge of chaos". It is at this edge, where uncertainty, difference and risk-taking have more space to generate creative thinking and action, that the propensity for emergence is thought to be at its greatest.

This, I decided, was where I wanted my group and its learning to be situated. I had spent my early years as a teacher in a further education college sited in the docks area of Newport in south Wales, and though I appreciated the benefits of a structured classroom which helped keep my students in order, I felt, almost viscerally, that the best classes that I had experienced were those where I had adopted a light controlling touch, and where we had discussed, as a collective entity, topics as diverse as the merits and demerits of rock 'n' roll stars, the value of local calypsos and carnivals, the state of Welsh rugby and whether the Vietnam war was a just or unjust conflict. There had been an element of uncertainty, there had been badinage, verbal cut and thrust, points scoring, adherence to "thinking on one's feet", acceptance of risk taking and inconsistencies, and a lack of any definitive script or even lesson plan - but there had been enjoyment, excitement and creative learning within the educational parameter of a Liberal Arts programme.

What was vital to the success of this approach was its spontaneity and humanity – attributes that underpin the belief of Martin Buber that an educator extemporizing out of his own experience can gain a pupil's confidence and, as a result, convince him that there is human truth and that existence has a meaning. And when the pupil's confidence has been won, Buber is of the opinion that *"his resistance against being educated gives way to a singular happening: he accepts the educator as a person. He feels he may trust this man, that this man is taking part in his life, accepting him before desiring to influence him. And so he learns to ask..."* (Hodes

1972: 137).

And it was asking questions that my pedagogy was designed to stimulate. I believed that my students needed to question and argue - but I also recognized that they should have even more from their course. I accepted that questioning alone guaranteed nothing, but that it was a vital step towards opening up a space of resistance toward authority, helping students think critically about the world around them, and getting them to recognize dialogue and questioning as conditions for social intervention in the service of an alternative collective and democratic order. I pointed out to my class that some educationalists, such as Zygmunt Bauman (2001:4), go even further in their belief in the value of questioning, and argue that the resurrection of any viable notion of political and social action is dependent upon a culture of questioning whose purpose, as he puts it, is to *"keep the forever unexhausted and unfulfilled human potential open, fighting back all attempts to foreclose and pre-empt the further unraveling of human possibilities, prodding human society to go on questioning itself and preventing that questioning from ever stalling or being declared finished"*. To reinforce the need for on-going questioning I then highlighted what Hannah Arendt had written in her book *The Human Condition (quoted in Foley 2010:125):*

> *"Behind all the cognitive questions for which men find answers, there lurk the unanswerable ones that seem entirely idle and have always been denounced as such. It is more likely that men, if they were ever to lose the appetite for meaning we call thinking and cease to ask unanswerable questions, would lose not only the ability to produce those thought-things that we call works of art but also the capacity to ask the questions upon which civilization is founded".*

## Controlled chaos, ground rules and creative conversation

What I was not advocating in this context was uncontrolled chaos. My colleagues felt that such a stance was contradictory, and that if

I advocated chaos as a teaching method - or an outcome of this method - then I did in fact believe in abrogating control of the class and letting matters take their own course. I replied by reflecting that in his classic study of *Chaos: Making a New Science* (1998: 303-17), James Gleick had reported some technical definitions of chaos in the scientific literature, including: "A kind of order without periodicity" (Hao Bai-Lin); and "The irregular, unpredictable behavior of deterministic, non-linear dynamical systems (Bruce Stewart), and that for all their technical differences, what these definitions had in common was a model of chaos as both unpredictable and yet far from disorderly - in fact, far from chaotic in the casual sense of the word - and it was exactly this type of chaos that I was hoping to achieve in my classroom.

Also, I had spent enough time in adult education to know that if left to its own devices, a group can suffer take over and control by its more assertive and articulate members. These people, I found, were generally middle class in origin who, in their domestic and working lives, were used to being listened to, and their views canvassed and respected. The great majority of the people who made up my classes did not fall into this socio-economic category; but there was a minority who did, and the individuals who made up this small grouping also possessed forceful personalities and strong opinions. As a result, some of them spoke loudly and at great length, some wandered off the point and others spoke merely to hear the sound of their own voice and to generate an argument. I realised, too, from my experience, that my classes often considered real life community problems that were complicated, and that because of this some of the students wanted to focus on one aspect of the problem while others wished to concentrate on other aspects. I knew that if trainees failed to get their particular point discussed, due to pressure from the voluble middle class element, they might give up trying to be heard and become bored and even hostile. If this happened, then I was certain that the discussion would cease to possess any relevance or value for them.

In order to counter these difficulties, I adopted three strategies. In the first I encouraged individual self-discipline by suggesting that all group members become more sensitive to the needs of the other members of the group, by learning to weigh their words before speaking them, and to speak only when they had something worthwhile to say. If this approach did not work, I chose my second strategy: I created ground rules that encouraged wider participation. In particular, I introduced the three-person rule which stated that once someone had made a comment during discussion they were not allowed to speak again until at least three other persons had spoken (unless the speaker was asked for further comment immediately by other group members).

I sometimes adopted a third approach - splitting the main group into sub-groups to allow a rapid and full exchange of ideas, opinions and experience. I found that even ten minutes spent in small group discussion, followed by five minutes reporting back, did a great deal to reduce the difficulties generated by many group members jostling for the opportunity to speak and be heard. After the sub-group discussions, in which it was easier for everybody to test the validity of their ideas against those of other individuals, members were less frustrated by their difficulties in breaking into the discussion in the full group and often increased their confidence levels significantly. I anticipated that by adopting these strategies I would provide all participants with sympathetic fellow learners who they could rely on while pursuing the fraught process of becoming accepted members of a new learning community. Such an approach, I calculated, would generate trust, care, commitment, and a common goal, that would bind my learning group together through a willingness to help each other. Along with Paulo Freire (1987) I was firmly of the opinion that:

*"Authentic help means that all who are involved help each other mutually, growing together in the common effort to understand the reality which they seek to transform. Only through such praxis - in*

*which those who help and those who are being helped help each other*
*spontaneously - can the act of helping become free from the distortion*
*in which the helper dominates the helped".*

I thus got the students to work as catalysts - helping, stimulating and guiding each other without dominating each other - and I intended to work in this way too. This methodology, I believed, possessed an integrity and an openness that I anticipated the students would appreciate, and I reinforced it by discarding the lecturing technique or "banking system" of learning. Not for me a reliance upon class passivity, a monotonous talking pace with which every student was obliged to work, a heavy dependence on verbal memorizing and a confusing reinforcement created by the reliance of students on detailed note taking during the class. Unlike many traditional colleagues, who still believed that appeals to the authority of student experience rarely advanced classroom discussion, and even provoked confusion, I saw talk about experience - the sharing of personal narratives about community work, home life and social activity - as pivotal to the course. In my eyes, focusing on experience allowed students to claim a knowledge base from which they could speak about community development with authority. Unlike the traditionalist classroom controllers, I did not deny that my students had experience and that such experience was relevant to the learning process, even though it might be limited, raw or unfocused. I did not believe that my students came to the course with blank minds. Each one of them brought with him a complex of his own values, beliefs, ideas and purposes. All this, I judged, I could direct and critically engage with - and move beyond by linking the personal with the academic to enhance my students' confidence to reflect and learn.

I realised that the acquisition of confidence was vital to improving my students' thinking and learning. I recalled reading in Robert I Sutton's book *Weird Ideas* (2002), about an experiment carried out by the Israeli army in which new recruits were arbitrarily assigned to three undifferentiated groups. Their instructors were falsely told that one group had been earmarked as having "high command capacity", whereas the other two possessed only average capacity. Only the instructors were aware of the rankings; the recruits had no idea at all that they were participating in a trial. Yet, by the end of the course, the "high potential" group were objectively better marksmen, navigators and tacticians than the other groups. The evidence from this example (and others quoted in Sutton's book), was that confidence makes people perform better; and by treating my class, and its members' ideas, views and experiences with respect - and laying out ground rules for dialogue that would prevent the group from killing off conversation before it had even begun - I was intentionally laying down the foundations for a confidence-enhancing process to take place.

## Accepting subjectivity

I also recognized that I had a personal and collective heritage which had molded the way I thought, taught and posed questions. I accepted that I was historically sited in an environment which influenced my views, ideas and actions - and I believed that my students should be made aware of these propensities while assessing my ideas and suggestions from their own individual, cultural and value locations. I also made clear my opposition to the strand of academic wisdom that upheld the ideal of a mind/body split and stressed the concept of knowledge compartmentalization. I saw this Cartesian tradition of the mind/body divide still dominating educational thought at my institution, and its impact is summed up well by Morris and Beckett (2004:123) who believe the connection between mind and body continues to "remain dualistic" today:

> "In Western European education, the highest status is reserved for the most abstract and immaterial learning, irrespective of its utility.

*The lowest status is accorded to concrete material learning, much of which we acquire in daily embodied actions. The utility of this latter learning has hitherto been under-recognized, although with "lifelong learning" there is a chance for giving it greater prominence in adult education pedagogy and policy".*

That a dismissive attitude towards concrete learning still existed in the institution in which I occasionally taught I could verify from personal experience. I remembered standing in the schoolyard of the local primary school waiting to take my granddaughter home at the end of the day. One of her classmates informed me, as he accompanied my granddaughter out of the yard, that his father had told him that the practical skills and learning acquired by plumbers and heating engineers was not real learning when compared with the theoretical learning undertaken by university lecturers (such as his father), and I also recalled the views of many of my campus-based colleagues who were very dismissive of practical learning, even though the courses they taught had their origins in training programmes initiated when the local higher education institution was a polytechnic. I viewed this dualistic separation of intellectual and practical knowledge as detrimental, because it forced teachers and students to disregard the connection between life practices, work experiences and the role of education. I believed that a strict adherence to objectivity, and a scientific approach to teaching, would miss the richness and subjectivity of individuals' experiences. I also believed that my own experiences, values and beliefs should not be discarded at the classroom door - and that there was no such thing as an objective mind free of preconceptions, prejudices and partialities.

My experience as a student, a higher education tutor, community volunteer and community development worker had convinced me that in many ways the academic belief in objectivity was antipathetic towards the concept of community in both its educational aspect and its social manifestation. In my eyes, objectivity held experience at arms length and created a world "out there" from which people felt excluded and detached. I believed that this aspect had been reinforced by the analytical aspect of objectivity, with its stress on analyzing, dissecting and departmentalizing. Furthermore, in my view, all these aspects had combined to further the ethic of competitive individualism, a process that turns people into objects and the world into an entity to be manipulated for individual and private gain. Because of these ways of operating, we have all been forced to look at reality through an objectivist lens: we see life divorced from our personal lives because we have never been invited to meld our experiences with the narrative of the world around us. Because of this, objectivity, to me, was often instinctively anti-communal.

On the other hand, I saw community as a capacity for connectedness within and between individuals, connecting people not just to their inner selves and other people but also to world events, events in history, events in nature and in the world of ideas, and I was bolstered in this view by remembering the words of Parker J Palmer who, in 1993, had written:

*"the way we know has powerful implications for the way we live. I argue that every epistemology tends to become an ethic and that every way of knowing tends to become a way of living. I argue that the relation established between the knower and the known, between the student and the subject tends to become the relation of the living person to the world itself. I argue that every model of knowing contains its own moral trajectory, its own ethical direction and outcomes".*

### Enjoyment and open learning

I wanted to combat objectivity, and reinforce a sense of community in my students and, through them, in society at large, by talking about collective ways of knowing that developed an inward capacity for relatedness, as well as an external capacity for the reweaving of community. By adopting this approach, I aimed to intellectually stimulate my students, to excite them and generate enjoyment in learning. I realised that by pushing to achieve this objective I was acting against another academic belief - that enjoyment in the classroom "goes against the grain", is flippant and potentially disruptive of the atmosphere of seriousness that is deemed to be essential to the learning process. Despite this, I believed that enjoyment could coexist with, and even stimulate, serious intellectual and academic engagement. I did not want my students "sleepwalking into knowledge" as one student succinctly put it.

But I realised that enjoyment alone was not enough, and that sometimes, before an enjoyable learning process could begin, there had to be some conscious diminution of the traditional notion that only the tutor was responsible for classroom dynamics. Accordingly, at the start of each course, I made it clear that I favored an open approach to learning - one where the students would work in groups to discuss their work, where their views and ideas, based on their working experiences, would be openly expressed and listened to, where agendas would be flexible enough to allow for spontaneous shifts in direction, together with an acceptance that students should be seen as individuals, and interacted with according to their intellectual and emotional needs - and that I would aim to implement this process through a concerted, collective class effort.

Remembering the wonderful metaphor used by Parker Palmer in his *The Courage to Teach* (1998) to describe what he tries to do in his teaching: "I have learned that my gift as a teacher is the ability to dance with my students, to co-create with them a context in which all of us teach and learn" (p. 72), I came out from behind my desk, entered the class - and brought my lecture notes with me. I had noticed that my students were very poor at taking notes as few of them had learned at school how to take the sort of brief, well organized notes which have real meaning after the class. I realised too that the process of note taking itself could form a distraction from understanding the tutor's words: an adult student who was frantically trying to cram down my every word probably understood less of the content than a member of the class who had focused totally on what I was saying and doing. Nevertheless, I believed that my students needed to have written reinforcement of the content of a new piece of learning, because this had the dual purpose of making them feel more secure and helping them retain new material. Consequently, at the start of each lesson, I distributed copies of my notes - spaced out in bullet point format, and containing the main points of his lesson - to act as a logical précis of my thinking on the topic under discussion, as a mental prompt and as an aide-memoir for student reflection and a template for any subsequent student note making.

By leaving my desk, physically becoming part of the student group, and distributing my lecture notes, I was abandoning my ethos of exclusiveness, aloofness - and power - in the class. I was putting into effect my belief that it was interaction - the context in which learning takes place - that was the key to my students' understanding and development, rather than the mere fact that they were acquiring knowledge. I was very pleased to find that I was not alone in adopting such an approach: I had just read Ira Shor's *Empowering Education: Critical Teaching for Social Change(1992) and* was relieved to find that my methods were not the thoughts of one operating "outside the box" but had support from an educational authority with prestige and influence. Shor, I believed, would have approved my system, and would have been glad that I was entering the class and taking with me a greater openness, thereby generating a new, face-to-face, relationship which signaled a respect for my students as individuals. By adopting this more informal approach, I made it clear that what I had to say was not now coming from behind a power partition with its implication of "from my side comes truth and sophistication which must be heard" and "from your side

73

comes ignorance and naiveté which is not worth consideration".
As in Shor's system (1992), by moving around, by eliminating a
psychological authority barrier, by acknowledging displays of
confusion, anger and joy, together with students' alternative ways
of thinking and knowing, I made it clear that I was offering
something of myself to the students, thereby heightening the
feeling of spontaneity and enjoyment, and the belief that everyone
was working together in the classroom for a common cause - the
good of their communities, their inhabitants, and the world as a
whole - and not just for the accumulation of academic grades.

## Assessing and researching

Concurrently with the questioning and discussing, the students
were encouraged to gather information by reading widely and
taking notes, studying extracts from recommended texts and
jotting down the themes, issues and ideas that arose out of the
intense discussion sessions and reading texts. These were used to
write a synopsis of the lesson, provide the core of a subject
portfolio and form the information base of any future essays that
were set. Such an approach was common in neighboring departments, but I suggested an additional, novel, element: taking a lead
from Shor's book (1992), I announced that any essay could be
rewritten up to three times, and that I would count the highest
grade the student got in any rewritten paper for assessment
purposes. By announcing this rewrite policy, I offered the students
a flexible, adjustable structure: I allocated grades but the grades
were not final if students chose to raise them. I did this because I
wanted the students to value revision, freshen up their thinking,
and accept that their thoughts and ideas about a topic kept
evolving even after they had completed an assignment. I knew that
many of my students' questioned their ability to write focused and
structured essays, and though they had a great deal to write about,
they did not always know how to express their thoughts fluently
and grammatically. Each rewrite I proposed was therefore

consciously designed to be one step in a confidence building continuum, each step of which increased the fluidity of the students' expression and the correctness and focus of their essays.

To encourage students to rewrite for a higher grade, I offered specific advice about revising their essays, often by e mail, as this method provided more confidentiality, especially for the shyer students, than a discussion in open class. Because I wanted my responses to their work to be positive, I responded to the ideas in their essays first, and then to grammatical errors and syntax. After commenting on the positive aspects of their writing, I encouraged editing for correctness. When highlighting incorrect usage, I brought standard usage to the students' attention by placing asterisks in the margins, next to specific passages, and suggested that the students correct those passages themselves. I did this to break their dependence on my knowledge, and to improve their confidence, by encouraging the correction of their work from their own knowledge reserves. Additionally, to get the students to value dialogue as part of the grading process, I also proposed that verbal contributions in class should count as part of the final grade - an option enthusiastically agreed by the whole class which decided that grades should be allocated (by the tutor) not on the number of times a student spoke, but on the relevance and originality of his or her contribution.

This policy was part of my belief that the grading process should go hand in hand with a transformed, non-traditional classroom. I took the position that I must observe and evaluate the work done in my class: I should not simply stand in front of the students and read from my notes. If I wanted to know whether a student was participating I had to listen, mentally memorize and anticipate beyond that moment. I wanted my students to think, "I'm here to work with all this information, and to work with it the best way that I can. In doing this I don't have to be fearful about my grade by trying to please my tutor by regurgitating his ideas and duplicating his views. I don't have to stay "in his good books" if I want to maximize my final grade". I made it very clear that the grade was something the students could control by their efforts in the classroom and was not dependent on slavish agreement with my views and ideas. I also drew a distinction between informal, or course-based diagnostic evaluations, and formal institutional, examination-based assessments. I believed the latter to be generally antipathetic to the creative development of many of my class so, to counter the negative aspects of the formal system, I decided to modify it and to turn it into a more collaborative and positive learning experience.

As a result, I introduced a course workbook and reflective diary into the course assessment techniques. My aim was to reassure my students, the great majority of whom had not written an essay since leaving school. I believed that to stop them being afraid of failure, I should introduce an on-going evaluative dialogue with them, to help them enrich their understanding of the learning they were undertaking. I believed in giving the class regular, individual feedback on their progress through comments in their workbooks - comments on which the students reflected and then commented on themselves. The final essay was still a formal requirement of the course, but the journey towards it now formed part of the final assessment grade - a move much appreciated by the students themselves.

Students were also encouraged to bring to the class cuttings from newspapers, books and articles on the subjects under discussion. These were kept in reserve until the need for them to illustrate a point arose out of the discussions: this process proved to be an effective introduction to critical reading for many class members, as well as creating a research database on community development on which the students could draw at any time in the future. Indeed, I used the classroom, and the programme as a whole, as a research base in its widest sense, because I wanted to move away from a narrowly defined academic research method-ology and relate research to the kinds of issues affecting people in their communities. To do this, I encouraged the students to examine and research the deep meanings, personal implications and communal consequences of the themes, techniques and topics that the class had discussed. In this sense, I saw the students as researchers who generated meaning and action through collective investigation, and not as inert, individual "units" of study who passively absorbed and recycled academic texts, figures and technical jargon.

# Chapter Four

## Developing Critical Thinking

What I was developing in my classroom was a transformative education based in an area between my own knowledge and experience and my students' knowledge and experience. My intention was to create what Vygotsky (1962) labeled a "zone of proximal development" (ZPD). This is a learning environment which entails development from "the known" to "the unknown" by the most readily accessible but not necessarily linear route; and is filled by myself and my students with specific subject matter, and a discussion-based learning process which consists of a mixture of themes and topics focused on the community work experiences of my students - together with a problem-posing dialogue directed by myself. What I was implementing here was based on Vygotsky's theory that learning is dependent on social interaction and that social learning actually leads to cognitive development. In other words, a student can perform a task under adult guidance or with peer collaboration that could not be achieved by working alone in a traditional lecture hall. I remembered that Vygotsky focused on the connection between people and the cultural context in which they acted and interacted in shared experiences, and that he believed that humans use tools that develop from a culture, such as speech and writing, to mediate their social environments. The fact that he further believed that the internalization of these tools led to higher thinking skills and that, as a result, thought and language could not exist without each other (Driscoll, 1994), was another component of the teaching beliefs that I held - a confirmation that made me even more determined to go down the unpredictable collective class conversation route.

While building my teaching practice around these theories, I concurrently wanted to generate what Kuhn (1962) called a paradigm shift - an intellectual move away by my students from the accepting, passive mindset often generated by formal academic education to the inquisitive, critical ethos developed by the best informal community-based courses. Such a conscious critical detachment from, and then counteractive interpretation of, accepted academic and social norms, placed my classes firmly within the collective learning parameters of adult educators such as Paulo Freire, Myles Horton, and Raymond Williams who believed that critical thinking included being able to:

- encourage people and communities to analyze the presumptions underlying their traditional values, behaviors, beliefs and social system;
- make them aware that their presumptions are "historically and culturally specific";
- help people and communities identify and explore alternatives to current ways of living and thinking;
- help them to combat and alter the processes by which a severely unequal society uses the dominant ideology to convince people this is a normal state of affairs.

I believed that for my students to reach this level of critical thinking my classes had to generate thought that was reflective, reasonable and responsible, and focus on deciding what a person should believe and do. A person who thinks critically, in my eyes, is one who can ask appropriate questions, gather relevant information, creatively sort through this information, reason logically from it, and come to reliable and principled conclusions about their community that enable him or her to live and act ethically within it. To me, critical thinking thus enables an individual to be a responsible citizen who contributes to society, and does not merely act as a consumer of its diversions.

I also stressed to my students that critical thinking was synonymous with critical enquiry, but I recognized that many of them would not naturally adopt such an attitude. In my experience, the average student was not especially curious about the world. S/he was conscious and, being somehow obliged to deal with this condition, felt the less effort it required the better. As a result, most students did not question, were not curious and rarely challenged authority figures (including tutors) who claimed specialized knowledge of the world. Most students, in my opinion, did not think for themselves but relied on others to think for them: many indulged in wishful and emotional thinking, believing what they believed was true because they wished it or felt it to be true. Most of my students therefore had to be taught to think critically and undertake critical enquiry. To stimulate such processes, I encouraged the class to investigate community problems, ask questions about these problems, pose answers that challenged the local status quo, discover new information that could be used for the good of the community, question authorities and traditional beliefs, and challenge received political and economic dogmas and doctrines.

**Provocative problems**

In one of our first classes, we all agreed that the students should work out their plan for future discussions, and that the class should divide into three groups to list the type of problems they have most frequently encountered in their work and which they would like to be discussed. After thirty minutes the groups returned to form the class again and listed each group's choices on the whiteboard. Usually we discovered that certain problems were listed by every group, some by two groups and some by only one. The full list was then thrown open for discussion to the class. Some problems were quickly challenged as being too limited in scope, while others were seen as reflecting a minority interest only. Eventually, after another thirty minutes, the class ended up with a list of five general problems which every member had encountered and often failed to solve. A typical list read as follows:

1. How to reach people effectively so as to diminish apathy and generate collective action?
2. How to generate sustainability once the initial community work has been completed?
3. How to develop an effective organizational structure that generates commitment among all staff?
4. How to obtain feedback on the effectiveness of community initiatives while they are being implemented?
5. How to create and maintain partnerships and coalitions?

The compilation of this list was only the start of a longer process: I then asked the class to search their individual work experiences for specific examples of situations in which they had encountered one or more of these listed problems, and to write a short summary of the problems. After the students had produced their examples, I edited them (we had found in the past that shorter statements tended to generate better discussions than very long ones), and duplicated one copy of each example to distribute to each student in the order in which they would be discussed, a fortnight before the start of the next series of discussions about these problems.

## Examples of Material Contributed for Discussion
### Example of Problem 1
*(How to reach people effectively so as to diminish apathy and generate collective action?)*

*A development worker had entered a community to help generate new social and economic initiatives in it. He had met representatives of the local voluntary and community sectors at a meeting arranged by the Council of Voluntary Service, had introduced himself to several local councilors, and had informed the residents of his presence at the local community centre on specific days of the week, where he was available to discuss his (and his organization's) plans for community regeneration.*

*All these moves had resulted in little apparent enthusiasm amongst the population, so the worker circulated, via an information pamphlet to each house, that he, together with the chief officer of the CVS and representatives of the voluntary/community sector, would hold a public meeting (on a specified date in a fortnight's time) at the nearby workmen's hall to explore future social and economic developments. Despite this move, only a handful of residents attended the meeting, with the result that nothing of any significance had been decided. What more could be done by the development worker to generate awareness, combat apathy and stimulate collective action?*

### Example of Problem 2
*(How to generate sustainability once the initial community work has been completed?)*

*A project had been in existence for three years. It had achieved some of its initial aims (its worker had helped local young mothers establish a crèche with funding from the local authority and the Welsh Assembly Government, and he had also helped several small groups become legally constituted). He had won the trust and support of the local people, too! The future looked bright, with groups having been directed to suitable funding sources and local councilors generally supportive of the worker's aims and his future development strategy. Despite these favorable circumstances, the worker was aware of the project's management committee's unwillingness to allow new members to enter the project, and that they were unduly suspicious of the motives and ideas of younger people within the community who wished to contribute to it. The worker realised that if "young blood" did not replace existing members as they lost their enthusiasm, or left the committee, the project would become inward looking, moribund and prone to failure. How could he make the current committee aware of the dangerous situation and plan for its future sustainability?*

## Example of Problem 3

*(How to develop an effective team ethos that generates commitment among all staff?)*

*A project had been successful in meeting the majority of its objectives. All staff had been paid well for their work, but there was a growing feeling that the plaudits and publicity had gone overwhelmingly to those at the top of the project. The manager, finance officer and senior development workers had been feted by local council officials and councilors, had received excessive publicity in the local and regional press - and there was even talk of the chair of the management committee being awarded an OBE for her "inspiring leadership and commitment". Although receiving some satisfaction from the reflected glory of their superior colleagues, a profound sense of disillusionment, even envy, had started to grow within the organization. The manager had recognized this, and was faced with the problem of generating a new team ethos that accepted the validity of all staff effort: how could he effectively achieve this before the internal atmosphere became too enervating?*

## Example of Problem 4

*(How to obtain feedback on the effectiveness of community initiatives while they are being implemented?)*

*A management committee thought it was doing a very good job at running its project. Although the great majority of the staff and volunteers thought so too, some staff were more wary of claims of success, while the feedback from local residents and users of its services seemed to indicate that certain staff and specific services were not meeting the organization's objectives. When a member of the public brought this state of affairs to the notice of one staff member, and she informed the committee of it, it was agreed that the committee needed impartial feedback on how the project was working in reality - and not in the biased views of insiders and outsiders who had an interest in "talking up" the project. How was such impartial feedback best obtained?*

## Example of Problem 5
*(How to create and maintain community partnerships?)*

*The community partnership committee that had initiated and maintained the neighborhood project was losing members. There was a feeling that the foundation capacity building phase of the project had been successfully established, and that it was time for the original members of the partnership to leave in order to allow new members with new ideas to replace them. Although this process was accepted as being valid by the remaining partnership members, they were at a loss as to whom to invite to make up the original numbers. Some members favored inviting two local councilors (one from each of the main parties); others felt that such intervention could place the partnership in the middle of a political spotlight with politics and party points scoring becoming more relevant than impartial, but informed, judgments. Other possible members were considered but rejected by the committee. What strategy could the partnership committee put in place to regenerate its work? Would it be better to dissolve the existing partnership and start again with a totally new committee?*

The value of this type of written exercise to stimulate verbal discussion was that by writing down their experiences the students had had time, without outside pressure, to think clearly about the essence of the problems they had faced. In the discussions that followed, what emerged were the different types of approaches to community development work that the students had adopted. Some of these had been successful, others had not, but they all provided real-life illustrations of the problems faced by community workers and the range of options open to them when it came to tackling everyday situations.

In subsequent classes, I suggested to the class that it compile a list of more general themes that had had an impact on their work, and had also affected the current condition of their communities. We all agreed that these more general subjects should not be prepared beforehand but, rather, be discussed without notice at the discretion of the class tutor. We all felt that an unprepared discussion would be far more exciting and revealing about the class's knowledge of external factors influencing their communities, and their own work within them, than a "scripted", more formal session. After a consultation session, the list of questions we agreed included:

1. Why does society at large, including academic society, undervalue the practical knowledge of ordinary people and marginalized communities?
2. Why do we spend very little time in our education system considering the ideas and actions of poor people and disadvantaged communities in economic and social policy making?
3. Why don't we learn more about the achievements of the British labor movement as opposed to the actions of bankers and celebrities?
4. Why are certain philosophies used to reinforce the power relations among certain groups in UK society?
5. Should the voluntary sector become closely involved with the implementation of central government policies?

By asking these questions and posing these problems, I was working to get my class to acquire what Marcuse (1978:7) has labeled "rebellious subjectivity", and what Mezirow (1981:6) has called "the emancipatory process of becoming critically aware" - by developing a new conceptual sensibility among the students. I believed this sensibility was best achieved by introducing provocative questions - concerning aspects of world politics, community work and their impact on local communities - into the on-going class dialogue, to challenge the politically and culturally limited knowledge of the students, to provide "a solid and thorough critique of the material and intellectual culture"

(Marcuse,1961:61), and to get my students to remember that, in the words of Max Weber (1967: 201):

> *"The primary task of a useful teacher is to teach his students to recognize "inconvenient" facts - I mean facts that are inconvenient for their party opinions. And for every party opinion there are facts that are extremely inconvenient, for my opinion no less than others".*

My questions, I believed, played a learning role similar to Paulo Freire's generative themes. These are themes that are inherently and integrally related to other generative themes, and they are contained in, and embrace, other contexts with national or even global parameters. My questions were issues that were central to, and manifested in, the working lives of the students, but which also overlapped with their social and domestic issues. Through the collective investigation of these provocative questions, it was my intention that the students would learn to "read" their world critically and creatively (Freire, 1972: 68-95). Such an investigation invited the students to make contact with concepts previously concealed from their experience, especially in regard to unequal power structures in communities and in society in general. It also allowed them to make broad connections between individual experience and social issues, and between single problems and the larger social system.

When dealing with these questions (and others, introduced later, such as, "is community work really effective?", "can we ever cure community apathy?", and "has collective action any role in an individualistic society?"), the class started from the personal accounts of their own encounters - as volunteers, full-time workers, part-time workers, committee members and fund-raisers - with the system and its structures. This process involved a two-way transformation of subject matter and talk. On the one hand, the subject matter, a body of knowledge, was introduced by me as a problem for students to reflect on in their own language: the students, who came to the class with their own bodies of knowledge, were challenged to go beyond themselves into new terrain not generated from their own backgrounds. This dual transformation of subject knowledge and student knowledge was also, on the other hand, a transformation of my role and the role of class discourse: the two separate universes of academic discussion and student speech ended their isolation and were fused into what Bruffee (1999:47) has called a "non-standard, boundary discourse".

### Using formal language

Students entered my class generally ignorant of the language that I spoke. In this boundary zone, in which expertise and knowledge were weighted in favor of the tutor, they did not yet know what the other members of the class would define as rational. Much of what I said initially was irregular and eccentric. Sometimes it sounded to the students as if I did not really mean what I was saying, or else it felt like the conversation was totally foreign. Sometimes the students thought that my responses were a measure of their ignorance or a result of my virtuosity. Sometimes it was either one or both. But it was more often attributable to significant differences in the knowledge and language that made up the separate learning communities in which we were operating.

One way I attempted to change the students' understanding of the structure of knowledge was by using my knowledge of the function of language and of symbolic structures. By making the students aware of the hidden complexity of language, and developing their linguistic fluidity by deploying certain words and phrases, and using unusual syntax, I was trying to realign the verbal relationship between myself and the class so that we both learned new speech or, as Richard Rorty (1989:7) has put it, both teachers and students were abandoning "old vocabularies" and acquiring "a talent for speaking differently". In these circumstances, Felman (1982, in Bruffee1999: 208) explains, knowledge

*"is not a substance but a structural dynamic: it is not contained by any individual but comes about out of the mutual apprenticeship between two partially unconscious speeches which both say more than they know. Dialogue is thus the radical condition of learning and of knowledge, the analytically constitutive condition through which ignorance becomes structurally informative; knowledge is essentially, irreducibly dialogic."*

The importance of my group and collaborative learning therefore was that it acknowledged differences, and created conditions in which the students could negotiate the boundaries between the language and knowledge communities they belonged to and the one that I belonged to. I therefore posed questions, introduced themes and assigned tasks to my class of collaborative learners that self-consciously generated discussion among them. This was irregular discussion to my students, but to me it was normal. My aim was to help the students learn fluidity in this discussion to make it become normal discourse for them too - and I did this by challenging the conventions of the communities that the students already inhabited, and by contesting those conventions implicitly with the conventions of the knowledge community to which I belonged.

What I was offering my students by following this approach to learning was a group apprenticeship. I was assisting them in acquiring the skills they required to behave as "insiders" in their chosen discipline. As Jim Gee (1989:7) has pointed out, the social nature of teaching and learning must involve apprenticeship into the subject's discourse in order for students to succeed in their aims - but he adds that these discourses are not mastered solely through teacher-centered and directed instruction, but also by "apprenticeship into social practices through scaffolded and supported interaction with people". Gee also stresses the point that an apprenticeship approach can be immensely useful with adult students if it generates the acceptance and valorization of students' prior knowledge through a mentoring process.

## Telling stories

I also realised that one of the most effective instruments I could use to generate fluidity, along with my attempt to stimulate thinking and establish connections between ideas and concepts, was storytelling. I quickly saw, in the words of Terrence Gargiulo (2007: 203) that:

> "stories can offer a wealth of opportunities for inciting insights in others. Stories are a powerful tool for experiential learning because they have the power to move participants safely away from their comfort zones and help them to encounter something totally new. In this way, stories act as transporters. They are low-tech virtual reality simulators capable of fabricating vast intricate worlds of discovery. Every time a story is told, listeners enter the realm of the imagination".

Stories, as imagination stimulators, therefore give us, in Gargiulo's view, the chance to examine our operating models of the world. Through stories we realize we do not always have to conform to the cognitive frames we have assembled during our lives. We build these constructs of the world from our experiences which are hoarded as stories, and our behaviors are often unconsciously guided by these cognitive frames. Stories often become theatres of imagination where individuals can play with characters and plots to fashion new possibilities for themselves and others. As we become more conscious of how our experiences have built our store of cognitive frames, we gain more control over our behaviors. Our experiences are then stored in the personal archive of stories. The act of remembering a story thus helps us to bring together parts of ourselves for greater introspection, and stories themselves, in the words of Gargiulo, (1997: 204) become "vehicles for experiential learning because they allow us to tap into the wealth and variety of personal experience and share it with a group".

I then realised that if I analyzed the stories I was continually telling during my classes, they fell broadly into the six categories that have been identified by Annette Simmons, President of Group Process Consulting (quoted by Gargiulo 2007) as the type of stories required to influence, inspire and persuade people. These categories were:

- "Who Am I?" Stories
- "Why Am I Here?" Stories
- "My Vision" Stories
- Teaching Stories
- Values in Action Stories
- "I Know want you are thinking" Stories

### *"Who Am I?" Stories*

I realised that before I tried to impart knowledge and information - and influence my classes - it was essential that I establish enough trust to successfully deliver my learning programme to them. Because I lacked sufficient time to answer the inevitable "who is this person?" and "can I trust him?" questions through personal experience, I decided the most effective way of establishing trust was by telling stories that simulated examples of my trustworthiness, thereby letting the individual members of my classes decide for themselves on my acceptability as a trustworthy and knowledgeable teacher.

I told the classes stories of my domestic, educational and vocational background, giving details of my academic and work failures as well as my successes. I accepted that such stories were purely subjective, but gambled that class members would base their judgment of me on this type of evidence, because cold objective data did not go deep enough to engender trust - whereas my personal narratives would allow me to reveal who I really was, flaws and all, to my audience. My reasoning was that if my students thought I trusted them enough to show my flaws, they would trust me enough to show me theirs - and they would accept that true strength of character is found not in perfection but in an understanding of, and sympathy with, a person's limitations.

### *"Why Am I Here?" Stories*

I had taught long enough to accept that people will not always co-operate willingly with an outsider - and an academic to boot - because they often feel such a person possesses hidden agendas. I therefore had to provide a plausible explanation of my good intentions early on in the programme. I did this by outlining the reasons for my belief in collective endeavor to counter economic and social disadvantage, by telling stories of my upbringing in the Rhondda Valley and how I had witnessed the efforts of poor individuals to better themselves and their communities through combined action, and how this action gave rise to personal creativity and collective commitment. I outlined my own commitment to community development as a force for personal and communal improvement by narrating my involvement with specific regeneration groups, funding initiatives, warring committees and thrusting social entrepreneurs, despite the numerous frustrations and small advances involved. I stressed that I was still "fighting the good fight" by passing on my experience through the medium of adult education classes, to individuals and groups such as themselves, and that I was still willing to take up the challenge of collective endeavor and on-going perseverance. In brief, therefore, I made it plain that I genuinely wanted nothing for myself, or the organisation which I represented, other than the satisfaction that I was making a positive contribution to my students' development and, through this process, to the improvement of surrounding communities.

## "My Vision" Stories

I then reasoned that if my students were happy with who I was, and why I was there in their class, then they were ready to listen to what I thought they could get out of my presence. I realised that to do this effectively I should not just parrot a list of targets backed up by an arbitrary timeline, but that I should grab their imaginations by finding a story of my vision for local communities that connected with their own dreams. I realised that if I wanted to influence my class of activists in a significant way, I needed to give them a vision story that would fit into, and correspond with, their own visions. I recognized that a vision story helped weave all the positive pieces of the community development process - and the negatives and the resentments - together so that they made sense, and concurrently offered hope for the future. I saw the vision story as an antidote to meaningless frustration, which helped community workers live and work with purpose and meaning in a world of deprivation and frustration. I accepted too that I would have to tell not just one story, but a series of stories, in order to reflect the struggle of a range of community groups to achieve their visions and which would give us hope in our efforts to overcome the obstacles in our path.

## Teaching Stories

I wanted to impart certain skills to my students, but did not have the time to demonstrate these skills in situ or in a community development context. I thus had to find stories that successfully delivered these skills in an educational environment. Often the message I wanted to put across was less about what I wanted my students to do and more about how I wanted the skill implemented. I thus told a series of stories about how I succeeded in defusing some interpersonal conflicts in specific community committees, how I failed to achieve positive outcomes in others, how these results were influenced not just by personality traits and individual characteristics, but how meetings where these conflicts

92

were worked through were influenced by other factors such as poor seating arrangements, poor chairing skills, poor communication channels and so on. All the students had experienced similar situations, so my stories gave us all opportunities to examine our successes and our failures - and to draw out from these opportunities appropriate lessons for future successful action.

## *"Values-in-Action" Stories*

The most effective way to teach a value is by practical example. The second best way is by telling a story that provides an example, for by telling a story the storyteller instills values in a way that keeps people thinking about themselves and their own values. But values are often regarded as ideals, and as such are often viewed by some individuals as intangible, invisible and, by association, unachievable. I saw that to counter this view, and to influence my class to embrace particular values central to community work, I would have to tell them compelling stories throughout the course. I realised that a discussion of values would be meaningless without vivid and relevant stories to bring these values to life and engage my class at a personal level. To do this effectively, I had therefore to draw extensively again on my experience as a community worker and community educator - and I was extremely glad that in my store of experience I had enough stories to influence the values of my class and, eventually, the behaviors they adopted in their communities.

## *"I know what you are thinking" Stories*

Sometimes when I told a story some of the students accused me of reading their minds. I deliberately prepared for this by conducting research into the working background of my students and the roles that they were undertaking in the community. After I had discovered the work they were doing, I told stories that contained my own work experiences in similar fields, thereby identifying myself and my experiences with those of my students. They recognized that I, who had a wealth of knowledge about the type of work they were carrying out, had thought the same thoughts and walked the same walks as they had, thereby giving me greater credibility as a teacher and a human being. Such an approach also confirmed my belief that I was teaching correctly and was in tune with the hopes and fears of my students. I was therefore doing more than merely transferring knowledge and skills to them: I was going deeper, and engaging with them on a psychological level, so helping them face up to, and dispel, their fears about the way they were working, thinking and feeling.

## Public stories and mega-stories

But telling stories was not just a role played by tutors, I pointed out. It is a role played by practically all participants in the community development process. An individual worker begins the development process by making contact with an interested individual who is concerned about the state of her community and wants to do something about it. The community worker tells his stories about why he is in that specific community, about his beliefs, his history and how he thinks the community could be developed – and how individuals such as his contact can institute action to consciously alter the state of the community.

This is initially therefore a "community of two" – the worker who is a storyteller and the contact who is encouraged to become a storyteller and keeper of her community's ideals and aspirations. But a good community worker knows that this community of two is not sufficient to generate sustainable collective community action. The two must become three (and more eventually) if they are to genuinely initiate widespread, effective and sustainable development. In other words, the community worker must tell his own stories, listen to the stories of others, encourage the stories of as many people as possible and understand the concerns, hopes and dreams expressed in them. Such a process is an integral stage of enabling people to move their stories into the public consciousness, thereby helping them stimulate a wider interest in social change and raise a more general awareness of collective community action while simultaneously weaving what Lederach (2005:101) labels "relationships and connections that create the social spaces that form the invisible fabric of human community".

Next, while discussing the role of storytelling, I highlighted that in class, in work, and at home we were all operating within a mega-story, or global narrative, and that the stories we told about ourselves reflected the ideals, values and norms of the currently dominant mega-story. At present, this story was neoliberalism, the message of which was that our individual and global salvation lay in following the creed of market economics and social individualism. This story, during the last thirty years, I postulated, had shaped our understanding of the world, how we fitted into it, who we were and how we made and ordered our experiences. This global story had also legitimized economic and political power and helped frame our allegiances, how we formulated our values, and how we created meanings regarding economic, social and environmental systems, and ways of living with them - just as previous generations had responded to the mega-stories of Christianity, socialism, fascism and communism.

Our individual, personal stories thus existed within global stories which stressed their effectiveness in bringing about a better world that would nurture better human beings and a better society. In reality though, in my view, these global narratives were promulgated by those in power to further their own political and economic agendas. As part of a strategy to combat the current narrative, we all agreed that in our work to generate community involvement and a fairer society, we needed a new mega-story that would help us all find our way out of the grip of the current market focused narrative. We agreed too that we needed a story of sufficient influence to realign people and communities, and transform the public imagination, in order to act to overcome the multiple problems created by market-driven mega-stories - and to demonstrate what possibilities were available for transforming these problems by revealing to people the role they, as individuals and community members, could play in the new global vision. In the words of Arran Gare (1995);

*"In order for such stories to "work", to inspire people to take them seriously, to define their lives in terms of them, and to live accordingly, such stories must be able to confront and interpret the stories by which people are at present defining themselves and choosing how to live in an environmentally destructive way. It is also important to reveal how power operates, and show why those individuals who are concerned about the global environment crisis are unable effectively to relate their own lives to such problems. The new grand narrative must enable people to understand the relationship between the stories by which they define themselves as individuals, and the stories by which groups constitute themselves and define their goals - ranging from families, local communities, organizations and discursive formations, to nations, international organizations and humanity as a whole".*

But, asked the students, what is this new mega-story? I stated that I believed it was already being written, and that it was about environmental catastrophe and how we must respond to counter it. Such a story was so vast, so intricate, that the students felt powerless when considering it, and very dubious about any potential role they could play in its creation or evolution. I stated that, to me, their role was clear - it was to constantly explain, in work and in society generally, through discussion and conversation, and by writing reports, pamphlets, books as community leaders, teachers and academics, what the new story was, and why it was vital for people to act if society was to transcend the myopic vision of the global marketplace, and combat the instrumental values of consumerism that had crept into every corner of community life.

## An Overview

Learning in this environment was therefore innately dialectical and experiential. Students were encouraged to act as storytellers, as interrogators, as participants in conversation who were encouraged to throw their experiences and themselves into the cut and thrust of collective thought. Passive reception of course information counted for very little - it was conversing, thinking, reflecting, comparing and evaluating that were valued, with the tutor focusing on learning as an activity rather than as the absorption of a static body of knowledge: the course was primarily about process, and only secondary about product. In essence, this learning involved the whole class questioning the conflicting evidence available to it regarding whether or not matters had been ordered the best way they could have been in their communities, and whether or not local authorities, government bureaucracies, business networks, global corporations and local community organizations had acted with the best interests of their communities in mind.

## Reviving Community Conversations

I then explained to the class the importance of such unpredictable discussion, or dialogue, for their roles as community workers in the wider community. I pointed out that many community settings where the people they were working with (and hoped to work with) used to meet to talk and learn were disappearing at an alarming rate. These informal "hangouts" or "third places" as Oldenburg (1989) has labeled them – pubs, cafes, community centers, barbers shops, post offices and small shops generally – were valuable not just because they provided access to community consumer services but also because they encouraged conversation – the essence of community life and democracy. Such places were the focus of good talk, provided a meeting ground midway between the home (first place) and  work (second place), and brought together people involuntarily united by the mere fact of proximity. In these settings, particularly in "the Bracchi's" - the Italian owned cafes of the Valleys vividly brought to life in the stories of Rhondda novelist Gwyn Thomas - this fusion of involuntary association and conversation gave the third place a quasi-political, sometimes even subversive, character. Here, where schoolteachers, miners, clerks, the unemployed, students, shopping housewives and even councilors met, conversation was paramount and individuals were respected not for their wealth or career status but for their common sense and decency. Conversations in this environment were wide ranging and provided many participants with the awareness that the world was much wider than the current locale. As a result, such settings and the conversations they generated, had often stimulated lifetime interests in community action, politics, economics, philosophy, and learning generally, among many habitués.

But, I pointed out, urban poverty, the closure of many small businesses (according to the Campaign for Real Ale - November 2008 - 39 pubs are currently closing in the UK every week), the creation of office blocks, housing developments and out of town shopping sites were destroying the third places and the opportunities they afforded for such talk - talk which historically had generated pamphleteers, agitators, politicians, newspapermen, revolutionaries and other verbal types. Because these new developments, particularly the shopping malls, were peopled not by browsers and conversationalists but by committed shoppers, who did not cast about for familiar faces, and the dedicated, time orientated serving staff of corporate organisations who rarely indulged in unfocused conversation, a whole series of vocal, interpersonal communities, was rapidly disappearing – as was a vehicle for day to day conversation, debate and argument and, therefore, informal community-based education. As John Dewey (1927) believed that our search for reliable information about a given course of action was guided by the questions that arose during conversations and arguments, this was a seriously negative phenomenon, especially as it was only by subjecting our preferences, ideas and views to the test of debate that we came to understand what we knew and what we still needed to learn. Until we had to defend our opinions in public, they remained opinions – half-formed convictions based on random impressions and unexamined assumptions. It was the act of articulating and defending our views that lifted them out of the category of "opinions", gave them shape and definition, and made it possible for others to recognise them as a description of their own experiences as well.

I underlined this process by reference to my experiences as a young person using the facilities of another vital third place in my town, the local workmen's institute. Although initially attracted to the institute by the promise of cheap snooker, billiards and Hollywood films, I soon discovered it had a conversational and educational aspect to its role in the community - a role that was essentially informal but none the less powerful for that! Here I found opportunities for discussion and argument with the management committee, working miners, retired miners, council workers, unemployed workers, local government clerks, school teachers, trade union officials and political activists. These committed citizens told me tales of struggles for workplace democracy and social justice which linked my sheltered, academic ideas to the real, rough, tough world of employers, accountants, trade unions, bankers and politicians, and to the struggles of individuals and collective groupings (such as trade unions and voluntary groups) for some influence on how their workplaces and communities should be constituted.

I highlighted too the mental conversations I had with the newspaper journalists, authors and their writings that I discovered in the institute library. Here I was introduced to newspapers I never previously knew existed or those I thought were not available for the likes of me to read (The Times, Manchester Guardian, Daily Telegraph and Financial Times). Here I discovered, and consulted for my school homework, the works of Marx, Rousseau, Carlyle, and the poetry of Wordsworth and Coleridge. But I also found enjoyment and instruction in the novels of popular authors such as Agatha Christie, Graham Greene, John Steinbeck and Raymond Chandler. The latter in particular, in the shape of his world-weary but philosophical private eye, Philip Marlowe, provided me with an example of a character with a cause who did not fear to walk down mean streets to complete his promises to his clients but who was "himself not mean". Marlowe, a "shop soiled Sir Galahad" who was true to his own personal values, exhibited an on-going reflectiveness that generated in me a similar, considered, even wary, view of society. I complemented the essentially individualistic, but honourable, values and actions of Marlowe with the more collective ideals of Steinbeck, and in particular his odyssey of the poor dustbowlers, the Joads, during the Great Depression, in his famous work *The Grapes of Wrath* (1939). The comment of Ma Joad to her son Tom: "why Tom, us people will go on livin' when all them people is gone. Why Tom, we're the people that live. They ain't gonna wipe us out. Why, we're the people, we go on" - summed up the determination of ordinary people to achieve social and economic justice, and in many ways characterised the beliefs and actions - and determination - of the individuals who I met, mixed with, argued with and talked to in the miners' hall.

The hall was therefore my informal learning site, a genuine community university where I learned to see that informal education and politics were seriously interlinked. My teachers were men, and a few women who worked in the cinema, who were all older than me who had experienced hard times. Despite this, they were determined to struggle together to improve conditions for themselves, their families and their community. The ethos they espoused stressed the virtue of communal effort and mutual aid, the reasons for, and the results of which, are highlighted in the following passage (Benney: 27), which though it specifically applies to a Durham coalmining community could equally well apply to the south Wales of my youth:

> *"Nothing had come easily to this village. When it felt a need it had tried to supply it for itself, and if anyone opposed the effort the village had fought. Every institution in the village, with the exception of the post office and the church, the people had built for themselves or struggled for through the union...Personal ambition was tamed to the Lodge office, the committee table, the pulpit and the craft of the pit. The customs of the community, both underground and on the surface were old and honoured for their age; the double isolation of craft and geography had turned these people in upon themselves, so that they took their standards from their forebears instead of from the strangers in the city".*

The people I learned from, and with, in my informal third place thus embraced the concept of collective self-help as the best way to help the community survive and progress within the existing economic, social and political environment: and, between 1928 and 1934 in particular, a great variety of initiatives was developed by individuals like them in south Wales for this purpose. Communities created work by means of co-operatives and community-based industries, established clubs for the unemployed, initiated community service groups of various kinds including sick clubs and friendly societies, as well as forming networks of mutual-aid groups and resource providers; and even after the depth of the Great Depression had passed, this tradition of communal solidarity and local initiative to cope with community problems was used to mitigate the social distress caused by enduring long term unemployment.

This collective attitude towards social and economic action reflected, I believed, the general feeling of trust in South Wales communities - a feeling that was engendered by the fact that these communities were places where the inhabitants knew most of the people living and working around them, and where informal networks of support led to a culture of collective security and individual self worth. I illustrated my point by pointing out that my father was born in the same street that he died in over 70 years later, that he attended school a few streets away with his contemporaries, that he worked in a local factory with many of these contemporaries, belonged to the same union, drank in the same local club as them, got married and started a family at the same time as them - and eventually retired and then died at roughly the same time as them too. My mother also spent her life within the same social and geographical boundaries, as did the rest of my relatives - grandparents and great grandparents - who lived only a few streets away (together with a legion of "aunties" who seemed to spend an inordinate amount of time in our house). This was a very settled community based around a colliery that guaranteed employment - albeit dangerous and poorly paid - for many years. It was a community that was open and often not easy to obtain privacy in, a community where one's business and family relationships were known by a great many people. Despite these weaknesses, it was also a community that was settled, strong on solidarity at work and at home and above all, a site of living which generated trust - trust in one's own beliefs and abilities, in the power of education for self and social improvement, and in other people's help and support in times of personal and economic strain and stress.

But with the closure of the collieries and steel works in the 1960 and 70s, the increased social mobility, the emasculation of the unions and rise of free market philosophies in the 1980s, families left to work elsewhere, poverty became more marked, and the community lost its sense of coherence and communal trust. The workmen's institute closed and so another bulwark of mutuality was lost. This situation was repeated across all the Valleys leaving their communities significantly poorer educationally and economically. This increased poverty and inequality was not limited to the Valleys though. Rather, during the 1980s and 1990s, it was a widespread phenomenon which affected large areas of the United Kingdom and even the USA. Indeed, the following description of the USA by Harvard professor Robert Putnam in his book *Bowling Alone* (2000: 359) - a survey of community life during the 1980s and 1990s in the United States - could have equally well have applied to south Wales:

> "*In terms of the distribution of wealth and income, America in the 1950s and the 1960s was more egalitarian than it had been in more than a century...those same decades were also the high point of social connectedness and civic engagement. Record highs in equality and social capital coincided...Conversely, the last third of the twentieth century was a time of growing inequality and eroding social capital... The timing of the two trends is striking: Sometime around 1965 - 70 America reversed course and started becoming both less just economically and less well connected socially and politically*".

Furthermore, one significant consequence of such inequality and diluted connectedness was, as American political scientist, Eric Uslaner, has pointed out in his book *The Moral Foundations of Trust* (2002) that "trust cannot thrive in such an unequal world" and that income inequality is the prime determinant of trust, having a greater impact on its viability than rates of inflation, economic growth or unemployment. He also believes that greater inequality leads to less caring people and less mutuality in relationships - with the result that mistrust and inequality reinforce each other.

Uslaner is also of the opinion - as is Putnam in *Bowling Alone* (2000) - that trust is a vital ingredient of a co-operative society. He shows that in the USA, people who trust others, including strangers, are more likely to do voluntary work and give money to charity. Such people also tend to see immigration as a benefit to society, believe that America is held together by shared values, and that everybody should be treated with respect and tolerance. Uslaner and Putnam also believe that high levels of trust mean that people feel secure, they have less to worry about, and they see others as co-operative rather than competitive. These views appear to be conclusively confirmed by the extensive data presented by Wilkinson and Pickett in their book *The Sprit Level; Why More Equal Societies Almost Always Do Better* (2009) which examines information from a range of sources to reveal that almost every modern social and environmental problem – lack of trust, lack of community spirit, ill-health, drugs, violence, mental illness, long working hours and large prison populations – is more likely to occur in a less equal society.

I therefore saw my class, and the focused conversations it encouraged, as going some small way to countering this loss of trust by creating a space where people could debate together and adopt methods of discourse in pursuit of consensual agreements. As well as a class, it was a meeting place, a new community-based third place, where committed activists could meet in a trusting atmosphere, to learn to converse intelligently, discuss matters that linked them with the outside world, and discover alternative ways of thinking and acting. In short, I was creating an environment which students could subsequently replicate in their own community centres - thereby initiating their own contemporary third places in which they could develop similar emancipatory conversations focused on questions such as: what is social justice? What is economic justice? What is the best way to distribute wealth? How should we value things? and, How can we cultivate in individual citizens and communities an ethical life of mutual responsibility and respect? The posing of such questions in non-threatening public third places would also help, I believed, to combat apathy, stimulate argument and so reignite trust in other people, interest in local collective action and belief in participative democracy.

# PART THREE:

# THEORY AND REALITY

# – MAKING CONNECTIONS

# Chapter Five

## Using Theory

In subsequent classes, linking critical thinking about local communities with an exploration of dominant ideologies, and how these ideologies, pervade and erode local attitudes, I introduced the students to the theories of significant writers and thinkers in the critical tradition. "Critical theory" has its origins in the theories of the "Frankfurt School", a term used to describe the work of the Institute for Social Research founded in 1923 at the University of Frankfurt. "Critical theory" became the term used to describe the social criticism characteristic of the diverse scholars - Marcuse, Adorno, Horkheimer, Fromm and Habermas - who made up the School, and of "outside" thinkers such as Antonio Gramsci, Myles Horton and Paulo Freire. One important strand of critical theory is the notion that criticism of ideology can eliminate "false consciousness" – an attitude or belief that interferes with an individual or group's ability to perceive the objective nature and source of its oppression - and so allow individuals and groups to resist oppressive power constituencies. Only by analyzing and criticizing false consciousness and common sense, notions that pass themselves off as value free, and which have constrained the world views of many deprived communities, can individuals and groups discern whose interests these notions really serve - and who might benefit if such notions, and the social structures they support, were disrupted and transformed.

My students were not initially enamored with my decision to introduce "theory" into the programme. They saw the concept as too academic, abstract, and complex to be of any practical use in tackling important social, economic and political issues. I responded by admitting that some academics did indeed treat theory in this fashion, but that such abstract theories were, as Thomas (2002) has pointed out, but one end of a spectrum of theorizing that consisted of ideas drawn from logical reasoning at the other end - and that it was this type of thinking and theorizing that I was concerned with. I also pointed out that theoretical analysis can form the foundation for thinking individuals to create their own critical analysis to help them to act collectively against the economic, neo-liberal theories and activities currently pervading society. In other words, theoretical analysis could be used as a resource for connecting community issues to those areas of conflict in which it becomes possible to open up learning spaces where people can challenge the actual conditions of dominant power, and create the promise of a future that contains a range of practical collective alternatives. Theory in this sense, I submitted, becomes a resource and both highlights and interprets – and thereby connects a broad range of community and educational conversations to previously unconsidered social ideas, practices and political possibilities. In the words of Henry Giroux (2004: 100), "While theory is not a substitute for politics, it does provide the very precondition for a critically self-conscious notion of individual and social agency as the basis for shaping the larger society".

Given the time constraints of the teaching programme, I decided to focus my discussions of theory and its uses on two representatives of the Frankfurt School and three outsiders who had been influenced by the School's ideas. I started the exploration of theory by reminding the students that the two questions most frequently asked in class were "why is public apathy, another term for passivity, submissiveness, and even numbness, reaching epidemic proportions when it comes to social, economic, environ-mental and political issues?" and "what can we as community workers do about it?" I pointed out that with the growth of capitalism, the spread of globalism and the move from an indus-trial to an information society, we are, according to John Ralston Saul (1995), an unconscious civilization. We are caught up in an environment where our knowledge does not make us conscious because information comes to us indiscriminately and is disconnected from usefulness. We are swamped with information and have very little control over it. As a result, we experience a loss of coherence because we no longer have a coherent conception of ourselves, our communities or our relationships of one to another. This situation, together with the workings of the education system and class structure, has splintered collective identities, forced people apart - and delivered them into more and more specialized roles, thereby leaving them isolated, their social experience detached and vicarious - and less prepared for participation in public discourse. As Zygmunt Bauman (1999: 65) has insightfully observed, "The public has been emptied of its own separate contents – it is now but an agglomeration of private troubles, worries, and problems".

## Jurgen Habermas

Next, I introduced a quote from Albert Einstein into the discourse: "the world is a dangerous place to live: not because of the people who are evil, but because of the people who don't do anything about it", and discussed how corrosive and negative apathy can be. I highlighted the horrific consequences of communal apathy from Nazi Germany and the Soviet Union, and further used the quote as an introduction to the work of Jurgen Habermas who had analyzed the growth of apathy, and its implications for society as a whole, in great depth. To him, the logic of capitalistic economic development was that "the unavoidable division of labor results in an unequal distribution of information and expertise" (Habermas, 1996: 325). Because of this, access to technical knowledge and use of IT were determined partly by people's education, income, occupation and status. These factors reflected the general organization of society for the benefit of specific groupings. Without access to or knowledge of communication technology, large sections of society were debarred from the public flow of information and, without membership of an influential group or association, people had no channel through which to voice an opinion.

What were some of the consequences of the decline of the public sphere? To Habermas, one was the growth of a destructive privatism, and an increased focus on the self. When people have no way to influence discussion and decisions in society or their community, they may as well pursue private goals without regard to the effects this pursuit has on others (Habermas, 1975). Another consequence of the decline of the public sphere is the increasing diminution of civil society. Habermas defines civil society as "composed of those more or less spontaneously emergent associations, organizations, and movements that, attuned to how social problems resonate in the private life spheres, distil and transmit such reactions in amplified form to the public sphere" (Habermas, 1996:367). In other words, the discussions people have within communities in groupings with democratic, egalitarian and voluntary structures - sports clubs, craft and art groups, local environmental associations, some religious organizations, play groups and community centers - about specific issues that affect them, help evaluate the topics and ideas that are subsequently transferred and considered in the wider public sphere are withering away, with the result that:

> *"the public (sphere) collapses into the personal, and the personal becomes the only politics that is, the only politics with a tangible referent or emotional valence, and it is within such an utterly personalized discourse that human actions are shaped and agency is privatized"* (Giroux: 224).

So civil society is being eroded as state power, and the capitalist pursuit of profit (*the system*), become ever more dominant. This erosion is most noticeable in what Habermas labels "the lifeworld". In his book *The Theory of Communicative Action* (1987a:131 quoted in Brookfield 2005:239), Habermas describes the lifeworld as all those assumptions that frame how we understand our experience of life and how we try to convey that experience to others - the vast stock of taken-for-granted knowledge and understanding that give people purpose and direction in their lives. The lifeworld always remains in the background but is all pervasive, unknowable and impenetrable. Additionally, in his book *Between Facts and Norms* (1996), Habermas states that the lifeworld is "a penetrating, yet latent and unnoticed presence...a sprawling, deeply set, and unshakeable rock of background assumptions, loyalties and skills" which provide a largely unconscious template for all we think and do.

When political and economic systems – power and money - operate independently of civil society, and increasingly eat away at the lifeworld then, in the words of Brookfield (2005:239), "all the discussions we have in the public sphere, and all the topics we raise for discussion in the organizations of civil society, are profoundly tainted and compromised without our ever being aware of that fact". Furthermore, when major decisions affecting communities are taken by those systems without any opportunity for dissention, or for modifications to be considered, our democratic society is facing an insidious and significant threat. Why join a community group or a neighborhood association if all its members can do is chose between options designed and delivered to it by the state's bureaucratic apparatus or corporate interests? In other words, the permeation of state political agendas throughout society, alongside the ability of capital to exploit new avenues for wealth creation, have resulted in more and more decisions affecting communities being based on the bottom line of power and profit. *The system* is standardizing the national (even international) environment in which individuals and communities exist. In this respect, the state and corporate interests are proactively instilling a common, uniform, accepting  mindset into people's heads - a process more likely to prove successful than any attempt to alter ideas already existing there. As a result of this process, as Mark Fisher (2009: 34) has commented:

*"Work and life become inseparable. Capitalism follows you when you dream. Time ceases to be linear, becomes chaotic, broken down into punctiform divisions. As production and distribution are restructured, so are nervous systems. To function effectively as a component of just-in-time production you must develop a capacity to respond to unforeseen events, you must learn to live in conditions of total instability, or "precarity", as the ugly neologism has it".*

Television and the press are powerful means of ensuring uniformity of belief in this system and, in the words of Smail (1998: 87), "the mentality which invented factory farming is not slow to appreciate the regularity and predictability to be achieved by standardizing experiential as well as nutritional diets". Furthermore, as Smail (1998:87) also points out:

*"used to it though one is, it is still quite an eerie experience to walk around any residential suburb after dark and to note the extent to which people are imbibing exactly the same impressions and information from the glowing screens: one only has to check the evening's programme to know what people will be talking about the next morning".*

The average UK citizen spends about one-third of his or her waking life watching television. The neurological implications are significant. In 1969 Herbert Krugman discovered what occurs physiologically in the brain of a person watching television. Very quickly the brain waves switched from predominantly beta waves (indicating conscious attention) to predominantly alpha waves (indicating lack of attention) due to the release of the body's natural opiates. Further research revealed that the brain's left hemisphere, which processes information logically and analytically, tunes out, so allowing the right hemisphere, which processes information emotionally and non-critically, to operate unimpeded. One implication of this process, in the words of Joyce Nelson

(1992:82) is that:

*"As real-life experience is increasingly replaced by the mediated "experience" of television-viewing, it becomes easy for politicians and market researchers of all sorts to rely on a base of mediated mass experience that can be evoked by appropriate triggers. The TV "world" becomes a self-fulfilling prophecy: the mass mind takes shape, its participants acting according to media-derived impulses and believing them to be their own personal volition arising out of their own desires and needs. In such a situation, whoever controls the screen controls the future, the past, and the present".*

The mindset generated by the TV "world", particularly its audience's acceptance of the status quo and the consequent loss, and fear of, critical thinking and discussion is admirably caught in a passage from the novel *The Long Lavender Look* (page 96) written by the novelist John D MacDonald in 1970 when his private investigator, Travis McGee (a direct literary descendant of Philip Marlowe), describes the disorientating impact of the loss of popular television series, and their heroic characters, on American families:

*"And the screens go dark, from the oil-bound coasts of Maine to the oily shores of Southern California. Chief Ironsides retires to a chicken farm and Marshall Dillon shoots himself in the leg, trying to outdraw the hard case from Tombstone. The hatchet bounces back off the tree and cuts down tall Daniel Boone. The American living room becomes silent. The people look at each other, puzzled, coming out of the sweet, long, hazy years of automated imagination.*

*Where'd all the heroes go, Andy?*

*Maybe honey, they went where all the others went, a long time ago. Way off someplace. Tarzan and Sir Galahad and Robin Hood. Ben Casey and Cap'n Ahab and The Shadow and Peter Rabbit. Went off and joined them.*

*But what are we going to do, Andy? What are we going to do?*
*Maybe...talk some. Think about things.*
*Talk about* what? *Think about* what? *I'm scared, Andy".*

Perhaps therefore, I suggested provocatively to the class, we really are not too far removed from what George Orwell wrote in his novel *1984* when describing how The Party controlled the nation's underclass, or proles, as follows:

*"So long as they (the proles) continued to work and breed, their other activities were without importance. Left to themselves, like cattle turned loose upon the plains of Argentina, they had reverted to a style of life that appeared to be natural to them, a sort of ancestral pattern. They were born, they grew up in the gutters, they went to work at twelve, they passed through a brief blossoming period of beauty and sexual desire, they married at twenty, they were middle-aged at thirty, they died, for the most part, at sixty. Heavy physical work, the care of home and children, petty quarrels with neighbors, films, football, beer and, above all, gambling filled up the horizon of their minds. To keep them in control was not difficult".*

This quote stimulated a great deal of discussion about working class stereotypes, especially those perpetuated by the more right wing popular newspapers. All the students pointed out that they considered themselves working class, and in no way did they correspond to "the proles" of Orwell's novel. They did concede that there did exist in their communities individuals and families who exhibited some of the characteristics listed by the novelist (even allowing for his use of exaggeration to create an effect), who's lifestyle had recently (during 2007) been satirized in the Channel 4 television series *Shameless*, but who, in their view, formed a very small proportion of their communities and society as a whole - but a proportion which they believed had also undoubtedly increased in size during the last ten years.

The group equated Orwell's proles with the current underclass therefore and thought that his description had some relevance. I said that I thought apathy and indifference to the state of society was currently common among both the underclass and the working class proper. From what I saw of local community life at first hand, and of UK society as a whole, from reading national newspapers and viewing national television news, the whole working class, with one or two notable exceptions such as the Miners' Strike and the Poll Tax riots, had temporarily lost its collective self-consciousness and its belief in itself as an effective political entity. It appeared to me that its involvement with service jobs, celebrity dreams, Lottery riches, credit cards, and devotion to cheap lager and televised football, meant that the British working class had lost its ability to identify, let alone fight for, notable causes. Perhaps, I suggested, all this explained why the British were so obsessed with watching endless replays of the second world war because, by doing so, they saw themselves as they might have been now - acting out collectively something they actually believed in, demonstrating a common commitment to justice, and making sacrifices to challenge a malignant power that threatened their distinctive way of life via the creeping asphyxiation of the public spirit, the intellect and the will to resist.

But I pointed out that I had used the word "temporarily" in my response because the idea that the working class was terminally apathetic, finished as an active, creative force in society was not a new idea. Talk about "the ignorant masses" had been expressed many times in the past, particularly among academics and the "chattering classes" - a point made by Raymond Williams in his 1958 essay *Culture is Ordinary* - when he refuted such claims and wrote in response:

*"There is a distinct working-class way of life with its emphasis of neighborhood, mutual obligation and common betterment, as expressed in the great working-class political and industrial institu-*

*tions; (it) is in fact the best basis for any future English society. As for the arts and learning, they are...a national inheritance...available to everyone. So when the Marxists say that we are living in a dying culture, and that the masses are ignorant, I have to ask them, as I asked them then (in the 1940s), where on earth they have lived. A dying culture, and ignorant masses, are not what I have known and see".*

My students replied to this point by highlighting that it was over 50 years since Williams had written this essay, and that during that time the great working-class political and industrial institutions that had fostered the basic collective ideal as the basis for a better society had largely withered away: the trade unions had been emasculated by labor laws introduced by Mrs. Thatcher, and successive Conservative and Labor governments, the co-operative movement had been marginalized, and the Labor Party, that had formed the spearhead of the working class movement for equality and social improvement, had "gone over to the enemy" and adopted a market orientated philosophy and eagerly embraced a neoliberal view of the economy and society. As a result, the students believed that if the masses were not ignorant, they appeared uncritically satisfied with the current individual-focused status quo - and that only a significant economic or political crisis would help stir the people from their consumer induced languor.

In our next class, we discussed the impact of television on children, and how the origins of apathy and indifference are sown early in life. I remembered how, talking in 2003, the creator of BBC children's programmes *Bagpuss, Ivor the Engine* and *The Clangers* - Oliver Postgate - mused on how childrens' television had become increasingly commercialized and, as a result, increasingly uniform and conventional in content and format. Postgate's view is worth quoting at length, for after pointing out that "children are no longer children, they are a market" in the eyes of television entrepreneurs, he added:

> "Finally, let me offer you the following thought. Suppose that I am part of a silent Martian invasion, and that my intention is slowly to destroy the whole culture of the human race. Where would I start? I would start where thought first grows. I would start with children's television. My policy would be to give the children only the sort of thing they "already know they enjoy", like a fizzing diet of manic jelly-babes. This would no doubt be exciting, but their hearts and their minds would receive no nourishment, they would come to know nothing of the richness of human life, love and knowledge, and slowly whole generations would grow up knowing nothing about anything but violence and personal supremacy. Is that a fairy-tale? Look around you." (The Guardian, 10 December 2008).

Views such as these, together with Habermas' ideas, made somber listening for my students as potential community activists, but they at least made clear the condition of the society in which the students would have to operate. It was one where the system was gradually imposing its values on communities, where former certainties focused on religion, the state, the community itself, and the family, had been severely weakened, and where competition was replacing co-operation in ordinary daily lives. Such an overtly somber analysis made some students question whether the picture was in fact really as black as Habermas had painted it. They pointed out that the writings of local authors such as Gwyn Jones (in *Times Like These*), Gwyn Thomas (in *The Dark Philosophers and All Things Betray Thee*), Jack Jones (in *Rhondda Roundabout*), Lewis Jones (in *Cwmardy and We Live*) and Raymond Williams (in *Border Country*) had stressed the solidarity of working class life in the south Wales Valleys during the 1930s and 40s. During this period there had been poverty and disadvantage in abundance, but there had also been hope, a sense of collective solidarity, discipline, institutions, a commitment to the power of community to generate change, and a belief in a better future - a belief in possibilities which could not then be foreseen, meanings not then revealed, and values whose worth could not then be measured in purely practical terms, but which would, many believed, surely triumph eventually for the benefit of all individuals and communities – as they ultimately did with the creation of a Welfare State.

I pointed out, in Habermas's defense, that he saw the struggle of civil society against this colonization by the system as a major mission for community activists such as themselves, and he believed that civil society was the site where this struggle should take place. I then quoted a passage from *Bowling Alone* (2000: 413) by Robert Putnam, which offered the author's view on how the decline of collective life, and the need to restore what he calls "social connectedness", can be achieved:

> *"Let us find ways to ensure that by 2010 many more Americans will participate in the public life of our communities - running for office, attending public meetings, serving on committees, campaigning in elections and even voting. ...Campaign reform (above all, campaign finance reform) should be aimed at increasing the importance of social capital - and decreasing the importance of financial capital - in our elections..."*

It was therefore by shoring up communities, by affirming all the groups and organizations operating on democratic and collaborative lines (and constructed by trust), by entering politics, by creating and sustaining grass-roots initiatives -  and by subjecting the forces of control to the consensus of active citizens who have rediscovered the power of critical reflection - that Habermas and Putnam believed activists could best defend their communities (and society in general) from the ravages of this impersonal, technocratic and meritocratic system. I also informed my students that if they accepted this role they had to totally commit themselves to it, even though they would not know, as they did so, whether this commitment would be an effective catalyst for genuine social change. But I stressed the fact that they could not predict a positive outcome should not, as Smail (1998: 131) has pertinently observed, prevent them from trying to achieve one:

> *"We have bought the belief that if one cannot change the world it is not worth trying and so we have become morally and politically paralyzed. Part of the process of growing up entails the recognition that "trying" is something to be done whether or not it has any degree of observable success. We have to reckon with the wastefulness of human society, to accept what is a fact as a fact; not only is it in most cases impossible to tell whether one's efforts in a given direction are or have been of any avail, but one must be prepared for the near certainty that they will have no measurable effect at all".*

I suggested that this view contained a great deal of truth, and that if the community did implement a development and action strategy, then it would be an act of faith in the ingenuity and determination of that community; and the implementers would have to recognize that often, during this process, they would certainly be in the business of small profit margins. The rationale for community action therefore, to continue the business metaphor, was, in my view, not that it guaranteed to make a fortune but that it would maintain an enterprise where no other action would, that it would create certain benefits for producers and consumers alike, that it would possibly yield a small profit year by year but, most importantly of all, if there was a reasonable profit to be made, it would create the right circumstances for making it.

In other words, communities and community workers must be prepared to make sacrifices if they have certain values and beliefs and are prepared to act on them - a view forcefully endorsed by a former community organizer from Chicago who is now President of the United States or "the most powerful man in the world":

*"After all, talk is cheap; like any value, empathy must be acted upon. When I was a community organizer back in the eighties, I would often challenge community leaders by asking them where they put their time, energy, and money. Those are the true tests of what we value, I'd tell them, regardless of what we'd like to tell ourselves. If we aren't willing to pay a price for our values, if we aren't willing to make some sacrifices in order to realize them, then we should ask ourselves whether we truly believe in them at all".* (Barack Obama 2007: 68).

I also pointed out that we should see community action as part of a broad educational strategy that influenced the wider society. I saw us all as members of society with interlocking interests and values and, though these were being eroded by the activities and individualistic attitudes of consumer capitalism, we were still interdependent citizens of the world - and that an appreciation of this interdependence at every level was essential to our human future. Indeed, in my view, this very physical, social and emotional interdependence made the need for critical thinking essential, and the need for community activists to spread such thinking as widely as possible throughout society, via community action, to combat a sense of defeatism, vital. What I was saying, in essence, mirrored the belief of Jacques Derrida (2001:7) that critical thinking provides individual activists and groups with an educational tool to challenge the presupposition that there are no alternatives to the existing social order, while simultaneously stressing the dynamic, still unfinished elements of a democracy to be realized. I also stressed that the "common ground" of everyday life is a space in which an emancipatory politics can be fashioned that, in the words of Alain Badiou (1998:11) "consists in making seem possible precisely that which, from within the situation, is declared to be impossible".

## Herbert Marcuse

When I was an undergraduate student in the 1960s, I reminisced, many left-leaning students were influenced by the music of folk singers such as Bob Dylan and Joan Baez, and the works of various political and philosophical thinkers such as Che Guevara, Frantz Fanon and Albert Camus, most of whom have subsequently fallen out of fashion and been replaced by "post-modern" or "poststructuralist" theorists such as Foucault, Derrida and Baudrillard. Another writer who had an impact on my thinking about society, and the ways in which people were influenced to act in certain ways, particularly as consumers, was the American psychologist Vance Packard. In the 1960s Packard published three books – *The Hidden Persuaders* (1962), *The Status Seekers* (1963) and *The Waste Makers* (1967) which revealed a society increasingly manipulated by commercial and political interests. I found Packard's ideas stimulating, but found my academic tutors rather dismissive. They felt that Packard's works "lacked intellectual rigor", overstated his case and were "rather journalistic" in tone. I believed, on the contrary, that the books described conditions and situations as they really existed, and that the conditions they described were pertinent and held lessons for the population as a whole – as well as idealistic students.

I later became acquainted with the work of the German/American political writer Herbert Marcuse, whose publications met with the general approval of my intellectual mentors. Marcuse expressed deeper insights into the contemporary world, and I soon regarded his ideas as raising critical thought about society, and how it could be changed, to a new level (while still valuing the thoughts of Packard). In his 1964 book *One Dimensional Man*, Marcuse elaborated on Hegel's belief that a thing possesses two dimensions: what it was at any given time (its positive side) and what it could become (its negative side). One-dimensional thought only sees what is and not what can and ought to be. This situation has been created by industrial society's generation of false needs which bind individuals to the existing system of production and consumption through the manipulation of advertising, mass media, scientific management techniques and popular ways of thinking. Marcuse particularly attacks consumerism as a form of social control because it distorts people's perception of freedom by only allowing them to choose products rather than ideas. In his view, modern capitalism is just as totalitarian as fascism. The difference is that it relies on "the scientific management of instincts", rather than on terror, to keep the working class docile. His belief therefore is that technical progress has not only made possible a non-repressive society of abundance, but has also provided the means for manipulating the mass of the population into accepting and being satisfied with the existing social and political system. (Marcuse 1964; Brookfield 2005; Kellner 1984 and 1989; and Wikipedia entries for *Herbert Marcuse* and *Totalitarian Democracy*).

My class thought that Marcuse was very significantly overstating his case. Although not born until later, many of them did not accept that western society in the 1950s and 60s was just as totalitarian as the societies created by Nazi fascism or Soviet Communism. My counter-argument was that Marcuse was using hyperbole to highlight his ideas - he wanted to shock people and so stimulate thought on the subject. I believed he knew full well that 1950s and 1960s capitalism was not comparable with fascist Germany and communist Russia, and that it was definitely not a conscious, systematic, tyrannical system. But, I posed the question, "what is the state of western, capitalist society today?" and backed this up with a lengthy quote for discussion from Benjamin Barber's book *Consumed* (2007):

*"there is considerable evidence to suggest that the ubiquity of consumerism, the pervasiveness of advertising and marketing, and the homogenization of culture and values around an infantilizing commerce together have created a cultural ethos which, although not totalitarian, robs liberty of its civic meaning and threatens pluralism's civic vitality. Combined with privatization and branding,*

*this commercial homogenization has made us less free as citizens and less diverse as a society than traditional liberals conceive us to be or than traditional capitalist producers and consumers think we are".*

I accepted straightaway that we still lived in a democratic society, but argued that the trends Marcuse described in the 1960s, and lucidly listed above by Barber, have accelerated significantly since then, so that his basic arguments are now more relevant than ever for students working in the field of community development. His basic premise, laid out in his *An Essay on Liberation* (1969), is that men and women are no longer conscious of their own oppression because technical progress has ensured a copious, on-going supply of commodities to satisfy the needs of the population. The philosopher Isiah Berlin in his *Four Essays in Liberty* (1969) also believed we are living in a time of "negative liberty" where individuals are shielded from radical ideas and so have little existential freedom, but are granted "internal" liberty to pursue recreational and consumer interests. In other words, commercial media and other social forces not only shape the population's beliefs, hopes and dreams, but its needs as well. Having convinced people that they are in some way deficient, the media then offer them ways to fulfill themselves, usually through the consumption of goods and services. This creation of false needs is central, in Marcuse's view, to the integration of the population into the social order (1969:11). Through advertising, through a mass of "sexy" images of affluence, people are shackled to a mechanistic and wasteful culture via promises of a share of its riches. As a result, consumer goods have formed a vital ingredient of social control throughout the twentieth century.

What surprised my students, after listening to my outline of Marcuse's thoughts, was how little the categories of commodities had changed in the last forty years. Substitute "Jaguar" for "car" and "fitted kitchen" for kitchen; substitute iPod for hi-fi set, and Mallorca and Florida for Barry Island and Porthcawl, and we all agreed we had today's dream list. By discussing Marcuse's ideas, especially those contained in *One Dimensional Man*, the students began to see that such services and devices, and the stimulated desire to own, and frequently update, them was repressive in the sense that they bound people to a corporate work environment that increasingly demanded their labor and souls. People are now forced to work long hours to pay for the goods that have become "essential", and they must conform in all respects to the corporate culture from which they draw their salaries (1964:159). Freedom to live alternatively - to explore less lucrative but more satisfying jobs - is severely restricted as a result. In this one-dimensional society, the conflicts and contradictions generated, and which Karl Marx predicted would stimulate revolutionary thoughts and ideas, have been safely assimilated into the status quo, thereby making "servitude palatable and perhaps even unnoticeable" (1964:24).

We identified a number of areas where this absorption was particularly evident: the assimilation of middle and working class workers in service and administrative occupations, the merging of the interests of workers and management by convincing the former that trade unions are no longer in their best interests, the merging of political philosophies and the subsequent loss of political partisanship, and what has been called "the mediated opening of private spheres of existence to public voyeurism" via an intrusive press and media obsessed with celebrity and sex. Most significantly, however, is the merger of business and government: the handing over of managerial and leadership roles in the National Health Service to US and European profit-orien-tated firms, the appointment of private companies to build public utilities via the Private Finance Initiative, the allocation of educa-tional establishments, such as city academies, to private engineering and car-sales firms, the railway system to individual entrepreneurs and their companies, and the reliance of a Labor government on the teachings and philosophies of right wing, neo-liberal think tanks such as the Adam Smith Institute.

But Marcuse goes further and considers the use of language in contemporary society as a tool of the dominant interests. He argues that the language of "the defense laboratories and the executive offices, the governments and the machines, the time-keepers and manager, the efficiency experts and the political beauty parlors...orders and organizes...induces people to do, to buy, and to accept" (1964: 86). In such an authoritarian setting, language itself becomes authoritarian, directing peoples thoughts and limiting their imaginations rather than serving as a means of autonomous expression and the exploration of alliterative realities. One-dimensional language, in other words, plays an important role in shaping thought into a one dimensional consciousness by extinguishing conceptual, critical thought, which depends upon sensitivity to nuance, contradiction and ambiguity (1964:174).

In addition, Marcuse points out that authoritarian language reduces a phenomenon to its present manifestation and, in so doing, it destroys other interpretations. He writes, "Remembrance of the past may give rise to dangerous insights...Remembrance is a mode of dissociation from the given facts, a mode of "mediation" which breaks, for short moments, the omnipresent power of the given facts" (1964:87-94). But, he also points out, authoritarian language is not only anti-historical, it is also anti-future because the ability to imagine a future that differs from the present is seen as dangerously subversive of contemporary society. This trend to stifle critical consciousness and thought has become even more pronounced in the fifty years since Marcuse put forward these ideas, so much so that as the critic Slavoj Zizek (2004, quoted in Barber 2007: 88) has pertinently observed, the consumer market now offers products that make choice easy, so by-passing any need for critical assessment - *"products deprived of their malignant property: coffee without caffeine, cream without fat, beer without alcohol...virtual sex without sex, the Colin Powell doctrine of war without casualties as war without war, the redefinition of politics as expert administration as politics without politics".*

Authoritarian language, and the techniques it utilizes, according to Marcuse, curtail the meaning of language and severely promote unreason in a system where everyday reality is posited as rationality. Because of these developments, one-dimensional man has lost his revolutionary consciousness: his ability to transcend the present, to negate it either in his individual thoughts and actions or in co-operation with others through collective action has largely disappeared. What Marcuse is saying in essence is not simply that the great majority of the population has been taught to accept capitalism, but that their psychological nature has been modified so that they now accept capitalism instinctively and have come to love their servitude – thanks to the consumer society's ability to create "the thorough assimilation of mind with facts, of thought with required behavior, of aspirations with reality" (1964:252). But, if this is really the case, certain questions inevitably follow for community activists and educators, such as: "how can we persuade the mass of the population to recognize their situation and take action to change it?" and "If the majority of the people are not free agents, but have been brainwashed into needing capitalism as part of their psychological make-up, what chance does community action and critical education stand in the face of such an ingrained scenario?"

The French psychoanalyst and philosopher Jacques Lacan has given us some hope however when addressing these questions. He suggests that ignorance, and acceptance of the status quo, is not a passive state but rather an active excluding from consciousness - a refusal by people to acknowledge that their subjective selves have been personally and actively created out of the social practices and consumerised information surrounding them, because they lack the critical thought necessary to reconstruct that knowledge that they choose not to know. Therefore, I pointed out, the situation was not entirely hopeless, because although the great mass of the population might be apathetic, brainwashed, and accepting of the current status quo, there were some individuals (such as Kanter's change masters) who did not accept that the existing cultural ethos and its values were the last word in how society should be arranged - and were willing to think critically and actively to reconfigure their subjective mindscapes.

I highlighted that the need for such people to come to the fore was pressing due to the oppressive weight of the bureaucratic direction and control that currently existed in UK society. I underlined this point by quoting the views of Max Weber on the domination of bureaucratic control in capitalist, Western societies. Webber recognized that modern bureaucracy generates problems, one of which is the threat of the "dictatorship of the official". He believed this threat could be combated by individuals communicating ideas of difference and choice to the population. In short, he hoped that informed debate would be translated into political action by the bureaucratic system. In reality, though, he saw it as far more likely that the bureaucratic system would impose itself on society and itself become an instrument of social control implementing, as he wrote in *On Charisma and Institution Building*, (1968: 28):

*"the consistently rationalized, methodically trained and exact execution of the received order, in which all personal criticism is suspended".*

I drew on examples from my personal experience of being a student at a university in the 1960s, and a working tutor in adult education during the 1990s and early 2000s, to highlight how significant bureaucratic control systems had become in the last 30 years in one sector of British society. I pointed out that my university tutors in the 1960s often commented on how independent they felt within their academic fields. Some published their research, others did not, and those who did not were usually more concerned with their standards of teaching and student pastoral care. In the 1980s this informal culture changed with the introduction into higher education of the Teaching Quality Assessment (TQA) exercise, the Research Assessment Exercise (RAE), "bench marking" and the internal audits (a process by which colleagues can scrutinize colleagues in their own university, in addition to offering their services for external scrutiny). These systems involved the imposition of regulations and the creation of significant numbers of personnel to enforce them. By creating such systems universities, I contended, had contributed to the destruction of their internal social connectedness by bowing to government policies that stressed the need for bureaucratic accountability to ensure the maintenance and extension of business-orientated, market-focused development strategies into the higher education system.

To reinforce how significantly bureaucratic procedures had mushroomed in academia, I used my experience as a module leader to illustrate the point. When I had originally created a two year adult learning programme in the early1990s, I had written out a proposal, submitted it to my departmental head and waited for approval. This came quickly after the agreement of the academic standards committee. Now, when compiling the current course, I had had to complete a module specification for each module in the course (10 in all), listing each module's aims and objectives, learning outcomes, methods of assessment, teaching methods, a content synopsis, and a module review in which the students give their individual assessments of the module's strengths and weaknesses, plus average marks and their dispersal. Furthermore, I pointed out that if I had wanted to compile a degree level course, the extra work involved would have included preparing a programme specification, and an annual programme report which tracked student performance through "progression rates", "withdrawal rates" and a spread of marks. All these marks would also have had to be graded against a "grid", while the marking of student assignments would have had to be monitored by external examiners.

Students too, I stressed, were therefore not immune from this bureaucratic scrutiny. They were now, via the use of numerous forms and paper trails, under greater surveillance than at any time in the past - but despite paying (as consumers) a high price for their involvement in higher education, it seemed to me that they did not seem to mind their servile status. My opinions provoked great debate and discussion. We agreed finally that perhaps Western society did not possess all the answers about individual and political freedom, but this provoked another query, how can we combine individual freedom with social justice? We returned to consideration of Marcuse's ideas, and I stressed that he saw hope of achieving progress by basing a future around four specific areas of action: firstly, by stimulating independent thought in privacy, away from the clamor of the popular, predominant culture; secondly, by providing opportunities for people to have powerful and stimulating aesthetic engagements. Marcuse believed in the transformative power of art, and argued that it could temporarily take people out of everyday reality and then allow them to renew it with a newly critical perspective – an approach I wholeheartedly agreed with and which I explored as part of the course: thirdly, by teaching reflective, conceptual thought which stimulates a new way of looking at life and society (and which formed a continuous motif in my teaching); and fourthly, by practicing liberating tolerance - an approach that involves exposing learners to alternative perspectives through which they can find greater self-determination and freedom. (Brookfield 2005: 195-219). This, I pointed out, is close to the view of the Dutch philosopher Baruch Spinoza who commented in his book *The Ethics* (1677), that when people acquire enough knowledge of the desires and emotions that are the internal causes of all their actions, when they understand why they do what they do, only then will they be truly free to reject the "sad passions" that captivate them.

I also highlighted Marcuse's view that committed activists should, against seemingly daunting odds, keep alive, through their actions and thoughts, the idea of an alternative society, even if by doing this they are labeled by the one dimensional majority as impossible idealists and utopian dreamers: "it is the task and duty of the intellectual to recall and preserve historical possibilities which seem to have become utopian possibilities". But why, asked my class, should they persist in advocating courses of action that have clearly fallen out of favor with the great mass of the populace? Because, I responded, in Marcuse's view (one which I wholeheartedly reinforced), which he explained in his *Essay on Liberation (1969)*, "what is denounced as utopian is no longer that which has no place and cannot have any place in the historical universe, but rather that which is blocked from coming about by the power of established societies".

What I was saying here was that as critical thinkers we should reject ignorance and delusion, and that as both teachers and learners we must, to make a difference, do more than just acquire a language of critique and possibility. In the words of Henry Giroux (1998: 215): "It also means having the courage to take risks, to look into the future, and to imagine a world that could be as opposed to simply what it is": a view reinforced by Bauman (1999: 8) who believes we need "to recall from exile ideas such as the public good, the good society, equity, justice, and so on – such ideas that make no sense unless cared for and cultivated in the company of others".

## Paulo Freire

I often distributed extracts from Freire's writings at the start of my classes, especially passages from his *Pedagogy of the Oppressed* (1972b). After allowing time for the students to consider these, and after lengthy discussion, we agreed that the core of Freire's liberating education is his concept of conscientisation. This is a critique of false consciousness, and can be understood as the process by which individuals become aware of the sources of their oppression. Freire stressed that human beings have the capacity to reflect on the world, and "name" its dynamics and problems, and choose a given course of future action based on reflection. But he also saw that the oppressed are not ideally placed to take up such a position. They may not have the intellectual confidence to "reflect upon the world" and formulate their own agenda for change. According to Freire (2001:83), such people are often trapped in "magical" and "naive" thinking, and their understanding of the world is affected accordingly. He writes:

*"Magical thinking apprehends facts and attributes to them power by which it (the world) is controlled and to which it must therefore submit. Magic consciousness is characterized by fatalism, which leads men to fold their arms, resigned to the impossibility of resisting the power of facts. Naive consciousness sees the causes of oppression as static, established facts and is, as a result, deceived in its perception".*

Furthermore, by maintaining these thinking modes, the oppressed may have internalized the "values of the oppressors" and so find themselves unable, or unwilling, to think critically about their situation in the world, and what actions are open to them to improve such a situation.

Conscientisation is therefore the process by which the capacity for critical thinking by the oppressed can be expanded. Thus, on one level, conscientisation, or the process of becoming aware, provides an opportunity to change one's perception of reality. But it is much more than a purely intellectual process and, at a second level, it is a dynamic and liberating process which generates critical action. In conscientisation action leads to further reflection, and so on, in a dynamic process of emancipation. Thus conscientisation is made up of two inseparable, mutually enriching and authentically human capabilities – action and reflection, or action based on reflection, and reflection based on action.

*"Meanwhile there are the enslaved human beings who must accomplish their own liberation. To develop their conscience and consciousness, to make them aware of what is going on, to prepare the precarious ground for the future alternatives – this is our task".*

This quote from the Marxist humanist Herbert Marcuse (1967) could well have been written by Freire, for to both of them the role of the educator is fundamental for the liberation of the oppressed. At its centre lies Freire's (1972b) concept of dialogue: the educator, rather than deposit "superior knowledge" to be passively digested, memorized and repeated ("banking education"), must engage in a "genuine dialogue" or "creative exchange" with the participants. In other words, the role of the educator is not to educate the oppressed in the traditional, formal sense, but to create "a space" in which the oppressed educate themselves, have time to identify or name the problems they face, reflect critically on their subjective experiences, and formulate plans to take action on them.

The space favored by Freire that must be created to generate this transformation usually takes the form of the small group. In the very deprived parts of Brazil, Freire (1972a) brought together groups of squatters in which participants described the themes that influenced their lives, offered these as problems to be examined by the group, chose several problems for dialogue and reflection on their root causes, and devised strategies to address the problems.

Writing in 1987, Werner and Bower highlighted a similar practice used by health workers in the western mountains of Mexico (quoted in Checkoway 1995:12). The workers brought together poor villagers to discuss the causes of illness through a problem-posing dialogue that moved from the individual to the community, and to society as a whole. The group began by discussing the illness of a single individual and listed its biological, physical and social causes, including the economic and political causes such as money and power. The workers recognized that social factors were often more potent than biological and physical ones, so they outlined a causal progressive link from the general to the particular, and then selected specific causes for dialogue and reflection for future action. The process of discovering the root causes is reflected in the following dialogue, (quoted by Checkoway: 12, from Werner and Bower 1982), between a health worker and a child in the village:

"The child has a septic foot".
"But why?"
"Because she stepped on a thorn".
"But why?"
"Because she was barefoot".
"But why?"
"Because she was not wearing shoes".
"But why not?"
"Because they broke and her father was too poor to buy new ones".
"But why is her father so poor?"
"Because her father is a farmworker".
"But why does that make him poor?"
"Because he is paid very little as a farmworker and must give half his harvest to the landowner".
"But why?" - and so on.

The comparison between the much exploited peasants of north east Brazil and Mexico, and adult learners in the south east Wales Valleys, seems rather drastic, but the comparison was not entirely far fetched in educational psychology terms, and the promotion of self-critical reflection not too outlandish, when one again considers the experience of the members of the class. These working class individuals, living and working in marginalized communities, found that their involvement with my community-based course gave them space, time and opportunity to move from a fatalistic consciousness to a critical consciousness. I therefore saw the classes as fine examples of conscientisation in progress, and my strategy was to encourage the students to reproduce this emancipatory process in their own action groups in their working environments. So, through critical thinking about, and reflecting on, their worlds and their own community, learners would come to understand the ways in which their thinking had been constrained by their political, social and cultural cultures and, from passivity and inaction, they would move constructively to a congruence, a fusion of critical reflection and community-based action. Here is an example, showing the stages of conscientisation of one of the students, a resident of a Rhondda mining village, reflecting on the economic situation in her community when a few vestiges of the coal industry still remained in south Wales:

**STAGE 1**

Magical/naming          *Lots of miners are out of work now*

Magical/reflecting      *The coal industry is in a downturn. Coal is going to pick up soon and the miners will go back to work*

Magical/acting          *We must wait for the coal industry to come back. I think coal is getting back to normal*

**STAGE 2**

Naïve/naming            *Engineering technology has changed. Coal is still being produced but with fewer workers*

Naïve/reflecting        *Coal is still booming: it's employment that's gone bust. The industry is working at full capacity; they don't need so many people*

Naïve/acting    *We're going to have to move away or bring in another industry*

**STAGE 3**

Critical/naming    *Coal will never employ more people and another industry is not likely to take its place in the valley. More people here now work in service jobs than in manufacturing*

Critical/reflecting    *The days of attracting big businesses to south Wales are over. Some of the people talking about how they survived made me understand that that was part of what kept the community going*

Critical/acting    *We are going to have to do it ourselves and I learned there were more people willing to do something. There are many poor people here…we could set up a community transport scheme to make them more mobile and travel to work outside the valley*

This critical process had been forged by the student exploring and discovering for herself the lived experience of the inhabitants of her community, and linking this process with the dialogical learning of my classes. This combined process of classroom learning, and first hand analyzing of the community's needs, was part of a staged progression of building validation of her own knowledge, and of her acceptance that society was not just an impersonal entity controlled only by local power holders and experts. As a result, she, and other community activists, could now see society as something which they themselves could act upon. This process of demystifying society, and affirming the place of the community within it, was essential for the worker and her colleagues to be able to critically assess future strategies for action and development - and develop their own plans and alternatives accordingly.

I then made the point that I believed that the acquisition of this type of liberating consciousness was a genuinely creative process, a view shared by Raymond Williams who, in the concluding words of his book *Marxism and Literature* (1977: 212), wrote:

> *"Creative practice is thus of many kinds. It is already, and actively, our practical consciousness. When it becomes struggle - the active struggle for new consciousness through new relationships that is the ineradicable emphasis of the Marxist sense of self-creation - it can take many forms. It can be the long and difficult remaking of an inherited (determined) practical consciousness: a process often described as development but in practice a struggle at the roots of the mind - not casting off an ideology, or learning phrases about it, but confronting a hegemony in the fibers of the self and in the hard practical substance of effective and continuing relationships".*

What Williams is describing here, I believed, is not just "consciousness-raising"; it is more a radical refashioning of consciousness. As Pope (2005:11) points out, Williams' "creative practice" involves an attempt by the individual to wrench from the contradictions he has internalized something that helps him live his life in a better way. Such a creative process must be a movement through the "known" into the "unknown". It can be started in the present but the results cannot be foretold - thus the invitation implied in Williams' final words (p.212): "For creativity and social self-creation are both known and unknown events, and it is still from grasping the known that the unknown - the next step, the next work - is conceived".

The class decided, after much discussion, that Freire's conscientisation process, and Williams's struggle to achieve the "unknown" after critical acceptance of the current "knowns", were both transformational processes that could act as reflective and action tools to help them view the everyday world in a new way, thereby creating new conceptual illuminations about society and its structures. These illuminations, they felt, could further be utilized to examine in detail these structures, and to consider how they could be modified and challenged. This, they finally agreed, could best be achieved by creating experiences of a truly collective nature, which communities could then effectively reproduce to engender a sense of "we together", and so regenerate a feeling of class consciousness and communal solidarity in local society.

## Myles Horton and Highlander

After stressing the importance of the ideas and thoughts of academics and philosophers, I thought it essential to introduce the students to a more practical approach to community development and community education – an approach that had influenced me a great deal in deciding how to deliver my programmes in communities and so effectively meet their educational needs. I therefore introduced my class to the work of Myles Horton. Horton was an educator based firmly in the tradition of Lindeman and Dewey, who believed strongly that genuine adult education only happened when adults voluntarily chose a programme of learning they had either designed or were interested in. He stressed how adult education could help learners develop skills and knowledge that would assist them in understanding and changing the communities in which they lived. Horton profoundly believed that this type of learning occurred through a collaborative analysis of adults' experiences during which the roles of teacher and leaner were interchanged among the participants. Adult educators who attempted to work in this tradition, in his view, did their best to replicate the features of participative democracy, with all partici-pants actively involved in deciding aspects of what and how to learn. As Horton explained in 1973 (p.331):

*"If we are to think seriously about liberating people to cope with their own lives, we must refuse to limit the educational process to what can go on only in schools. The bars must come down, the doors must fly open; non-academic life - real life - must be encompassed by education. Multiple approaches must be invented, each one considered educative in its own right".*

The basic principle of Horton's philosophy, and that of the staff at the Highlander Folk School which he established in Tennessee in 1932 (and which I had visited in 1990), was that people know the solutions to their own problems and that the role of the teacher is to get them talking about those problems, to raise and sharpen questions, and to trust people to come up with the answers. The belief was that the answers lie in the experience and imagination of people as communities as well as individuals. Horton also culti-vated leadership, because, as he wrote in 1947:

*"though it is, of course, impossible to bring together more than a small percentage of the people, that is all that is necessary. Leaders are aroused people, who, like the aroused atom, start a chain reaction which is self-propagating. It is the multiplication of leadership that gives power to the people and enables them to make reality of dreams..."*

As a result, potential leaders from poor local communities and company towns coping with the same problems were identified, brought to Highlander, and taught how to analyze their situation in a group environment. Through story telling, peer teaching, discussions and vision sharing the participants would compare their actions, make connections and generalizations, and draw out conclusions. In the course of this process, Horton and his colleagues would encourage the participants to consider future actions and therefore future learning, too. Then the leaders were taught how to go back and take other community people through the same process in accordance with "training the trainers" concepts (see Glen 1988; Horton 1989, 1990).

This philosophy, together with his moral purpose, ensured that Horton, and his Highlander staff, intentionally focused their educational efforts on community problems. In 1933 Highlander brought timber workers and their families together to research the logging industry in the area and to develop a model of sustainable logging that would protect both the forests and workers' jobs in the long term (Adams, 1975). In the 1950s, in addition to promoting worker education programmes, Horton and Highlander became involved in the civil rights movement and, later on, in the promotion of adult literacy skills initiatives in the southern states. Indeed, during the period 1957-1963 Adams (1972:515) has estimated that nearly 100,000 adults had learned to read and write because of Horton's efforts and the impact of the literacy programme. Highlander was involved in racially integrating labor organizations, as well as laying the groundwork for the 1954 *Brown v. Board of Education* school integration decision. After the floods that devastated Appalachia in 1977, Highlander helped local residents, community organizations and academic researchers investigate the conditions that produced the endemic poverty in the region, with the intent of bringing about changes through community action. In the process, local communities learned development skills and actively participated in civic politics to bring about changes in local tax regimes that had been impoverishing the regional economy in favor of absentee landowners, mostly coal mining companies (Horton, 1990).

Horton's philosophy therefore laid its emphasis on respecting people's ability to educate themselves, and I pointed out to my class that his social action initiatives had achieved just this type of learning. I highlighted how one group had undertaken a research report into local housing and how, by doing so, they began to understand their own situation better. Community members who looked at the data on home ownership in their neighborhood, and drew maps showing where the home owners lived, began to ask other questions arising from their own experiences in the community. They started enquiring about the quality of housing where home owners were concentrated versus where absentee landlords owned more property, or about the incomes of home owners versus renters. From their research, they identified areas where home ownership was rare and correlated this with their own personal knowledge of the quality of housing in those areas, or the incidence of crime there, or the neighbors' perception of safety. Through this process, community activists became more comfortable, more knowledgeable and more skilful at asking and answering their own questions - a very fine example of a community-controlled social enquiry initiative in which learning through collective investigation occupied the central role.

What Horton was putting into effect at Highlander was a linkage between collective problems and individual concern - an approach that has close links with the later work of C Wright Mills who was concerned with the connection between private troubles and public issues. Mills believed (1959) that micro and macro levels of analysis could be linked together by what he termed "the sociological imagination" which enables the individuals who posses it to understand the wider world and its history in terms of its meaning for that individual's inner life and the social activities of other individuals. In Mills' view, individual people can understand their own experiences properly only if they place themselves within their own, and society's, environments. The vital element is the combination of personal troubles and public issues: the combination of problems that occur within the individual person's immediate environment and relations with other persons with concerns that have to do with the organization of many institutions of society as a whole. Mills saw that American society was deeply divided and constantly shaped by the on-going interactions between the powerful and the powerless - and that the exercise of the sociological imagination could lead to conflict with the power elite (see Wikipedia entries for *C Wright Mills – Works*).

Despite the positive outcomes associated with his approach, Horton was realistic enough to recognize that his type of learning also involved risk for the educators and the students involved, a view he expressed well in his book *The Long Haul* (1990: 183) when he stated:

> *"It's dangerous to do this kind of education, to push the boundaries to the place where people might be fired, or get in some kind of trouble. But you've got to get on that line, as close as you possibly can, and sometimes you'll analyze it wrong and get clipped. If people don't take chances, they'll never keep pushing. They must explore and push as far as they can. People get the exhilaration of liberating themselves, pushing the boundary line until they push it to the place where they're challenged, and they either have to back off or go further…"*

To Horton therefore education is essentially a political endeavor and a servant of the democratic process: and he would have been sympathetic, I believe, to what Mills wrote in The Sociological Imagination in 1959 about the role of the educator:

> *"It is the political task of the social scientist - as of any liberal educator - continually to translate personal troubles into public issues, and public issues into the terms of their human meaning for a variety of individuals. It is his task to display in his work - and as an educator, in his life as well - this kind of sociological imagination. And it is his purpose to cultivate such habits of mind among the men and women who are publicly exposed to him. To secure these ends is to secure reason and individuality, and to make these the predominant values of a democratic society".*

## Horton and Freire – the similarities
I pointed out the parallels and links between the work of Horton

and that of Paulo Freire, two educators focused on the everyday implementation of their ideas and beliefs. I emphasized these linkages by reference to the book, *We Make the Road by Walking*, published in 1990, which is a dialogue between the two popular educators. Both agree that the role of the educator is one of supporting communities and acting as catalysts for them. "You have to know something: they know something. You have to respect their knowledge, which they don't respect, and help them to respect their knowledge" (page 55). "You have to keep out of the act, and get them to act" (page 43). The educator's role therefore is only to give the information when asked, and to let the people themselves decide how to use it. The educator can, though, "provoke the discovering of a need for knowing, but never impose the knowledge where the need for it has not yet been perceived" (p.66). Alongside this action, both Horton and Freire concur that the expert must create a space for dialogue and generate possibilities for learners to envisage change. As Horton says, "it's like planting seeds, where the planter does not immediately see the fruits of his labors" (p 99).

Both men also accept the importance of understanding "the soul" of the culture in which they are working. Freire states that as an outsider, if the vision of the educator does not match that of the community, it's "not unethical to put the possibility of change on the table" (p132). However, both agree that it would be unethical to impose this idea on the people. They thereby reiterate the importance of having values, while making sure that they do not recreate a colonial experience as occurred when Western Values were imposed on "Third World" communities in the eighteenth and nineteenth centuries.

Essentially, Horton and Freire's basic philosophy is that educators must start their work with their learners' experiences, and accept that knowledge and change "grow out of what they do" (p 7). Therefore, both believe that positive change, although difficult to achieve, is possible. They talk about the centrality of vision in guiding action in the present, and use the analogy of ever higher mountains to climb in the future (p 56). They also suggest that community educators and activists do not start social change action from scratch – rather they should find "pockets of hope" that already exist: "finding the pockets is not an intellectual process. It's a process of being involved" (p 94). Conti (quoted in Brookfield, 1983), succinctly sums up his thoughts regarding the similarity between the two educationalists as follows:

*"Using a learner-centered approach which emphasizes discussion, dialogue and communication, they get the curriculum to make use of (and to enhance) the life experiences of their learners…Both also encourage their clientele to test their learning in real life situations".*

Overall, after reading *We Make the Road by Walking*, I am left with feelings of hope, of determination, of commitment, and am reinforced in my belief that collective action can change society (albeit initially on a local scale) – and that as well as having ideas on how to start the whole process rolling, I have in my consciousness the knowledge that theory and practice can be combined to help people and their communities change their lives through reflecting on their own experiences, and by taking action on that reflection. To reinforce this belief, in one class I told the story of a specific student who had had links with the education courses offered by Myles Horton's Highlander School. I read out the Guardian newspaper's obituary of Rosa Parks (October 2005) and gave a brief précis of her life. I underlined that in the summer of 1955 she had studied sociology at Highlander along with non violent strategies for action to combat racism in the southern states of the USA. On 1 December of the same year, Rosa Parks sat down in the whites-only section of a segregated bus in Montgomery, Alabama and refused to give up her seat to a white person. The reason she subsequently gave ( Parks,1992: 116) for her action was:

*"People always say that I didn't give up my seat because I was tired, but that isn't true. I was not tired physically, or no more tired than I usually was at the end of a working day. I was not old, although some people have an image of me as being old then. I was forty two. No, the only tired I was, was tired of giving in".*

Rosa Parks thus made it clear that she was not only dissatisfied with the system which valued her as less of a human being than someone with white skin, but also with herself for having complicity colluded with it over her lifetime. After a long period of reflection on the injustice of Alabama's apartheid system, and of her tacit acceptance of it, she acted to regain her integrity, without any guarantee that her beliefs and education would yield positive results, and refused to move to the rear of the bus. As a result, she was arrested, but her action initiated a public transport boycott led by Martin Luther King Jr, precipitated a federal court ruling that bus segregation was unconstitutional, and provided an inspirational impetus to the civil rights movement - and her action still remains a beacon of light to community activists after all these years.

## Antonio Gramsci

Several classes later I introduced the class to the work of Antonio Gramsci, one of the major social and political theorists of the twentieth century, who devised his theories while in prison in an Italy controlled by the fascists in the 1930s. I paid particular attention to his theory of hegemony. This, to Gramsci (1971) is not just dominance by force, but a set of ideas by which dominant groups secure the consent of ancillary groups to their subordination. He maintains that the dominance of the established powers is asserted in society through moral persuasion: and that specific ideas are disseminated as common sense, or the accepted norm, through the institutions of civil society such as schools, television, newspapers; and in political life by political groups shielding the population from certain ideas and information and by teaching particular economic, political and social values. Hegemony therefore permeates all aspects of life and is constantly learned and relearned by the mass of the population during their lives. To Gramsci (1971:356) the hegemonic relationship exists *"throughout society as a whole and for every individual relative to other individuals. It exists between intellectual and non-intellectual sections of the population, between the rulers and the ruled, elites and their followers, leaders and led, the vanguard and the body of the army"*.

Some students expressed their difficulty in getting to grips with this concept and found it complex and confusing. I explained it by referring to some of my own teenage and student reading about the use of power, notably the *Foundation Trilogy* and the *Robot* novels of Isaac Asimov. In these works, Asimov created the science fiction stereotypes that subsequently influenced such modern works as *Star Wars, Alien* and *Bladerunner,* and explored power and its use to decide the destiny of mankind. But power in Asimov's books is never just about brute force. It is far more subtle in that it is the cogent robots which succeed in bending human thinking in their, and their masters', preferred direction, always keeping one step ahead of the humans who do not realize how they are being manipulated. I also made reference to the more recent film The Matrix, starring Keanu Reeves and Lawrence Fishburne, which I knew all the students had seen. I pointed out that the premise of the film was that being subordinate is a desirable state of affairs, and that those who are subordinate are enthusiastically embracing beliefs and practices that are slowly destroying them. Indeed, the state of subordination is actively sought out and regarded as desirable.

This is a situation, I stressed, that is very close to Gramsci's concept of hegemony and its impact on individuals. The active pursuit of self oppression is what happens when hegemony is working effectively - a situation which some observers see as occurring today in many parts of the world where the governing classes are succeeding in persuading the governed to accept the moral, political and cultural values of their rulers. "But how are they doing this?" I asked. Essentially, by implementing a neo-liberal agenda that stresses the need to privatize, reduce government expenditure and allow the market to decide economic affairs. I then illustrated in more detail how this philosophy had permeated western society and, by doing so, had helped to subordinate individual freedom to commercial and government interests.

I highlighted the role that the privatization of public services had played in the neo-liberal agenda, and gave my view that privatization destroys the bonds that link us all together in a democratic community. By appealing to our basic instincts to do what we please, privatization was helping dissolve our ability to collectively secure those services to which we have a right. Private choices I claimed rely on individual power, personal skills and a great deal of luck, whereas public choices rest on social rights, common responsibilities, and presumed equal rights for all. Public liberty is what the power of collective action creates, and so presupposes that we have constituted ourselves as public citizens by opting into the social contract. On the other hand, as Benjamin Barber (2007: 144) has written:

*"With privatization we are seduced back into the state of nature by the lure of private liberty and particular interest, but what we experience in the end is an environment in which the strong dominate the weak and anarchy ultimately dominates the strong and the weak, undermining security for both - the very dilemma which the original social contract was intended to address".*

So, I believed privatization was being used as a strategy to undermine and discredit not just the practical functioning of public services but the principle behind their very existence. All this was being done by twisting the rubric, by using words such as "freedom", "choice", "liberty" and "enterprise" to draw invidious comparisons between the "efficient" private sector and the "inefficient" government sector. The privateers thus offer the public a false choice, one that appeared obvious, even commonsensical to individuals, but which in reality was used primarily to push for greater freedom from government control for those groups with vested interests - the private companies and corporations - in order to generate greater profits for the people who controlled them and the shareholders who financed them. The belief in the efficacy of the free market was the prime thrust of the discreditation strategy, and that it has proved amazingly successful can be seen from the current state of the global economy that overproduces goods and targets children as well as adults as consumers because there are never enough shoppers - and never enough profits.

All this vindicates Gramsci's belief (1977: 12) that what enables the ruling elite to gain and sustain power is not just force but also the attainment of cultural domination through its ability to saturate society with its values, tastes and philosophies. In other words, the consumer society is not a spontaneous process - rather it is the consummation of a process of commercial insight, personal cupidity and the flow of economic ideology. As a result, we are now in the age of consumerism and of the marketeer whose role has subtly enlarged the scope of private power at the expense of the public good. In his book *Consumed*, Benjamin Barber quotes Douglas Atkin on how marketeers aim to make "customers become true believers". This is a lengthy quotation, but it makes plain how insidious the marketing industry's aim is, and how it helps push forward the agenda of disinformation, manipulation and control:

*"We've reached a unique intersection in society that favors marketeers. On one side, established institutions are proving to be increasingly inadequate sources of meaning and community. On the other, there has been a growth of a very sophisticated kind of consumerism.*

*Marketing is reaching its maturity in terms of shrewdness and artfulness. Billions are being spent on gratifying a discriminating audience with complex and subtly crafted brands. The confluence of these two trends is leading to these commercial creations being embraced by a population disillusioned altogether by less satisfying, and often less trusted organizations. Alongside alternative religions, brands are now serious contenders for belief and community".* (*The Culting of Brands: When Consumers Become True Believers*. New York: Portfolio. 2004. p. 202)

Such a situation could be regarded as typical of what market-focused conditioning and cultural hypnosis could achieve and, given this situation, it makes what Aldous Huxley, the author of *Brave New World* predicted, in 1949, in a letter to George Orwell, author of *Nineteen Eighty Four*, very prescient indeed:

*"Within the next generation I believe that the world's leaders will discover that infant conditioning and narco-hypnosis are more efficient, as instruments of government, than clubs and prisons, and that the lust for power can be just as completely satisfied by suggesting people into loving their servitude as by flogging them and kicking them into obedience".* (Smith: 1969).

Indeed, a comparison between the dystopian visions of Orwell and Huxley regarding the future state of society make interesting reading - a point forcibly made by the social critic Neil Postman in his 1985 book *Amusing Ourselves to Death*, when he wrote:

*"What Orwell feared were those who would ban books. What Huxley feared was that there would be no reason to ban a book, for there would be no one who wanted to read one. Orwell feared those who would deprive us of information. Huxley feared those who would give us so much that we would be reduced to passivity and egotism. Orwell feared that the truth would be concealed from us. Huxley*

*feared the truth would be drowned in a sea of irrelevance. Orwell feared we would become a captive culture. Huxley feared we would become a trivial culture...As Huxley remarked in Brave New World Revisited, the civil libertarians and rationalists who are ever on the alert to oppose tyranny "failed to take into account man's almost infinite appetite for distractions". In 1984, Orwell added, people are controlled by inflicting pain. In Brave New World, they are controlled by inflicting pleasure. In short, Orwell feared that what we fear will ruin us. Huxley feared that what we desire will ruin us".*

Closely linked with the trend towards what Christopher Hitchens (1998: 37) has called "the hedonistic nihilism of Huxley", which encourages "a painless, amusement-sodden, and stress-free consensus", is contemporary society's encouragement of a sense of living in a present-tense culture, a trend which Hitchens believes is far more insidious and effectively described in Huxley's account of the future rather than Orwell's. He writes:

*"Orwell's was a house of horrors. He seemed to strain credulity because he posited a regime that would go to any lengths to own and possess history, to rewrite and construct it, and to inculcate it by means of coercion. Whereas Huxley...rightly foresaw that any such regime could break but could not bend. In 1988, four years after 1984, the Soviet Union scrapped its official history curriculum and announced that a newly authorized version was somewhere in the works. This was the precise moment when the regime conceded its own extinction. For true blissed-out and vacant servitude, though, you need an otherwise sophisticated society where no serious history is taught".*

Are we close to a society that faces Gramsci's hegemonic power? Are the fears of Huxley and Orwell now being realized? If so, "how can this situation be combated?" My questions stimulated a discussion that ranged over a series of alternatives, but finally arrived at a general consensus that the best option for countering the hegemonic force of the power holders was by getting people to learn to think critically. This, in Gramsci's view (1971: 323-4), requires the learner *"to work out consciously and critically one's own conception of the world and thus, in connection with the labors of one's own brain, choose one's sphere of activity, take an active part in the creation of the history of the world, be one's own guide, refusing to accept passively and supinely from outside the molding of one's personality"* - a process which I believed I was currently reinforcing in my students, and in myself, in my classes.

In the class dialogue that followed my use of this quote, I emphasized the need for students to always remember how the dominant powers, and their ideologies, even at local community level, often deceive, fragment and distort the interests of the many in favor of the power and privilege of the dominant elites - and how a study of Gramsci's theories can help effect the critical thought, and subsequent action, necessary to transform current local, social and economic relationships. I used this approach because I believed that a study of relevant theories would reinforce the critical thinking of my students, while simultaneously helping them identify aspects of their own experience that had previously eluded or puzzled them: when they read an explanation that interpreted a difficult experience in a revealing way, the experience became more comprehensible. In other words, when someone else's theories and ideas illuminated a personal insight, the students felt vindicated and confirmed in their own views - and grew significantly in confidence as a result. My students and I thus saw the study of theory as having practical implications - an attitude that had a great deal in common with the views of Cornel West (1991:34) who believes that theory is *"an indispensable weapon in the struggle because it provides certain kinds of understanding, certain kinds of illumination, certain kinds of insights that are requisite if we are to act effectively"*, and which chimed with the conviction of Gramsci who held that theory which could not be translated into fact was useless abstraction, while political action not guided by theory was fruitless and impulsive.

A particularly fine example of theory helping students to learn to perceive and challenge prevailing attitudes arose after the class's study of Gramsci's theory of the "organic intellectual". For Gramsci (1971:10) a "traditional" intellectual is educated to maintain the status quo of the different classes in society, but an "organic" intellectual is the one who is engaged in public life and acts as "constructor, organizer, "permanent persuader", and not just a simple orator" or mouthpiece, for the working classes in order to help them become self-reflective, and so "empower them with a voice in the larger body public". Gramsci thus believed that organic intellectuals had to develop not only intellectual capital to distribute to the masses, but also the social capital of trust and collective effort necessary to bring about community-wide reflection which would result in liberating engagement. In other words, Gramsci was calling for a general change of culture because, as he observed in his pre-prison writings (Berman 1994a: 9-10):

*"Culture is...the mastery of one's personality; the attainment of a higher awareness, through which we can come to understand our value and place within history, our proper function in life, our rights and duties...And this awareness has...developed through intelligent reflection, first on the part of a few, then of a whole class, on the reasons why certain situations exist and on the best means of transforming what have been opportunities for vassalage into triggers of rebellion and social reconstruction. Which means that every revolution has been preceded by a long process of intense critical activity, of new cultural insight and the spread of ideas through groups of men initially resistant to them, wrapped up in the process of solving their own, immediate economic and political problems, and lacking any bonds of solidarity with others in the same position".*

By discussing the role of the organic intellectual against the background of their own experiences of working in communities where local power-holder attitudes, especially the personal prejudices and machinations of individual councilors, often militated against genuine community-based participation, the students realized that they themselves could, with some justification, be classified as organic intellectuals, and that local authority members should sometimes be realistically identified as part of the current hegemonic system and so be labeled their "enemies" - opponents of community action who, in the words of Baptiste (2000) "intend, on principle, to frustrate the goals of their opponents because their opponent's goals stand in opposition to theirs" and, because of this attitude, adult educators should, in the words of Newman (1994: 144), as well as helping students look at themselves, also:

> 'help them look at the people who do not care, the people who intrude, the people who misuse their authority…by doing this we can encourage people to be outward-looking, to be active and activist. We can help them focus their anger on the cause of their anger. And we can set up situations in which we and the people we are working with think, plan, learn and decide action.'

## Some questions

At the last session on the usefulness of theories and ideas, I asked the class to form into three groups of four to discuss their reactions to the theories and ideas we had analyzed, and their readings from the works of Marcuse, Habermas, Freire, Horton and Gramsci. Some of the questions I suggested they consider in these groups included the following:

### Hegemony
- What are the main elements of the dominant belief system in the United Kingdom today?

- What hegemonic beliefs and actions have you personally adopted?
- Do you think the critical ideas and collective responses we have discussed can help individuals and communities counter the current dominant value system?
- How did you find the language and the teaching methods used in the classes? Clear?/Confusing?/Coherent? /Incoherent?

*Power*
- In what ways does your experience of power match or contradict the ideas and theories of power we have discussed?
- Have you discovered ways of challenging power?
- Do you or your community at any time feel threatened by the power of the state, local authority or other interests?
- How did you find the language and the teaching methods used in the classes? Clear?/Confusing?/Coherent?/ Incoherent?

*Critical Thinking*
- Which discussions on critical thinking were most relevant and most irrelevant for you?
- What pressures do you feel in your life are encouraging the loss of critical thinking in looking at society?
- Can the belief in critical thinking be put to positive use for yourself and your community?
- How did you find the language and the teaching methods used in the classes? Clear?/Confusing?/Coherent?/ Incoherent?

Out of these group discussions generated by Gramsci's ideas, and reinforced by the thoughts and views of Habermas, Marcuse, Horton and Freire, came a request by the students for the inclusion in the course of an examination of the theme of "community confrontation", and an exploration of the tactics and procedures necessary to effectively oppose power-holders by playing them at their own game: by learning about, and applying, techniques of manipulation, confrontation, manoeuvring, misinformation and even deception. As I believed that the course I was teaching should help its students develop the skills and knowledge that would help them understand and change the communities in which they lived and worked, and that genuine learning occurs through a collaborative analysis of students' experiences and wishes, and teacher's expertise, I readily agreed to their request to include a section on confrontation later in the programme.

# Chapter six

## *More Useful Ideas*
### Albert Camus

Before providing the students with information and advice about community confrontation, I gave them an insight into another writer who had influenced my ideas on community education and commitment as instances of social and political action – the French writer and philosopher Albert Camus. I pointed out that Camus had, during and after the Second World War, made a philosophical/political journey from his original view that the individual cannot make rational sense of his/her existence in the face of the "benign indifference of the universe" so, as a result, adopts an attitude of total moral indifference to the ills of society (as expounded in *The Stranger* 1942), to something like a humane stoicism as expressed in his 1948 novel *The Plague*. This, I believed, is a work in which the important achievement of the characters who fight the plague lies not in their limited success but in their assertion of human dignity and on-going perseverance - acts of defiance and statements of their personal morality which they have constructed in order to make sense of an uncaring world.

Later, in the essay *The Rebel* (1954), Camus criticized what he regarded as the dangerous tendencies of monolithic philosophies – Christianity and Marxism in particular - that demand unquestioning belief from their adherents. In place of these intransigent, all-embracing beliefs, he argued in favor of humanism, advocating decency and moderation rather than historicism and violence as appropriate avenues for social improvement. Camus, it can be claimed, thus took a journey that led from Marxist utopianism to Manichean dualism; from a belief in the necessary creation of a new social order by overthrowing current structures, to an acceptance that evil will always exist in society, and that it must be constantly combated by good works because the maintenance of goodness is never guaranteed. The end of the journey can, I believe, be summed up in the words of Dr Rieux in *The Plague* who tirelessly treats the disease-stricken citizens of Oran without any guarantee that his work will be successful: "We refuse to despair of mankind. Without having the unreasonable ambition to save men, we still want to serve them".

So, ultimately, Camus' existentialist pessimism harbors a sense of hope. What he is saying is that you can make something out of what you've been made into by society; and that this sense of optimism, however limited, can be harnessed for the good of that same society - an essentially humanistic view which slides easily into the wider view of his fellow existentialist Marcel Merlean-Ponty (quoted in Flynn, 2006: 103) when he wrote:

*"The human world is an open or unfinished system and the same radical contingency which threatens it with discord also rescues it from the inevitability of disorder and prevents us from despairing of it, providing only that one remembers its various machineries are actually men and tries to maintain and expand man's relations to man".*

This emphasis on humanistic optimism, to me, reflects Camus' journey from self-centered introspection, and unquestioning adherence to political dogma, to a desire to combine political action and social commitment with a strict attachment to moral values – a move that reflected my own political journey, but which I supplemented by a recognition of the need for individualistic humanist values and actions to be linked to collective strategies and analyses to combat the tactics used by people who were opposed to community-initiated renewal, and more generally to a culture even partially based on collective values. To clearly identify my position on this point, and my view of society generally, I then highlighted a quote from Paulo Freire's 1972 book *Cultural Action for Freedom*, a quote that is full of moral force and political commitment and with whose sentiments I thoroughly concur:

> *"The Right in its rigidity prefers the dead to the living; the static to the dynamic; the future as a repetition of the past rather than as a creative venture; pathological forms of love rather than real love; frigid schematization rather than the emotion of living; gregariousness rather than authentic living together; organization men rather than men who organize; imposed myths rather than incarnated values; directives rather than creative and communicative language; and slogans rather than challenges".*

I thus encouraged the class to consider the path I had taken, and to research and practice the counter-manipulation techniques used by contemporary community activists; and, as a parallel response, I also encouraged my students to initiate research and inquiry into the whereabouts of the members of the local power elite. I stressed that community activists should enquire: "Who are these people, which organizations do they represent, what positions do they hold?" and vitally "can we name them and do we know where they work?" To further equip the students with some techniques to counter hostile situations and attitudes, I presented the class with two instruments I had utilized to some effect in my own planning and organizing for community change activities - the innovation diffusion theory devised by Everett M Rogers (1995), and the thirteen rules for radicals compiled and listed by Saul Alinsky (1989).

## Rogers and Alinsky

The main reason for considering Rogers' diffusion theory was to alert the students, as community activists, to actions that can help generate positive change in communities. These actions include promoting an innovative initiative in a community; refining the goals of community organizations; increasing participation in community action; and increasing the effectiveness of community group activity. In addition, I believed that a study of this theory would also enable the students to gauge the probable rate of adoption of an innovation - a new worker, new development strategy or idea or concept - in a community, and to highlight the specific characteristics of communities on which they should focus in order to maximize the potential for change.

I pointed out that in his 1995 edition of *Diffusion of Innovations*, Rogers catalogues five vital characteristics that reinforce the rate and effectiveness of diffusion. The first focuses on the relative advantage of the innovation over the "idea it supersedes" (15), emphasizing the imperative for the innovator - in this case the community activist - to demonstrate that any new idea is more effective than the one it is replacing. The second characteristic concerns gauging compatibility of the new idea or action with the "existing values, past experiences and needs of the adopters" (15). The third characteristic relates to the level of complexity or the ease with which an innovation can be understood, while the fourth and fifth related characteristics are based on "trialability", the extent to which adopters can implement an innovation (16) and observability, the extent to which "results of an innovation are visible to others" (16).

Roger's ideas are also useful when it comes to community activists answering the question, who best to target to stimulate innovation in communities? Prior to my reading his book, I had focused on comparing local leaders against a list of characteristics possessed by many leaders and assessed how each of the local leaders compared with them. My list, based on that compiled by Desmond Connor (1966:22-23), consisted of the following types of leaders:

1.  **General Leader** - followed in many areas of community life, e.g. politics, business, health, sport
    **Segmental Leader** - followed in one or very few segments of community life, respected in this but not in others

2.  **Formal Leader** - holds office, familiar with accepted ways of tackling public affairs
    **Informal Leader** - avoids office, ill at ease in public meetings but nevertheless his advice is sought and respected when decisions have to be made

3.  **Altruistic Leader** - seeks the well-being of the community as a whole, rather than direct personal advancement; rather rare
    **Self-Seeking Leader** - seeks personal progress by attaching himself to projects or persons likely to succeed; may well attach himself to a community worker with valid contacts beyond the community. Should not be written off by a snap value judgment as he is often willing to WORK for a successful outcome; protect your back as he may well exploit you when the opportune time comes

4.  **Authoritarian Leader** - dictatorial style, may be technically effective but provides little involvement for others
    **Democratic Leader** - acts in an egalitarian manner; creates much involvement and learning for others, but may not get the technical job done as well or as quickly

5.  **Goal-Orientated Leader** - very much concerned with the task at hand, but may cause disruptive interpersonal relations
    **Socio-Emotional Leader** - more concerned with developing and maintaining a warm and creative relationship between those involved than in the specific task at hand

6.  **Charismatic Leader** - dramatic and dynamic figure who sweeps up his followers in a tsunami of emotion; may be short in staying power and technical knowledge
    **Technical Leader** - followed because he is competent in subject matter; may loose followers because of purely rational and factual approach

7.  **Local Leader** - has his full life in terms of the local community
    **Cosmopolitan Leader** - followed locally, but is in touch with affairs at regional and national levels

8.  **Majority Leader** - rank in terms of size of following
    **Minority Leader** - smaller size of following but may have characteristics offsetting mere numbers

I then set my class an exercise, and asked them to select those characteristics which appeared to be significant for their own communities and, if necessary, to add characteristics that I had not listed. Then I asked the students to consider three community leaders they knew and to estimate where he or she stood on these characteristics (this is expressed diagrammatically below in figure 4), and I pointed out that the students would find that some of these characteristics tended to go together - and that the information to make such a classification required detailed knowledge which is critical for subsequent social action. All this underlined my belief that it is well worthwhile to make as thorough a case study of key community leaders as possible if future action is to be based on sound foundations.

**Plotting the Profile of a Leader**
**Figure 4**

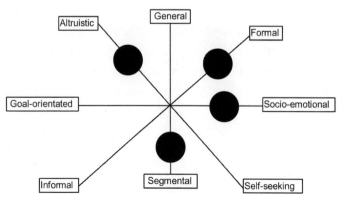

**Some Leaders I Know**          **Characteristics**

...............................................................................

...............................................................................

...............................................................................

...............................................................................

...............................................................................

...............................................................................

...............................................................................

Source: Connor 1968

I found the use of such a list very useful in my community work, especially when tackling a range of problems or dealing with individual situations that required specific leadership characteristics. But I recognized that using this approach took a great deal of time and effort, and that most workers are under great pressure from their agencies to produce "hard" results as quickly as possible. I thus found Rogers' ideas very useful in that he had researched in depth (a luxury generally unavailable to community workers, including my students) the characteristics of leaders, and had come up with evidence for the most effective approach to getting things done - and who to focus on in implementing this process. Rogers believes the answer is "opinion leaders", key players in the interpersonal aspect of the diffusion process which also includes the activist or worker sent by a community agency to influence community attitudes and actions. Rogers' characterization of these leaders can help activists identify the best allies in their pursuit of change. In his view, opinion leaders have more credibility than their more innovative counterparts, and they remain more receptive to change than their conservative peers. Also, they are usually recognized in communities for their "technical competence, social accessibility, and conformity to the community's norms" (27). In addition, compared to their followers, opinion leaders are generally "more exposed to external communication" and "more cosmopolite" (27) - in other words, they are interested in, associated with, and open to, external information and influences.

What Rogers is saying here is that the essence of the diffusion process is its essentially social nature. So, although mass media is useful in creating knowledge about an innovation, interpersonal contacts are more useful in changing attitudes about a new idea - and subsequently changing behavior. *Diffusion of Innovations* reminds us that "face to face exchange between two or more individuals is extremely effective in persuading individuals to accept new ideas" (18). Accordingly, it is useful for community workers to note that when making innovation decisions, most people are not influenced as much by statistics or consequences as they are by word of mouth from others who have already adopted the innovation (18).

Although I stressed the usefulness of Rogers' ideas for community workers acting under pressure, I emphasized that if they had the luxury of a working timetable that gave them sufficient scope to observe, assess and plan before they acted, then they should seriously consider using the assessment methods outlined by Desmond M Connor in his books *Understanding Your Community* (1964)), *Diagnosing Community Problems* (1966) and *Strategies for Development* (1968). I then highlighted how I had found Connor's ideas extremely effective when I had been working on my own in poor, isolated communities in south Wales because they offered me an action template I could study, reflect on (and modify if necessary) and apply in real life situations - and that I would be sharing these ideas, and offering them as examples of good practice for their consideration, in subsequent classes.

## Types of Residents

This brought the class onto consideration of those everyday agents of innovation who are frequently influenced by word of mouth communications - the residents, the individuals who actually live in communities, who form the driving core of any community development strategy and often act as informal change masters and "opinion leaders". During our group sessions, the students who already had "hands on" experience of community work highlighted how difficult it was for them, when entering a community and attempting to work with people on an initial project, to sort out, in their minds, the different types of residents and the relevance of their attitudes, ideas and skills for future development. They accepted that each person was unique, but realized that a worker cannot work completely on a one-to-one basis - so they had to find some way of looking at those residents who possessed dynamic characteristics and attitudes that could be vital for the community's developmental process.

In a brainstorming session of 30 minutes I then posed the question: "But what are these dynamic characteristics?" We eventually agreed that classifying inhabitants by sex and age will not provide the worker with much guidance, nor do education, occupation or income, or classifying individuals as traditional, transitional or modern citizens, shed much light on how people will involve themselves in the development process. Finally, after considering all these points, the class came to the conclusion that three vital characteristics should be borne in mind at the start of the community worker's resident assessment process:

**Place of Birth:** If an individual is a native of the community it is likely that the community has more relevance for him than if he had been born and raised elsewhere.

**Community Experience**: A person who has been a continuous resident of the same community all his life is likely to be less familiar with alternative ways of acting than if he has lived elsewhere and been exposed to alternative ways of taking action.

**Identification**; The people who live in the community willingly, who want to remain in it for the rest of their lives, who think of it as home and a valuable place, are likely to invest time and effort in working to better the condition of the community. Those people who are unwilling residents are not likely to support any developmental action.

From their experience, the students knew that this type of information can be easily acquired - in casual conversations with local residents and with key individuals - without anyone feeling threatened. Gathering information on whether individuals are willing or unwilling residents they accepted was more problematic, but was worth pursuing tactfully as it was a vital piece of knowledge. Also, they pointed out, while it was feasible to classify all the adult residents in a small valley community, this method was not feasible in a large urban community: information here, they suggested, can more efficiently be gathered on key individuals, while an attempt is made to assess the general composition of the main formal and informal groups of people.

When place of birth, community experience and strength of identification with the community are considered together, this core information can suggest some types of residents who have interesting characteristics from the viewpoint of the development worker's plans and strategies. The class then compiled a list, based on one suggested by Desmond Connor (1966: 26-9), of the types of residents it considered central to any community development initiative, and came up with the following categories - and their reflections on their characteristics, again stimulated by the ideas of Desmond Connor:

| Type of Resident | Place of Birth | Community Experience | Identification |
|---|---|---|---|
| Satisfied Resident | Local | Continuous | Willing |
| Reluctant Resident | Local | Continuous | Unwilling |
| Returned Migrant | Local | Interrupted | Willing |
| Disappointed Migrant | Local | Interrupted | Unwilling |
| Immigrant Professional | Non-Local | Interrupted | Willing |
| Transposed Resident | Non-Local | Interrupted | Willing |

## Satisfied Resident

This person was born and brought up in the community and has lived there all her life. She is an active member of it, viewing the advantages of living there as far outweighing its disadvantages. Her education, income and occupational class are likely to be below the average level of the community as a whole. This individual's viewpoint focuses on her own community rather than on any larger social or political grouping. Personal, informal and face-to-face kinds of communication are those she usually uses. Satisfied residents of this type generally make up the stable emotional and physical core of many south Wales valleys communities - in contrast to the more mobile and more "radical" types that are parachuted in to help them. Also, the class noted with interest that this resident category in the valleys was overwhelmingly filled by women. They formed the heart of any community action for community betterment - the driving force behind the creation of crèches, playgroups, regeneration forums, environmental initiatives and a host of other activities. As a supplementary comment on this state of affairs, we all posed the question for workers to seriously consider, "why are so few men involved in all these activities?"

## Reluctant Resident

While being a native of the community and a continuous resident, this individual remains in it unwillingly. She is often stopped from leaving by family obligations, the possession of unsalable property or the lack of up to date job skills. She sees events in national rather than local terms. She is likely to be a source of destructive discontent for any development initiative - the dissatisfied voice from the back that shouts: "Why bother - it'll never work here!" There are a surprising number of such residents in local communities. Indeed, in the eyes of many of the class members, they are currently so significant that they form a bedrock of communal apathy that is providing workers with their greatest development challenge.

### Returned Migrant

This person has much in common with the Contented Resident but, unlike her, she saw she could not establish herself in her native community to her own satisfaction without some additional capital, experience or education. She thus left the community for a while and then returned and settled where she was born, usually for motives to do with emotion rather than economics. Many view this resident as successful - someone who made her mark outside, but who still believes in the values of the local community. With her breadth of knowledge, she has seen alternative ways of solving traditional problems and is thus a potential innovator. She will empathize with a great amount of the development worker's thinking more easily than some other local people. Her experience, capacity for empathy and commitment to the community make her a pivotal person for the worker to identify and get to know - she is somebody who could have a great deal to contribute to the process of development.

### Disappointed Migrant

This individual has much in common with the Reluctant Resident, being a native and unwilling resident who views life in national rather than local terms. She left the community intending to migrate from it permanently. However, she failed to establish herself elsewhere and was forced to return home because her abilities failed to match her expectations. Many see her as unsuccessful. Like the Reluctant Resident, this individual can often act as a negative force in the process of development.

## Immigrant Professional

This person is not a native, and therefore not a continuous resident, but lives in the community willingly: she also belongs to a skilled or professional occupation. Her viewpoint is usually that of the national society: typically she has an above average income, education, social rank and formal leadership skills compared with other members of the community. Whilst she has some commitment to the community now, it is often not as powerful as many other residents. She is likely to be regarded as an outsider until several generations have passed. Although she is often found at the head of various organizations because of her special skills, this does not mean she is necessarily a power in the community - she may be acting as a front for a powerful leader who hopes to remain anonymous. The Immigrant Professional, like the Returned Migrant, often has a breadth of experience and capacity for empathy that the development worker will appreciate. She may have a useful part to play in the development process, but does not have the same appeal for local people as the native-born daughter.

## Transposed Resident

This is usually a very similar type of person to the Contented Resident we have just discussed. She came from a community nearby because she wanted to continue the sort of life in which she was raised, but perceived this to be impossible in her community of origin. Apart from this, the Transposed Resident shares many of the characteristics of the Contented Resident, and may with time seem almost indistinguishable from her. But to the native born, she is likely to remain an outsider. She usually views the world in terms of the local community and can add some weight to the stabilizing influence of the above resident.

I followed up this analysis of resident characteristics by pointing out to the class that their list was meant to stimulate their thinking about the community; it was intended as a point of departure rather than an academic exercise or a final destination. I stressed that students should add other characteristics from their experience if they felt it necessary, and to adapt them to a new community situation if required.

After discussing and analyzing the resident categories, the students split into groups to consider each type of resident we had listed and to implement three exercises in assessing the relevance of our listing to future development action. Bearing this in mind, I then asked the groups to consider:

- The names of three persons in the communities in which they worked for each of the resident categories we had identified.
- Note some differences it might make to their development work if the leader of the local council fell under each category listed.
- Consider what would be the implications for their development work if their community was made up predominantly of one type of resident - taking each of the six categories.

In a subsequent session, I asked the class to again divide into groups to think through the problems of getting their ideas and information over to the residents they had previously identified. They were encouraged to think about what were the most favorable situations in terms of time, place and medium of communication in which they could hope to reach the residents, how best they could select and present their messages (verbally or with audio-visual aids), and what they could do to ensure, as far as possible, that their messages would be understood, accepted and acted on.

After considering leadership characteristics, Rogers' views on innovation and its implementation, and the characteristics of helpful residents, the next element in my strategy was consideration and reflection on the grassroots strategies and tactics devised by Saul Alinsky, and their relevance to community activists. Alinsky is concerned with the acquisition of power. In his handbook *Rules for Radicals* (1971) he makes it clear that "my aim here is to suggest how to organize for power: how to get it and how to use it". His goal is to use power to encourage positive social change by equipping community activists with a realistic view of the world, with a kind of pre-emptive disillusionment: if a person already knows what evil the world is capable of, then perhaps the surprise factor can be eliminated, making the person a more effective activist. According to Alinsky, "the first step toward a solution (acquiring power) is the development of a people's organization", through escalating conflict, and "rubbing raw the sores of discontent". In addition, Alinsky devised thirteen tactical rules for use against opponents vastly superior in power and wealth, which were:

1.  Power is not only what you have but what the enemy thinks you have
2.  Never go outside the experience of your people
3.  Wherever possible go outside the experience of the enemy
4.  Make the enemy live up to their own book of rules
5.  Ridicule is man's most potent weapon
6.  A good tactic is one that your people enjoy
7.  A tactic that drags on too long becomes a drag
8.  Keep the pressure on
9.  The threat is usually more terrifying than the thing itself
10. Major premise for tactics is development of operations that will maintain constant pressure upon the opposition
11. If you push a negative hard and deep enough it will break

through into its counter side
12. The price of a successful attack is a constructive alternative
13. Pick the target, freeze it, personalize it, and polarize it

In Chicago, where Alinsky put his rules into practice, and influenced many people, elderly citizens created organizations to represent their concerns about poor housing and transport. These organizations, which held monthly meetings to stimulate community interest and widen their support base, also consciously used confrontation to increase their influence. When the mayor of Chicago refused to recognize an issue, they organized demonstrations and mobilized the media against him in ways that increased their influence even further, demonstrating that implemented with commitment and skill group action can create positive change. Alinsky, therefore, by encouraging groups to take advantage of the patterns of weakness, arrogance, repeated mistakes and miscalculations of large organizations, helped convert the emotional energy of community groups into effective anti-government, anti-institutional and anti-corporate activism. By studying Alinsky's rules, together with the ideas of Everett Rogers and the development methods of Desmond M Connor, activists could, I believed, allocate blame and productively develop and target empathetic counteractive strategies which would help to level the local power playing field, a development long overdue in many geographical areas of the UK.

The impact of these theories reinforced my belief that the study of theory was vital for stimulating the students' critical thought and their community action, because it consciously situated learning in the themes, cultures, knowledge and idioms of the students, started where the students were, and then developed exponentially. This empowering education adapted the subject matter and learning processes of academia to the students' ideas so as to develop the critical dimensions missing from their own knowledge and speech. I wanted to match critical thought to contemporary experiences by examining workday community issues and academic scholarship. This approach contrasted with traditional pedagogy that expected the students to adapt unilaterally to the offered curriculum with its academic themes, and the formal language of both tutor and texts. Course implementation could thus be described (and was by one student) as "controlled, constructive, conversational confrontation" - and its content was nearly always confrontational too.

I therefore symbiotically linked critical thinking with the identification of power, of partiality, of conflicts of interest and the allocation of blame. With this linkage came an explicit commitment to one side - the community and its inhabitants - and a belief in the validity of an on-going struggle on its behalf. This type of critical thinking gave substance to abstractions such as authority, power and oppression by analyzing local and personal experience and by highlighting how such abstractions are made real - and, more significantly, how these realities could be identified and confronted - and by remembering during this process the exhortation of Chrita Paulin (2007) to her fellow African-Americans:

*"If we begin to read and think crucially about the information that we receive on a daily basis we will begin to recognize how our society attempts to control our economic spending, our thought processes, and our actions. We will begin to think more critically about how we are being targeted and will make more educated decisions when spending our hard earned money. We will begin to see how we are used in the political arena. We will begin to see how advertisers target our children in an attempt to convince their parents to spend money on frivolous items. And, hopefully, we will begin to see that we truly do have the power. If we...begin to exercise our power as a collective whole, there are no limits to changes we can make in this country".*

## Contested Values

While delivering the curriculum and commenting on its content, especially the need to oppose many current corporate and governmental policies, I stressed that such opposition was based on my value system that had at its core a preference for a way of life that stressed mutual action, collective working and a belief in the efficacy of the post Second World War consensus that accepted the correctness of the Welfare State and the mixed economy. My belief, and its obvious opposition to the ideas and policies of the neoliberal elite, led to discussions surrounding the importance of values in community action and in political life as a whole. During this discussion I pointed out that my personal values had remained broadly consistent throughout my working life, but that maintaining them had become increasingly difficult because they had conflicted markedly with society's values which had changed radically during the last thirty years, and were now, as Foley (2010: 40) has noted: "favoring change over stability, potential over achievement, anticipation over appreciation...opportunism over loyalty, transaction over relationship, infantilism over maturity, passivity over engagement, eloping over coping, entitlement over obligation, outwardness over inwardness, and cheerfulness over concern".

I then explained that, to me, a value was a condition that a person preferred to the extent that she was willing to make sacrifices if necessary to obtain that condition. I believed that a value was important, and that by definition, for a person to have internalized a value, that person must have had some experience of the absence of the conditions suggested by the value. For example, if a person valued collective action, then that person had had some experience of working alone in a system that stressed the importance of individual effort, opportunism and competition. In my eyes, it was the preference that was important, and the willingness of the person to make some sacrifice to obtain it.

My view, and my explanation of it, led on to a discussion about how people obtain their values. I made it clear that I believed that values such as trust, honor, freedom, justice, honesty and duty, were learned, and that they were not genetically implanted. I did not think that values were deliberately instilled in school, but to remind students of them I pointed out that they form a tacit part of the general culture by being "chiseled in marble and inscribed in historical, civil, and religious documents" (Kizlik, 2008). Also, I stated my belief that values were symbiotically linked with motives. These links were complex and essentially personal, and so not entirely explainable. In other words, I saw values as the context, the cognitive and emotional template, that was different for each person, but which possessed enough universality to have general application. I believed, as a consequence, that each person, affected by the common values of others, could change and improve communities, and even the world.

Although I did not think I could teach values as a core subject on the programme, I was determined that my students should be helped to understand personal value systems; to think about when, where and how value systems are formed; and to reflect on the formation of personal values as well as those values formed by others. In addition, I wanted to have the students analyze their own values and determine how values affect both behavior and decision making – and to relate this understanding of values to dealing with people as community leaders. To encourage this process, I introduced an exercise in Values Clarification entitled "Alligator River", compiled by the Cooperative Extension Service at the University of Georgia USA (1990), which took the form of a fairytale:

*"Once upon a time there was a woman named Abigail who was in love with a man named Gregory. Gregory lived on the bank of a river, and Abigail lived on the opposite bank of the river. The river which separated the two lovers was teeming with man-eating alligators. Abigail wanted to cross the river to be with Gregory. Unfortunately*

*the bridge had been washed away. So she went to ask Sinbad, a riverboat captain, to take her across. He said he would be glad to if she would consent to go to bed with him preceding the voyage.*

*Abigail immediately refused and went to a friend named Ivan to explain her plight. Ivan did not want to be involved at all in the situation. Abigail felt her only alternative was to accept Sinbad's terms. Sinbad did fulfill his contract and delivered Abigail into the arms of Gregory. When she told Gregory about her sexual escapade in order to get across the river, Gregory cast her aside with disdain. Heart sick and rejected, Abigail turned to Slug with her tale of woe. Slug, feeling compassion for Abigail, sought out Gregory and beat him brutally.*

*Abigail was overjoyed at the sight of Gregory getting his due. As the sun sets on the horizon, we hear Abigail Laughing at Gregory".*

After reading this story, I posed several questions to the group to elicit their values:

- What values do you think directed the actions of each person – Abigail, Gregory, Sinbad, Ivan and Slug?
- Do you think the actions taken demonstrate the individual's values?
- Were there conflicting values?
- Did values change during the course of events?
- Whose values were most appropriate?
- Who was the best person? The worst? Which person was right/wrong?
- Did individual values justify the actions?
- Did each person seem to weigh the consequences of his/her actions?
- Who held true to his/her values?

I used this exercise to get students to see that their acceptance of a clearly defined and relevant set of values would help them to do the right thing, especially when doing the right thing was difficult. In other words, when they had the values they needed, they would understand that these values had costs associated with them, and that they would have to be prepared to meet these costs when acting upon them. So, I pointed out, the values and processes I encouraged were not neutral, rather they were very likely to generate resistance and conflict from the established authorities. I remembered how even working at arms length from direct state power - in the voluntary sector - could involve punitive counter-action: the Community Development Projects of the early 1970s, which were initially accepted as genuine attempts at "bottom-up" regeneration, were subsequently closed down when they developed a practice and analysis that ran counter to the original intention of the state. This view is underlined by Gaventa (1980) who has highlighted in his work on Appalachia that this can be a very uncomfortable approach, as student discussions and explorations may generate resistance from people in the community who wish to keep the status quo intact, and who are unaccustomed to adult education dealing with real life economic and social issues.

In Appalachia, for example, resistance to transformative education has come from corporate institutions that have mining interests and operations in many communities. Since Gaventa wrote his book in 1981 the influence of corporate interests has grown significantly, not just in Appalachia but across the world as a whole. As Naomi Klein has vividly illustrated in her book *The Shock Doctrine* (2007), neoconservative economic policies based on the beliefs of Milton Friedman and his associates at the University of Chicago, have influenced the acceptability, and spread, of market-orientated policies that stress the effectiveness of privatization, reduced social spending and the deregulation of government controls – with devastating results in many communities in the developing, and developed, worlds. Because of this, the need for transformative education to act as a counterweight to the asset-stripping and community destroying activities of the neoconservatives has grown exponentially - and what has made the situation even more urgent in the United Kingdom is the attitude of the Labor government since its entry into power in 1997. While expectations were high that this left of centre government would reverse the neo-liberal measures introduced by previous administrations, the reality has been that post 1997 it has introduced market-driven policies of its own that stressed the need for private and corporate involvement in the delivery of services such as education, health and administrative programmes.

This failure to construct a concerted alternative to the pervasive neoliberal economic system, even from traditional supporters of working class interests, has prevented people thinking creatively about the relevance of alternative systems based on collective values. I explained that research in anthropology had revealed that our ancestors did not always live in a permanent state of individual conflict, because they generally used non- hierarchical and non-confrontational methods of living to promote harmony, including systems of gift exchange, food sharing and collective living - all elements that serve to minimize conflict and generate equitable living conditions where forms of exchange that encouraged personal gain were generally seen as socially unacceptable (Sahlins 2003: quoted in Wilkinson and Pickett 2009:198).

So, despite the current belief in the permanence and efficiency of our individual focused, competitive based society, in the timescale of human history it is the contemporary, highly atomized culture which is exceptional. Over the vast majority of our history, as Christopher Boehm (1999) has pointed out, human beings have lived almost exclusively in highly egalitarian societies. For the great majority of the time humans have lived on this planet, they have lived in egalitarian hunting and gathering groups. Modern competitiveness, and its resultant disparities of wealth and power, arose comparatively recently, with the development of agriculture which stimulated a more individualistic and less egalitarian approach to living.

I pointed out to my class that there is therefore a historically authentic, alternative value system to the competitive culture of neoliberalism. It is called mutual aid and, in the words of the social philosopher Colin Ward, it is "the essential characteristic of the human species in spite of appearances" (*The Guardian* March 2010). Such aid is a vital, in-built element of our humanity that stresses equality and collective living - and the existence and validity of this element should be propagated and spread through educational programmes as well as via informal conversations as widely as possible. In south east Wales, opposition to the use of education as a counterbalance to consumerism and the power of the corporate sector has come primarily from local government agencies. Such organizations have a long tradition of seeing development as a process done on behalf of communities, not by the people themselves. As one disillusioned community worker commented, "rather than embrace the people and their expertise, councils carefully create and maintain the illusion of meaningful community involvement, knowing that their actions will eventually destroy the community". Over time, the separation of the economic and the political, at least at local level, meant that ordinary people saw the economy as something to be dependent upon, not act upon themselves. But with the failure of the traditional model of development from above, and the increasing confidence of communities to act for themselves, many local groups have turned to creating their own alternative development from below. Local authorities are often very wary of these new found confidence levels and actions because many councilors see them as a threat to their long-standing culture of authoritarian service and paternalistic control. Despite this, more and more communities in south east Wales are taking the view of education and learning as expressed by Keep and Rainbird (2000:173), and accepting its often uncomfortable consequences:

> *"Learning is, in essence, a political process in that it leads to change and the disorganization of existing patterns of influence and control (and)...disrupts the continuity of power relationships and hierarchies".*

I, too, accept this viewpoint, and firmly believe that community based education is not limited to the lecture room: that the ideas that are generated in class should go home with the students, should go to their workplaces, and should also be spread throughout the community - a view supported by Raymond Williams who saw adult education as helping to refashion the social structures created and buttressed by conventional education, rather than reinforcing them in the name of selective and commercial interests, thus creating what he labeled a "newly mobile and varied elite" (Williams 1993: 223).

But if the adoption and propagation of collective values puts the students in opposition to the defenders of the status quo, it often puts them in opposition to their own values as well. A striking example of this is found in the students' responses to the theory set out in Jane Jacob's book *Systems of Survival: A Dialogue on the Moral Foundations of Commerce and Politics* (1992), in which she argues - drawing on sources ranging from medieval law and anthropology to current business practices - that human society has developed two ways of generating work and wealth: "trading" or "commerce" on the one hand and "taking" or "conquest" on the other. Linked to these two systems, according to Jacobs, are two moral syndromes - the "trade syndrome" and the "guardian syndrome". The trade syndrome is the domain of entrepreneurs and is based on values such as competition, innovation, honesty, initiative, willingness to collaborate, adherence to agreements, and avoidance of force - all designed to materially advance communities. The guardian syndrome, on the other hand, is relevant to people who work in the government and public sectors and who are led by values such as duty, honor, obedience, discipline and loyalty and the distribution of largesse, all designed to preserve society. Jacobs labels both systems "syndromes" because she sees their elements as having an inner connection which has been built up over time through tradition and legal precedent.

Jacobs believes that for a healthy society to be maintained the traders and guardians need each other: they operate in a symbiotic relationship. But though the two systems need each other, they must be kept apart because if they mix they will harm society due to a clash of values. Jacobs therefore is skeptical about the effectiveness of a mixed syndrome approach. I eagerly grasped this opinion to stimulate discussion in my class: and the mass of students thought that the mixing of values from each syndrome was worth trying. As one put it: "the mixture of the two systems would surely provide the necessary flexibility and ingredients - the best of both worlds - needed to generate community development", while another thought that adherence to a theory devised by an academic was missing the point because "peoples' worlds are created from their own, bottom up experiences, not from academic, top down abstractions".

But, I pointed out, the situation is not that simple, because the syndromes are complex structures that have evolved practically over time: they are what works, and they have not been imposed as artificial entities. Furthermore, though they are separate systems, they are also interdependent: trading needs government to police the rules, and guardians must have commerce to instill initiative and drive into society. Furthermore, and crucially, I stressed that the syndromes are systems, with the vital attribute that all their elements operate together and are self-reinforcing. Because of these characteristics, Jacobs believes that it is impossible to remove and transfer individual elements between syndromes without causing unintended consequences in the system. If transfers do take place, they produce not an effective fusion, but what Jacobs labels "monstrous hybrids" (p 93), transforming positives in one syndrome into negatives in the other.

I gave examples from my own experience of how this dangerous situation already existed, and how it was negatively affecting community groups: I provided an overview of local groups who had taken government money to further their objectives, only to find that their initial activities had been diverted into new developmental avenues. As a result, their original enterprising ideas and actions had been slowed down and slewed towards government policies and targets, their structures hierarchically bloated, and their organizational and strategic nimbleness lost – as was their accountability to the local community. In other words, government money had turned exciting, enterprising/ trading community organizations into bland, guardian/bureaucratic ones, thereby changing their motives for their actions from intrinsic ones (which focused on the organization's work) to extrinsic ones (which focused on outside inducements).

Consideration of Jacobs's two syndromes made the students think about the wisdom of community organizations taking the "government's shilling" (as one student put it) and entering the bureaucratic world where their beliefs were often compromised, even if such a move led to increased funding in the short term. As well as altering the internal structures and attitudes of individual organizations, the acceptance of the government's money also modified the structure of the voluntary sector. Recent research by one of the students showed that the 150,000 strong sector has enjoyed a huge growth in income over the last decade with an average increase of 5.4% per year from 2000 to 2007. In 2000/01 charities received £4.6 billion in grants from statutory agencies and £3.8 billion in contracts. By 2006/7 contract income had more than doubled to £7.8 billion. Although three-quarters of charities in the UK still receive no government income, medium-sized and large charities now make almost 40% of their revenue this way with hundreds of voluntary organizations delivering employment and training, housing and social services. The result of this process is that just 0.5% of charities with incomes of more than £10 million now absorb more than 50% of all charity income - a development that has led to fears of the "Tesco-isation of the voluntary sector, with a few hundred public service deliverers, thousands of micro-organizations at the grass roots, and nothing in between" (The Guardian 23 December 2009).

More importantly, in many ways, discussion about the two syndromes and consideration of the impact of government funding, also forced the students to think deeply about balancing the reality of community against the ideal of community, about the clash between traditional values concerning their community and the new values that they realized they had already adopted to help turn their community into a more dynamic entity – values which, if Jane Jacobs was to be believed, were incompatible and extremely damaging to community efficiency and coherence. Many students thus reported a struggle of conscience - a clash between the foundations of personal morality (reflected in the concern for one's community and the good of its inhabitants) and the foundations and values required for effective action, especially if this action was translated into bureaucratic ways of thinking about community development. Many students felt their new ways of seeing the world, their new awareness of reality, were leading to a conflict between a familiar, comfortable mindset and a new, unfamiliar and threatening one. Though the great majority reported that they were very glad to have learned to think critically about community and society, a minority felt that they had lost their grounding in local society, had compromised their beliefs, and had become far more cynical. "The obtaining of wisdom has come at a high price and, as a result, made me view education as a threatening as well as a heartening experience," was one typical response.

## Local Educational and Economic Initiatives

This approach to community education is particularly necessary in south east Wales where community and lifelong learning have traditionally enjoyed a close, almost symbiotic, relationship. During the heyday of industrial development, and its subsequent rapid decline, the depressed conditions of south Wales acted as catalysts for change. Class and community struggles led to a rich history of grassroots social, political and economic developments - credit unions, neighborhood action schemes, tenants' associations, citizens' rights groups and mutual societies - and although these groups existed for other than pure educational ends, nonetheless their activities contained within them an active learning component.

In addition, the area generated, in response to its social and economic deprivation, a wide range of purely educational initiatives aimed at individual self- improvement. These were focused on local community venues such as miners institutes, libraries, church halls, community centers, workmen's clubs and temperance halls and contained such subjects as Art, History, Philosophy, Political Philosophy, Classical Music, Chess, Antique China, Economics and Ornithology. There was a general belief in self improvement, with working people bettering themselves by reading the classics of English literature, creating book clubs and reading circles, going to concerts, learning to play instruments and joining choirs and libraries. Self-help became mutual improvement and was institutionalized. The miners' institutes of South Wales were, as Rose (2001) observes, "one of the greatest networks of cultural institutions created by the working class anywhere in the world". By the 1930s there were some 100 miners' libraries in the South Wales coalfield, with an average stock of 3,000 volumes. Indeed, given the scope of both social and educational initiatives in the region, the south Wales Valleys during this period could, with some justification, be regarded as one intense "learning community".

But the changing modern economy, linked with the services of the modern Welfare State, has presented new obstacles to these traditional modes of adult and community education activity. One of the most significant impacts of the decline of the mining and heavy manufacturing base of south Wales has been the loss of the wide range of adult educational initiatives previously activated by community groups and the labor movement. Perhaps of even more significance has been the marked decline of a general workplace "learning culture". In this, working conditions generated a world of labor which was highly organized through the trade union movement and a shopfloor ethos which generated its own norms, values, rituals and informal learning structures that stressed such concepts as group solidarity, group action, teamwork, meeting procedures, debating skills and public speaking techniques. An everyday learning culture that was seen by many as essential to working class learning and development has now been swept away, and a "grass-roots" educational hiatus exists which is being partially filled by collective initiatives dedicated to changing the society through educational activity.

The work being implemented by the students attending the classes was therefore embedded in a local educational tradition committed to Enlightenment values of reason for bettering society and sustaining social progress. These students were (according to Welton 1993) also representative of a range of world-wide social movements which were selectively radicalizing social and political values. They were involved in protecting the life world from its enemy, the system world, epitomized in the hegemony of the market and the ambivalent role of the state. Welton proposes these movements have a more holistic view of what it means to be human, and possess a sound understanding of the connections between individuals, and between individuals and their communities. The systematic distortion of communication generated by system world priorities and interests over those of the lifeworld, makes the need for critical learning education, together with social action education to address such debilitating trends, essential in areas such as south Wales which have been poorly served by conventional political action.

To reinforce the action element of the programme, I allocated several lessons to a consideration of local social enterprises and their impact on their communities. I started by listing the successful initiatives that I had either worked with, or had some in depth knowledge of, during my days as a community development worker in the South Wales Valleys. Next, I drew out of their histories the advantages that I believed these collective initiatives had clearly demonstrated in their attempts to bring local people together to address issues that they were all concerned about, but which the public and private sectors had failed to resolve. I pointed out that these enterprises worked through people rather than through structures and systems. They allowed staff the freedom to be proactive and to respond quickly to ideas within a collective and supportive framework that helped the whole organization generate a sense of direction, while they also encouraged their staff to be socially entrepreneurial. In short, the enterprises employed their workers not just to manage the work of the organization, but also to create environments which would encourage a sense of commitment and communal motivation.

I then threw the discussions open to the views of the students, many of whom were actually employed by social enterprises of one sort or another – i.e. community businesses, co-operatives, credit unions, development and regeneration trusts, housing associations and the trading arms of charities. They were honest enough to admit what they saw as the disadvantages of their organizations (the occasional sense of insecurity generated by lack of long-term funding, low levels of pay and the hostility of the local authority and local councilors in particular) but, overwhelmingly, they stressed the advantages of their organizations and the benefits of working for them. As one student said: "we are committed, practical visionaries. We are not hamstrung by strategies – rather we'll see an opportunity and take it by adapting our work to new market niches – and by mobilizing local people around this new mission". As another pointed out: "we're very good at forming partnerships. We recognize that often we cannot stand alone – we need a wide spread of support – and to achieve our aims we often have to work across sectors. We think we are more flexible than the local government sector without embracing the extreme individualism and commercial ruthlessness of the corporate sector. We therefore have an evolving relationship with our supporters and, as a result, we can swiftly offer services which meet new community demands and needs".

Next, I highlighted the point that social enterprises were just one element within a wider phenomenon focused on collective action and its opposition to the dominant culture of competitive individualism and the maximization of profit - an element generally referred to as a social movement. Such a phenomenon points up another approach towards communal change: one based on the belief that resistance to the dominant organizational struc-tures is the area where actions begin, and that the social movement mentality is one that takes energy from opposition. In short, the social movement approach believes that opposition validates the dangerous idea that the status quo is not immutable and that change is possible - and that the students would do well to adopt such a belief when dealing with local power holders.

I then explained, from my experience of working in the community, and from my reading of the relevant literature, that social movements, although often loose and unstructured groupings, develop through four definable stages, and that by understanding these stages my class would see more clearly that they also belong to a valid, contemporary movement, that they hold power in their hands that has generated genuine change in the past and in more recent times – and that knowing about this power will provide them with the belief to combat the despair of believing that the victory of the *system* is preordained. I then outlined the four stages and explained their relevance:

The first stage occurs when individual citizens decide to stop leading isolated lives and to act on their inner beliefs instead. The decision to stop leading an isolated life is often less a strategy for altering other people's values than a surge of the basic need for one's own values to come to the fore. The power of a social movement lies less in attacking some opponent's belief than in naming and claiming a belief of one's own. There is immense energy for change in such internal decisions as they jump from one person to another – and then outwards to society. With these decisions, individuals may set in motion a process that generates change from the inside outwards.

But these decisions are often tenuous, as the people who make them are surrounded by seemingly massive, unmoving obstacles. So the second stage in a social movement occurs when the people making these decisions begin to discover each others existence, and start entering into relations of mutual support and advice – relations which help convince them that although they see themselves as outsiders, they are not crackpots or eccentrics, and that they can combine to consider alternative futures. Also, by then, they may have even heard and acted upon the advice of Margaret Mead: "never doubt that a small group of thoughtful, committed citizens can change the world: indeed, it's the only thing that ever has".

The third stage of a social movement occurs when support groups and individuals translate their private concerns into social issues. It was a process such as this, I point out, occurring in small groups in pubs, chapels and churches, through pamphlets and songs, which transfers individual and private ideas and beliefs into the communal discourse. By doing this, private ideas are projected so that a wider public can hear them, consider them, respond to them and be influenced by them. But, because this transfer does not always have a direct political impact, some doubters often call it an artificial transaction. I countered this argument by pointing out that by transferring private beliefs to the public sphere we can create something more fundamental than political change – we are crating social and cultural change. When people obtain a place in public discussion for phrases such as "community work" and "collaborative action" they are following in the footsteps of reformers who coined phrases like "affirmative action" and "equality of opportunity" and not only made them common but also eventually brought them to life and had them implemented.

I reinforced this point by giving the class a précis of my time working in the community development field. I underlined the point that twenty years ago the idea of community work being an occupation, and process, valued by government and local councils was inconceivable. Then, community workers were found in only a limited number of areas – the Community Development Projects scheme in Pill, Newport, was one of the few that I actually encountered in Wales – and the concept of community development as an instrument of social and economic regeneration being accepted generally was risible. However, due to the persistence of a few individuals who believed in the efficacy of collective responses to communal problems, the creation of a limited number of community development education programmes in local universities by a small number of committed academics - and the transfer of these education programmes into their adjacent communities under pressure from concerned activists - the desert of community-focused initiatives was gradually transformed. Today in Wales, funded by the Welsh Assembly Government, the Communities First programme, with its tranche of development workers and co-ordinators, covers over one hundred disadvantaged areas, and is regarded by central and local power holders as a vital strategy in their efforts to regenerate some of the most deprived parts of the country. (Whether or not such a system can be classified as genuine community development provided the students with a question that was discussed at length in subsequent classes).

I then moved on to explore social movements in general. I explained that as a social movement moves through its first three stages, it develops ways of rewarding people for sustaining the movement itself. These rewards are integral to the nature of each stage: they are rewards that arise from belonging to a community and from discovering a public voice. But in stage four, a more systematic pattern of alternative rewards emerges, and with it comes the capacity to challenge the dominance of existing structures. What exactly are these rewards? I pointed out that as a movement grows, the meaning participants do not find in conventional work is found in the meaning of the movement. Also, as a movement grows, the support and praise workers do not receive from co-workers is received from movement colleagues. Also, as a movement grows, careers that no longer satisfy may be revived in forms and images that the movement has inspired. It is a fact, of course, that these rewards are fragile when compared to the promotions and financial inducements offered by conventional organizations – but the type of person drawn into a movement is not totally focused on conventional rewards, and is far more likely to be concerned with "old fashioned" values such as truth, honor and integrity.

What local social initiatives offer therefore, I summarized, and what community activists must always bear in mind, is that they represent an alternative opportunity for the development of ideas and actions that might otherwise be extinguished or lie dormant for ever. In short, they offer their participants a positive alternative to the bleak, cynical professionalism of organizational existence and a new methodology for developing one's inner self and forging durable communal commitment and action. They also, of course, given the current state of information technology, provide local initiatives with the opportunity to become part of a wider, potentially global, political movement (See Capra pages 188 - 194).

# PART FOUR:

# ACQUIRING ACTION LEARNING SKILLS

# Chapter Seven

## A communal learning overview

The acquisition of skills geared to getting practical outcomes in the community should, I believed, be placed within a wider learning context that stressed the communal nature of reality and the centrality of community in the learning and teaching process. I realized that in most academic environments the individual student is the focus of knowing and, as a result, the inevitable focus for teaching and learning. Given this focus on the individual learner, competition between individuals for knowledge becomes inevitable. Our conventional pedagogy thus emerges from a principle that is essentially anti communal. As well as focusing on the individual learner, it also, In the words of Parker J Palmer (1998:116): *"centers on a teacher who does little more than deliver conclusions to students. It assumes that the teacher has all the knowledge and the students have little or none, that the teacher must give and the students must take, that the teacher sets all the standards and the students must measure up. Teacher and students gather in the same room at the same time not to experience community but simply to keep the teacher from having to say things more than once".*

But, to me, knowing and learning were essentially communal activities: they required many perspectives, many experiences and observations, continual cycles of discussion, disagreement and consensus over what has been experienced and what it all means. This, I believed, was the essence of the oft quoted phrase "community of scholars" – and, in my eyes, it had to be the essence of my classroom too.

I also believed that at the centre of this communal way of knowing and teaching was the need for creative conflict. I encouraged my students to confront each other honestly and critically over disputed facts, imputed meanings and personal biases and prejudices. I recognized that an effective learning group should include conflict at its core, checking and correcting and enlarging the knowledge of individual members by drawing on the knowledge of all the group. I knew such a process often generated the fear of appearing ignorant and of being ridiculed, but I countered this by creating a hospitable environment in which every comment, no matter how incorrect, naive or stupid, was treated with respect and consideration. Within this environment I used an approach, based on my belief that every effort to acquire the truth, no matter how far off the mark it is, is still a contribution to the search for collective truth: students were therefore encouraged to say what they need to say, to expose their ignorance and be willing to appear foolish - in short, to do those things without which learning cannot happen, but without feeling personally and psychologically threatened by doing them.

### Reflection tools

One of the first exercises I set my class to en courage reflective thinking about their work in the community was the Count the Squares exercise (see figure 5). In this exercise, participants were shown a large square divided evenly into sixteen cells (themselves squares) and asked: How many squares are there?

**Figure 5**

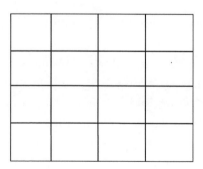

Most people responded with the answer sixteen, but a few said seventeen because they included both the one large square and the sixteen small squares. Eventually, participants realized that you could divide the large square into four quadrants and obtain four more squares. Then some people recognized that you could adjust the way you find quadrants (2 x 2 cells) and identified five more squares. Finally, the participants saw that there were four squares containing nine cells each (3 x 3 cells), culminating in a count of thirty squares. I used this group discovery process to bring out several interesting learning points, and highlighted these to generate discussion and reflection about:

- seeing more than meets the eye
- our assumptions blocking our view of things as they really are
- some people seeing things that others fail to see
- that big problems often have lots of small ingredients

Afterwards, to equip it with a suitable armory of tools for communal learning and problem solving, I introduced the class to the learning system theories of Argyris and Schon (1974, 1978 and 1982). These highly regarded academics distinguish between two different types of learning: single loop and double loop. Single loop learners are disposed to externalize problems by attributing these problems to forces beyond their control, and to resort to counteractive strategies as the treatment for problems that are perceived as dysfunctions. In single loop learning, the focus is on re-establishing stability and normality by enacting corrections and eliminating errors. Solutions that come from single loop learning focus on the external manifestations of the problem and leave internal values, norms and beliefs intact – hence the tag single loop.

Double-loop learning, on the other hand, focuses attention on the root causes of a problem and the changes that need to be made in the attitudes, values, beliefs and practices of individuals (and organizations) to bring about enduring results. Looking inward is the capacity to reflect on how practices (and beliefs and expectations) at the individual and institutional levels produce unreal situations. In particular, according to Argyris (1991: 2), individuals "must learn how the very way they go about defining and solving problems can be a source of the problems in its own right". In essence, I pointed out to my class, the difference between single-loop and double-loop learning is that in the former, change is at a surface level, whereas in the latter, the change is in underlying norms, beliefs and principles. We do not have to be restricted to our traditional attitudes, preconceptions, behaviors and mental models because reflective practice fractures unproductive patterns and reveals new options for future actions.

**The GURU process**
But I stressed that we need to do more than just spend time thinking about what we have done. Our reflection must be purposeful, and the good news is that it is possible to combine reflection in the moment with reflection about the moment to create a highly effective learning/action culture. In his book, *The Fifth Discipline Fieldbook (1994)*, Peter Senge talks about "moments of awareness". This means paying attention to what is happening with enough focus that we can analyze our actions and thoughts and change them while in mid-step. To further this process, Saeger and Remer (2001) detail the GURU process which combines reflection in the moment with reflection about the moment. This is a process of self-questioning that is easy to learn and which dovetails with the experiential learning cycle proposed by David Kolb in 1984. In the GURU process, the learner asks a series of questions that help him analyze the current situation, come to a conclusion, make a plan, and implement the first action step of that plan.

GURU stands for four categories of questions: *Ground, Understand, Revise* and *Use,* When the learner encounters a situation ripe for learning he can ask questions in each category. *Ground* questions aim to help the learner remember the event and recall the basic facts associated with it - questions that will help the individual discover the common ground of the experience. The questions asked focus on the learner's thoughts and feelings at the time, and help him identify his emotional response to the situation. The second category of questions is designed to help the learner *understand* the event or situation in a wider environment, and encourage him to identify similarities and differences within and between events, ideas or actions. The questions in this stage encourage the learner to articulate what he learned and to make generalizations or hypotheses. After understand is *revise*, in which questions are asked which impel the learner to think how he would react if the event, or the information gleaned from it, were slightly different. The purpose is to prompt the learner to think about what aspects of his thoughts, attitudes or behaviors he would revise if given the opportunity. Finally, in the last phase of GURU reflective process, questions are asked that will help the learner plan his next action and *use* what he has learned in various personal and communal situations.

The GURU process is particularly useful in eliminating the unproductive blaming that often accompanies highly charged group working situations. Rather, the emphasis is on identifying problems, analyzing the situation and inventing solutions. Learning thus becomes a process of two-way discovery which ultimately puts the onus of changing behavior on individuals. With GURU therefore, Saeger and Remer believe that individuals and group members can infuse any situation, incident or event with an element of reflective practice to accomplish many different purposes, including:

- assessing a new situation to determine how to begin their interaction with it
- stepping back from an emotionally heated situation to start anew
- adjusting rapidly to changing interpersonal or social factors

- changing course in the middle of a situation to take advantage of new information
- slowing a process to make sure all relevant information has been considered
- evacuating past performance to determine effectiveness
- making a plan for future social and communal encounters

The authors also recognize that one of the prime difficulties of reflective practice is remembering to use it. They realize that to be really effective it has to become a habit. The good thing though, in their view, is that there are many good indicators that can become reminders of when reflective action might be helpful, and these they list as follows:

- when you find yourself making the same mistake over and over
- when you are stuck and don't know what your next move should be
- when emotions run high - anger, fear and nervousness are particularly good indicators
- when you experience cognitive dissonance with a clash of values or attitudes
- when you experience a critical incident - any threshold or watershed situation
- when you fail or succeed - both have great potential for learning
- when you've only completed a portion of the experiential learning cycle
- when you want to learn more about something
- when you unexpectedly find yourself in a teaching role - you can become the expert that others are waiting for

**Espoused theory and theory in use**
In another session I introduced another useful theory of Argyris

and Schon – their distinction between espoused theory and theory in use – and how knowledge of this theory could help community workers and activists construct a realistic picture of the community within which they were operating. I pointed out that organizations and individuals usually proclaim their values and their actions: individuals announce how they live and work, while organizations produce vision and mission statements and set themselves strategic targets and goals - and Schon and Argyris label these public pronouncements "espoused theory". Despite these public expressions, the same organizations and individuals often operate in contradictory ways, seemingly guided by alternative values and criteria. In effect, there is often a shift in the nature of the individual's and organization's actions and values - and Argyris and Schon have labeled these operating actions and values "theory in use". In the words of Argyris (1999:131), people "consistently act inconsistently, unaware of he contradiction between their espoused theory and their theory in use, between the way they think they are acting and the way they really act".

The class then exchanged stories of local individuals and voluntary organizations they had encountered where they felt there was an obvious distinction between their formal objectives and their public actions. I contributed to the discussion by highlighting the case of a small community group that had originally set itself up to campaign on behalf of homeless people but had, over the years, taken government funds to build new accommodation for such people becoming, in the eyes of many other local community groupings, not an increasingly effective advocacy organization, but a market-orientated, money generating business with a contingent mindset. This example, along with the others quoted by the class, underlined my point that when espoused theory and theory in use split apart, an organization often becomes dysfunctional, and often fools itself that it is still maintaining its original objectives, goals and values. I rounded off the session by suggesting that if class members ever worked in specific localities, then their assessment of the problems in those areas should contain a study of all the key individuals and organizations involved and, one by one, a comparison should be made of their stated goals and objectives with their everyday actions and practices.

## Phenomenological reflection

We then turned to a consideration of a new way of thinking about society and how to influence it. We started by considering the ideas of the American anthropologist Clifford Geertz (1973:5) who, when thinking about society and culture, wrote *"believing...that man is an animal suspended in webs of significance he himself has spun, I take culture to be those webs, and the analysis of it to be therefore not an experimental science in search of law but an interpretive one in search of meaning"*. In essence, Geertz believes the concern is with connecting individual action to its sense rather than behavior to its determinants. Furthermore, he believes (1975:10) that society is a shared structure of events and practices - a public "acted document" - that has significance and meaning. So, because humans are agents of their own realization, in Geertz's view, they construct as symbolic models the particular capacities that characterize themselves. They complete themselves through these constructions of cultures, ideologies and symbol systems in general, which in turn act as feedback controls over their behavior.

The phenomenological view of society, as originally proposed by Edmund Husserl, and later developed by Martin Heidegger, opposed this subjective worldview and proposed a new one based on reflection, or a disengaging of an individual's subjective experience through the suspension of beliefs and presuppositions about what is being experienced. Husserl suggested that we must return to the understanding of phenomena. We must isolate the preconceptions we have created directly from our everyday participation in the world, and instinctively "perceive a phenomenon", establishing ourselves as "disinterested onlookers" of both the phenomenon and the perception of the phenomenon (Husserl 1995:35). By adopting this reflective process the field of experience becomes more vividly present, and the individual's capacity for on-going reflection is heightened. Such a disciplined examination of personal experience has similarities with the meditation practices utilized by religions such as Hinduism, Sufism, Taoism, Christianity and Zen Buddhism. These faiths have developed and refined rigorous techniques for examining and probing the mind for centuries, and this applies particularly to Buddhism. Buddhists regard the undisciplined mind as an unreliable tool for observing different states of consciousness, and, following the Buddha's instructions, they have developed a great range of techniques for sustaining and refining reflective contemplation.

While not expecting the students to obtain enlightenment on the scale of Zen Buddhists, I did see phenomenological enquiry as helping my students supplement their conventional approaches to the study of the relationship between individual understanding and the lived world. I thought that the phenomenological way of understanding oneself and one's place in the world more objectively was a way that could generate change in both the individual and the community in which she was working. To me, therefore, learning and thinking about community development could not be seen exclusively as commonsensical, inter-personal processes, but also as contested and extremely complex practices – a view reinforced by Peter Willis, who has extensively explored the impact of phenomenological thinking in relation to education, and who believes that "as a phenomenon, adult education practice...has a constant element of judicial and prudent dealing, compromising, clarification etc, like the sound of the drone in bagpipe music that permanently colors whatever melody is being played" (Willis, 2002:121 quoted in Newman, 2006: 157). I applied the same detached, pre-interpretive approach to the phenomenon of community development. I became an outsider, an external observer of my own mental processes (a process rather like standing back from a painting on a gallery wall in order to see it more clearly). As a result of this intense mental engagement I saw community development as possessing the constant themes of: reaching out to people; meeting them in their own environment; talking to them in their own language; respecting their culture, experience, ideas and views; encouraging them to set their own priorities for action; helping them decide social priorities, choosing if and when to work in partnership with other groups or agencies; being free to reject or accept new knowledge and skills, and being free to compromise and clarify their activities.

I compared this phenomenological approach with the interpretive approach of my college colleagues who saw the community development process through their pre-existing concepts formed by management-speak, authoritarian values and formal language, and so viewed it as a "command and control" system which consisted of on-going elements such as profiting, targeting, directing, imposing, manoeuvring and obfuscating. Many of the individuals operating this system used technical language in their reports and lectures, but possessed few technical skills to match such language. Most of them did not know, and did not know that they needed to know, the inhabitants of the communities they were studying. Most had never even worked in communities. As a result, I was inclined to believe that the task of inducing or persuading them to adopt a more phenomenological view, and change their attitudes and behavior, was one that called out for recognition and implementation as quickly as possible, especially when the individuals involved started labeling their questionnaire findings and surveys "community development", despite having had minimal contact with the inhabitants of the communities they had just surveyed.

I saw this misinterpretation of community development by the "experts" as a good example of how people, even educated people, were able to choose to act in certain ways, but always within a restraining situation of which they were only partially aware. I was determined to make my students conscious of this state of affairs, to open their eyes to the potential consequences of thinking and acting in this limited way, and to encourage them to take a more phenomenological view of society by reflecting and looking beyond their preconceptions when considering communities, educational relationships, events and especially themselves.

**More action tools**
These cyclical and phenomenological models of learning via reflection proved intellectually stimulating for both myself and my students. When I distributed extracts of the writings of Argyris and Schon to the group though, the subsequent discussion revealed how dense and academic these ideas often appeared to my learners. They felt that they needed additional, more accessible models for their group learning and community-orientated purposes ("please give us a more human and down to earth example that we can relate to!"). To meet this demand, I presented them with two alternative concepts of action learning. The first was Action Learning, a system developed by Reginald Revans (1998) in the UK in the 1940s, which stood in marked contrast to traditional teaching methods by bringing together small groups of activists with the following intentions:

- Of working on real problems
- On working together to check individual perceptions, clarify issues and explore alternatives for action
- To take action in the light of new insight
- Bring an account of the consequences back to the group for further shared reflection
- To focus on learning, not only about the issue in question but also on what is being learned about oneself. This is essential to turn developing understanding into learning

that can be transferred to other situations
- To be aware of group processes and develop effective ways of working together
- To provide the balance of support and challenge that enables each individual to manage herself and others more effectively

The core methodology of Action Learning is the formula L=P + Q where L is learning, P is programmed (traditional) knowledge and Q is questioning to create insight. Furthermore, Q consists of four "major" questions, which are:

- Where?
- Who?
- When?
- What?

and three "minor" questions which are:

- Why?
- How many?
- How much?

This Action Learning methodology has proved widely influential, especially in the business world, and I believed that its more straightforward, less complicated structure could provide my students with an extremely handy tool when reflecting on, and reviewing, their actions while carrying out their community work. In addition, I offered the class a second technique: a collaborative learning process that I thought they could utilize in their community groups to help them learn while working – the AGENDA mnemonic compiled by Richardson in 1991, in which the influence of Paulo Freire can readily be seen. The mnemonic breaks down as follows:

**A** Acknowledging, accepting, affirming, aims and the actual situation

**G** Getting to grips with the group's grievances and its activities

**E** Enquiring into experiences, experiments, endeavors and enterprise of group members

**N** Noting notions and ideas

**D** Deliberating, debating, disagreeing, drafting, declaring and demonstrating

**A** Agreeing on action and acting – and starting over again

I made it clear to my students that Action Learning is essentially an educational process whereby the participants study their own actions and experience in order to improve performance and see more clearly what they are about. This is done in a small group setting, and is particularly suitable for adults as it enables each person to reflect on and review the actions they have taken and the learning points that arose out of them. This learning will then, I anticipate, guide their future actions and improve group performance.

### Learning from experience

The community development worker, as I constantly stressed to my class, needs skill in working with people. Every work situation she encounters is likely to be in some way different from every other. In each new situation, therefore, the worker has to chart her own specific course of action in the light of whatever diagnosis she can make of the characters, attitudes and relationships of the people with whom she is working, and of any additional factors she may categorize as important in relation to the strategies and objectives she has in mind for the community. Even if a worker's principles are sound, she will fail to achieve her objectives if she diagnoses the situation incorrectly; or if, having diagnosed it correctly, she chooses on inappropriate action; or if, having chosen the appropriate action, she lacks the skill to implement it. So, if she fails, she will not only have failed in her immediate purpose - she will also have done inestimable harm by souring the local people's relationships with herself and with each other.

The students who attended my course had experienced both success and failure in their community work, and it was their failures that indicated their need for greater skill levels and more learning. I accepted therefore that one of my priorities was to encourage my students to examine their experience in order to help them identify the types of situations with which they were often insecure and nervous, and in which they were most conscious of their lack of skills. These areas of concern, I believed, then provided me with the foundation on which I could build more skill training strategies for them.

One student contributed to the class discussion by admitting her previous shortcomings in dealing with a specific development work situation. By doing this she was not only volunteering her own failures but was simultaneously questioning the skills of the other members of the class and challenging their ability to diagnose where she went amiss and what she should have done. She had failed, so something had to be wrong with her methods. To tackle this problem, class members posed such questions as: did the worker diagnose the initial situation correctly? If so, just what factors did she fail to consider? Was her reasoning inappropriate and, if so, why? Were the difficulties she faced self-inflicted? What did she actually say and do? Could she, in fact, have said something different and acted in an alternative manner?

In this type of discussion, I believed that members of the group, sometimes for the first time, stopped focusing on their own problems as workers and attempted to think themselves into the minds and thoughts of the inhabitants of their communities. Once they did this they began to see themselves, their aims and actions from a different perspective: and they realized that in many instances they had been creating their own problems by using technical language, adopting abrasive attitudes and initiating inappropriate action strategies. By attempting to see things as local people saw them, and drawing on their own experience of working with such people, they could generate a wide range of ideas about why the community rejected the worker's aims and objectives. It became increasingly clear during the discussion that there were several vital elements in her situation which the worker had ignored because she had been too focused on her own problems, and too little concerned with the effect her distraction was having on the attitude of the local people towards her. Once this fact had been recognized and accepted, the way was open for the next stage of the learning process - to discuss what the worker should have done in the light of the insights gained from the earlier discussion.

If such a discussion had only trained the members of the group to work more efficiently in a single situation its educational value would have been limited, but in reality it helped them to develop a range of ideas and a new learning mindset. In effect, each discussion helped clarify the key decisions made at each stage of the development work process, assessed the suitability of the worker's objectives in the light of the mistakes committed, and decided on more suitable courses of action. In each case, the discussion linked the worker's mistakes to specific examples of her lack of sound judgment, and to a general over-emphasis on her own perceptions, which lead to confused comprehension, faulty diagnosis and unsuitable action on her part. In every problem that was discussed the group's members sympathized with the worker's faults because they were willing to admit to similar errors in their work, while recognizing their own lack of expertise in perception, diagnosis and action.

We allocated fifteen discussions of this type during the first year of the course, with each discussion lasting approximately two hours. The discussion started with myself summarizing the main points of the problem to be tackled, and asking whether everyone was clear about what the development worker was attempting to do and in what respect she failed. The group then split into two sub groups with four or five members each to clarify their ideas about two things: first, diagnosis – the reasons for the problem occurring: and secondly, action - what should the worker have done or have avoided doing, in order to anticipate it or resolve it. After half an hour the full group reassembled and the sub groups reported their findings. These were listed on the whiteboard with related points grouped together. The listed points were then considered - some were quickly rejected while others were assessed and considered in great detail, with members expressing their views and contributing ideas based on their own work experiences in similar situations. After another half an hour, when members had usually reached an acceptable diagnosis, they then discussed, in light of this, how the worker might have acted differently in tackling the situation.

The account that follows outlines the course of discussion at an actual meeting. The meeting started at 2 p.m. and ended at 4.15 p.m.

## Outline of a Discussion No. 1
### The Problem

*A community development worker had worked in a small valley community for nine months. She was employed by a regional charity whose objective was to help local people regenerate their communities. The funding for the project that employed the worker was time-limited, and the charity expected positive results within the three year timespan of this funding.*

*The worker had entered the community with the brief of creating three community-led initiatives within the first twelve months of its operation.*

*She had initially made contact with several local community groups to ascertain what they felt the community needed, but had met with a very limited response. Nevertheless, she had pressed ahead with her work by establishing contact with one of the community's councilors who supported her ideas. Within four months the worker had raised enough money (or had it promised from several sources) to build a new community centre within three years. Despite this success, the development worker found that she still could not generate any significant level of support from local people to develop more social initiatives.*

## The Discussion

*The problem was first very briefly discussed to ensure that everyone had got it clear. It was agreed that:*

*The community development worker had made contact with several persons and, working with a local political leader, had generated a substantial amount of money to facilitate the building of a community centre in the near future. Despite this, the worker could not generate any substantial level of public support for her work.*

*The members then broke up into small groups to discuss a) just why the worker failed to generate support, and b) just how she could have tackled the job better. The sub-groups reports made a number of points from among which, after further discussion, the following were agreed:*

*Diagnosis (why the worker failed)*
1. *The development worker had allowed pressure from her employing organization for quick results to influence her actions.*
2. *She had allowed insufficient time for consultation with local people to ascertain exactly what the felt needs of the community were.*
3. *She had failed to analyze the attitudes and values of local residents, and had also failed to assess which residents could be used as partners in her development strategy*
4. *She had taken a consultative shortcut by linking with a local leader, without assessing the state of personalities and politics in*

*the locality, for expediency.*

5. *She had, in the eyes of the local people, ignored their views and ideas in favor of the ideas of one individual who, in their eyes, was putting forward the ideas of the local Establishment - she was imposing initiatives from above.*

6. *The local people felt slighted and became very distrustful of the worker's development agenda, viewing her as a tool of authority - and not to be trusted.*

*Action (what she should have done)*

*The development worker should have resolved this dilemma by observing systematically the community which she had entered, and then used a needs assessment survey to collect more information – especially the opinions of individuals – to consider the question of community needs and the potential for action. Using the information gathered by the survey, and drawing on her reading of one of my book recommendations, Desmond Connor's Diagnosing Community Problems (1966:14), one group member suggested she could have used an analogy with an iceberg, one-ninth of which is seen above the surface and nine-tenths below to discover what the community really felt. Figure 6 illustrates how community needs may be visualized by using this device:*

1) *those felt by both the worker and most of the people*
2) *those felt by the people*
3) *those felt by the worker but not present in the community*
4) *those felt by neither the people nor the worker*

*The worker should have started by co-operating with the people in resolving some of their felt needs (i.e. No. 2 in the figure), ideally those which she shared (i.e. No. 1 in the figure). By doing this, as the people experienced small successes in dealing with some felt needs, they would become aware of needs previously unrecognized, as the iceberg rises when "needs sections" are removed from its protruding surface. Vitally, too, the development worker would have taken the population with her and*

*maintained its trust, thereby generating more public support for future*
*social initiatives.*

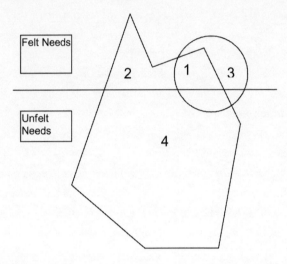

**Figure 6**

1. *Needs felt by both the people and the community worker*
2. *Needs felt by the people only, not yet recognized by the community worker*
3. *Needs felt by the worker, but not either felt or unfelt needs of the people i.e. results of the worker's own biases*
4. *Needs not felt by either the people or the worker at the present time*

*As time goes on, the community worker should recognize more of the felt and unfelt needs of the people i.e. circle increases in size and moves to the lower left in the figure above. As felt needs are successfully dealt with, unfelt needs rise to consciousness as felt needs i.e. move from No. 4 to No. 1 and No. 2.*

*Source: Connor 1966*

*The groups made it plain in their reports that this felt needs approach to community development should have been adopted by the worker for a number of reasons, which they then listed and explained, again drawing heavily on the reasons given by Connor in his 1966 publication (pp. 14-17):*

*Firstly, because it respects the prevailing situation in a community, the wishes of its inhabitants, and their judgments based on their experiences; whereas the development worker, who personally assesses the community and defines its needs with reference to only a single, or limited number of individuals, is often operating on the basis of very restricted and shallow knowledge.*

*Secondly, this approach respects the cultural values of the inhabitants in a meaningful manner, recognizes that their values and motivations are genuine, and reflects the fact that to ignore them is often the initial step to failure and alienation.*

*Thirdly, this approach realistically builds on the people's awareness of a problem and accepts that this is the first step in the process of the community adopting a new idea. To overlook this advantage, and start instead the often slow process of creating awareness of a currently unfelt need, or accepting the view of a politically motivated individual, seems a very weak approach in comparison.*

*Fourthly, psychologically, the felt needs approach has sound analogies with personal experience. Most people are aware of their own problems but are shielded from awareness of more than they can cope with by psychological defense mechanisms. If they are made fully aware of all the problems they face, this would be too much for most people to cope with, thinking that their weaknesses far outweighed their capacity to cope with them. They would probably feel fearful and angry towards anyone responsible for upsetting their mental equilibrium in this way - and the same principle can be applied to people living in communities and their attitude towards problems implicit and explicit.*

*Fifthly, the ethical approach towards felt needs has a great deal to* commend it, because community workers, wherever they are based, are invariably challenged with the question: "What right do you have to enter our community and interfere with our way of doing things?" The answer to this question will undoubtedly be easier if the worker is co-operating with the local people to find solutions to problems which they have identified. If the community worker chooses what she considers to be an important problem, and works at it for some months without much sign of success, it can become increasingly difficult to justify her actions to herself - and to the local population. This is a situation which it is better to avoid.

Sixthly, at the start of her involvement, a community is often divided into cliques so that an effort to create a unified front only generates interest in a very small percentage of the population. The people often have little confidence in their own ability and even less in the ability of the development worker. The confidence to co-operate grows with the lessons learned in early and successful experiences in dealing with the felt needs which may have little technical significance. People, as a result, are only then likely to become aware of more demanding issues which were previously unrecognized.

Finally, the felt needs approach distinguishes between priorities in time and of importance. It is often poor strategy to tackle first the most important problem in a given situation, yet this is a frequent temptation to the worker who wants to make an impressive start in the community. While communities do sometimes tackle something beyond their existing capacity, they are less likely to do so than an eager young development worker. Also, the felt needs approach is the first step in a development process that minimizes the dependency of the local population and maximizes its self-reliance.

Summary
The main points of the reports were summarized by the main group as follows:

- *The development worker should have resisted pressure to create initiatives as quickly as possible. She should have taken at least three months to observe the community and then diagnosed and ascertained its needs. In this phase, she could have utilized active citizens to compile and carry out a community-wide needs assessment to reinforce her findings (or modify them should the outcome of the assessment provide a different picture). After this phase, the worker, in conjunction with the community, should compiled strategies for development and finally stimulate community action to implement these strategies.*

- *Her reliance on a single individual and his ideas (probably politically orientated) to get things done was a vital mistake that cost her the trust of the local people and meant that she found herself lacking any adequate level of support for her future action plans.*

- *The worker forgot that one of her key roles was to act as a catalyst of ideas, attitudes and actions for the local population. Once she had compromised her position (even for genuine reasons to "get something going"), she had failed in her role as a community development worker because she had jettisoned respect for the people she was supposed to work with.*

This way of working through problems experienced by class members caught the imagination of the whole class. As a result, I decided to introduce another session soon after the first one, and we adopted the same system of group discussion and sub group reporting back with recommendations.

## Outline of a Discussion No. 2
### The Problem
*This problem was closely associated with the problem highlighted in the first discussion. It centered around the relationship between the community development worker and her employer. The latter had a timetable and targets, and it expected the worker to conform to these as closely as possible. The employer, a voluntary organization funded by*

*government moneys and deeply into modern management systems which stressed budgets, obedience and time-limited outcomes, pressurized the worker to select and implement a suitable initiative in the targeted community as quickly as possible - in order to produce something tangible that could be shown to its paymasters as proof of their effectiveness. It appeared that this was a workplace problem that was common to a significant number of the students, and was therefore one of which they all had experience. As a result, deep and heated debate followed in the session allocated to the problem.*

## The Discussion
*The problem was first very briefly discussed to ensure that everyone involved had got it clear. It was agreed that:*

*The essential problem was the relationship between the development agency and its worker, and their disagreement over which project should be tackled first in the community. The agency was driven by commercial considerations to create and establish something from a limited field of activities in order to attract future funding and maintain its operation. The worker, on the other hand, was operating with the best interests of the community at heart, and believed that she should take some time to carefully observe, diagnose, plan and act to produce what the community really needed, for the betterment of its population, from a much wider range of activities.*

*Again, the class broke up into small groups to discuss a) just what the worker could do, and b) how what she did could be reconciled with the objectives of her employer. The sub-group reports made a number of points, from which after discussion, the following points were generally agreed:*

## Diagnosis
*The general view was that the community worker had been placed in an impossible situation by her employer. The situation represented a clash between two sets of values - those of the worker who saw her work as being focused on the local people, and her agency which was more*

*concerned with generating a profit. The agency was still a voluntary body, but had accepted the neo-liberal view of the government that voluntary organizations could provide services for local communities by adopting more commercial and business-orientated systems and methods of working. The agency's original commitment was still operational, but had become submerged among its desire to expand its activities by producing outcomes that met the agendas, policies and targets set by central government.*

### Action

*All the group agreed that the worker's first task in a community was to survive. To achieve this she had to be accepted, and remain accepted, by both her community and her agency. Moving close to one, at the expense of the other, would jeopardize her effectiveness for both.*

*The group believed the development worker had three options she could pursue:*

a) *she could draw up a list of the major felt needs (those felt strongly and widely) and relate these to the acceptable goals as defined by her agency. Several of these items would be both felt needs of the people and acceptable to the agency; the first project in the community should be chosen from amongst these.*

b) *she could ask her agency to reconsider its priorities and allow her to work on this problem with the local people because of the particular circumstances involved, or as an experiment or pilot project.*

c) *she could explain her situation to the community, suggest that there might be another agency which was better equipped to co-operate on this specific problem, and work with them to make effective contact with this organization.*

*Other topics were also primary goals of the agency but not felt needs of the people. In this case, the worker's dilemma was either to reluctantly push the agency's agenda onto the people or to ignore the clearly defined agency policy. One way out of this was for the worker to play for time - she should take up the community's concern with several other agency goals and state her intention, to the agency, of working with the people on these; to suggest that she would be more than busy with these problems, but that once she had made some progress on them, she was sure the people would become aware of the importance of the agency topic currently under consideration.*

## Summary

*The worker should not have been placed in such a difficult situation. The future of community development as a genuine collective process of regeneration will be put in doubt as long as employers adopt more commercial attitudes to working in the community. Despite the dilemma faced by the development worker, all the group agreed that the first project tackled by the community must be successful, otherwise it was likely to be worse off than it had previously been. Drawing on its own collective experience, the tutor's knowledge, and the views of Desmond Connor (1966) again, the group agreed that a first project in a community should therefore meet the following criteria:*

1.  *be based on a generally felt need of the whole community or a significant proportion of people within it*
2.  *be concerned with a piece of work agreeable to the worker's employer*
3.  *be technically straightforward, dependable and practicable in the local situation*
4.  *can achieve physical and visible results quickly*
5.  *contain some learning element for future initiatives - this is almost unavoidable, but must always be consciously built into the project.*

These discussions were very popular with both myself and the students. They reinforced the collective learning processes - visioning together, acting together, building a sense of community, developing energy, leading together and learning together - that I anticipated when I included them in the course curriculum: and they bore out what the McMaster example of small group learning had illustrated - that giving students problems based on their own experiences to solve, and to ask some key questions about these problems and their solutions, is a far more effective learning tool that merely loading them with masses of information.

Furthermore, by adopting this approach the students discovered the causes of their colleagues' (and their own) failures, and also, concurrently, found themselves discovering, testing and affirming basic community development principles for themselves in a far more meaningful way than I could provide through lectures. Also, in discussing how they could have avoided or solved their problems, they were pooling experience of many situations in order to assess what applying these principles meant in terms of day to day work. In addition, the discussions had a cumulative effect. Each discussion further reinforced some of the principles affirmed in earlier discussions and provided yet another opportunity for investigating how to apply them in the field.

## Listening skills

I constantly stressed the vital importance of collective discussion as a learning tool in this development process, but I also recognized that effective discussion depended on the capacity of its participants to listen - and that many conversations were not discussions, but rather the half-listening of one person waiting for the other to finish, and the half-listening of the other waiting for the first to do the same. Little in the practices of everyday conversations fostered the critical consultative elements of discussion - those pauses, questions to the other person, and general attentiveness and interest which encourage discussion's vitality rather than its reduction to monologue. Indeed, I had come to the conclusion that my students were often not engaged in genuine discussion at all, were not establishing a trusting relationship with the other speaker, but were, in the words of Allman, (2001: 175) engaged merely in "the sharing of monologues". The ability of my students to generate focused discussion could not then be taken for granted, and I realized that to get them to use focused, relevant language - what Allman labels dialogue - I would have to include a number of training sessions on this topic.

In the first of these sessions, I introduced Allman's (2001) concept of dialogue to the class. I pointed out that to Allman dialogue is different to discussion because it is a creative exchange in which new understandings are generated. To Allman, true dialogue consists of a collective examination of a topic under discussion. Each participant can set out the reasons why she believes what she does about a topic, together with a justification for her values, ideologies and assumptions. This process is designed to allow the participants to obtain a clear reading of their world and its meaning. The objective of the process is to expand the knowledge, develop the thinking and alter the consciousness of the whole group, so radically changing its collective ways of knowing and seeing.

In subsequent sessions, I focused on Habermas's (1984) theory of communicative action, especially his ideas on "criticisable validity claims", in which he argues that whenever there is a conversation between individuals with the intention of reaching an agreed position, all parties are making a number of validity claims, whether they are aware of this or not. Habermas believes in "fair play", such that all parties have a right to expect each other to speak with sincerely, truthfully, and with legitimacy (Habermas, 1984:99, 317). He further believes that the validity of these claims can be assessed by the listener posing a yes or no answer to the claims by asking herself: for sincerity, has the speaker made clear his vested interests?; for truth, has the speaker included all the relevant information on the topic?; and for legitimacy, is the speaker operating in the appropriate context and role? Habermas suggests "an ideal speech situation" occurs when everyone involved in the conversation tries to meet these three criticisable validity claims. By doing this, they are seeking consensus – a consensus that accepts differing interpretations but which generates genuine or "true" knowledge. In this type of emancipatory conversation therefore each person can speak frankly, test her own, and the other person's, view of the world, revise her ideas and act on, and change, both herself and the world of which she is a part. This does not mean there will always be a consensus after participating in a conversation – one can agree to disagree as well as agreeing to agree. Also, when a consensus is achieved this does not mean that it is a definitive consensus – it can always be rediscussed in the future.

To make explicit the effectiveness of the validity claims process, and to stimulate a genuine interplay of talk and ideas, I divided the class into four groups of three persons and encouraged them, by following the three validity claims in every utterance they made, to conduct a collective enquiry into an idea I had written on a whiteboard, and to simultaneously generate new ideas and knowledge about the idea provided. To reinforce this belief in the power of dialogue, in the next lesson, I introduced Allman's views about monologue sharing, and asked the reconvened groups to spend 10 minutes considering Allman's idea - and then report back their views to the whole class. After reporting, I asked the same groups to reform and take a further 10 minutes to reflect on their past classes, and the language they used in them while discussing community development tactics, strategies and histories.

Later, to reinforce the impact of this approach, and make even more explicit the effectiveness of the validity claim process, I introduced more articles by Habermas and Allman and, in a subsequent class, introduced the latter's ideas regarding "objects of thought" - those topics that form the core of a group dialogue - and their role in generating focused dialogue exchanges (Allman,

1987: 2001). In this class, I wrote a problem concerned with community development ("Is there such a thing as genuine partnership in community development") on the whiteboard, and asked the students to tackle it as an object of thought, to help each other explore their responses, and to try to generate new ways of thinking about the problem.

The students reported that though they found the exercises I had used useful as "scholastic tools", and concluded that though towards the end of the course they had moved away from the sharing of monologues to a more reflective, "ideal" dialogue situation, they believed that this process had more to do with my constant chivvying of them to focus on whatever topic we were discussing, on insisting on the three-person speaking rule, and by them duplicating my attempts to stick to the subject under discussion. While generally accepting the potential utility of Habermas's criticisable validity claims and ideal speech situations, they pointed out that such processes were likely to be implemented really effectively only in a controlled environment, such as an academic seminar, where people with equal power and knowledge debated philosophical issues.

The students did not believe that Habermas's ideal speech situations did in fact generate optimum conditions for creative conversation. Habermas, in his later writings, also shows a certain degree of caution on this topic. In fact, in 2005 (2005: 89) he supplemented his "ideal speech" process with an additional ingredient – four pragmatic presuppositions - to make conversations approximate as closely as possible to the ideal: a) no one capable of making a relevant contribution to the conversation should be excluded, b) all participants should have equal input, c) all should be free to speak their honest opinion without self-deception, and d) there should be no coercion during the process of the discourse. Such controlled situations and dispassionate procedures are not easy to create in everyday community affairs, but if such presuppositions are followed, Habermas believes that they will have an "operative effect" on the actual discourse and will genuinely prevent suppression of arguments, manipulation, self-deception and exclusions (2003:108). My class, while accepting the need to, as far as possible, achieve equal input and access, still thought that in reality true discussion was far more "messy", uneven and chaotic - and all the better for being so.

I countered this view by noting that if the result of "messy" was really chaos and uneven participation, then though excitement may be generated, the outcomes of such interaction were frequently opaque and confused as a result of the pressure from the conflicting and haphazard voices in the discussion. I, while admitting that reality often fell short of the ideal, pushed the view that community group members in particular should endeavor to create ideal speech situations by asking fellow members to explain and make comprehensible and truthful their assertions and proposals. I also pointed out that genuine attempts to adhere to these rules were what had granted legitimacy and efficiency to my educational methodology and, more importantly, to the broader workings of society in general and democracy in particular; and I underlined this point by using the words of Habermas (1996:4) who believed that "those aspects of validity that undergird speech are also important to the forms of life repro-duced through communicative action" – especially the democratic way of life.

# Chapter Eight

*Group Development Processes*
**Task and people elements**
As well as introducing Habermas's and Allman's ideas into the programme to further the impact of critical collective discussion - or dialogue - on community problems, I also stressed the importance of the students recognizing that there are two basic components of group development: the people component and the task component, and that the classic dilemma for community groups involves getting the job done while maintaining a humane group existence. Drawing on the work of Rohs (1984) and Bolton (1986), I emphasized that as groups form, inter-personal relationships must be established (the people component) and the job to be done must be defined, organized and accomplished (the task component). In order for both of these components to be successful, it is important for group members to monitor the development of the group. Too often members assume that this role should fall to the chair exclusively. I stressed that, in fact, all members had a responsibility to monitor and intervene if the group appears to be loosing cohesion. By doing this, they can influence the group by using discussion in such a way as to ensure completion of the task and maintenance of positive human relationships. So I introduced the class to group roles that would implement the two tasks: by emphasizing that for the task to be completed participants must:

- give their opinions regularly,
- seek the opinions of other members,
- direct and channel the work of the group,
- energize it when its enthusiasm tires and
- check its methods when confusion arises.

As for maintaining a humanistic relationship with other members,

I stressed the need to:

- encourage even participation,
- facilitate open communication between all participants,
- relieve potential emotional "flashpoints",
- help defuse interpersonal tensions and
- give everybody support and encouragement.

## Being assertive

But some students pointed out that open communication between all participants was often not possible due to the fact that on some groups, indeed on many community committees, there were councilors with strong views and personalities who were used to getting their way due to the strength of their personalities. Such people were often difficult to deal with, so the students asked if I could give them some training in assertiveness in order top help them counter these individuals and their often aggressive attitudes. I responded by pointing out that assertiveness was not the same as aggression. Rather, it was a technique halfway between aggressive behavior and passive behavior, where people stand up for themselves, express their true feelings, and do not let other people take advantage of them (while at the same time being considerate of the other person's feelings). After exploring these basic concepts in more detail, I offered the class some tips on behaving assertively:

- Keep what you want to say clear and to the point. Avoid long explanations.
- Look directly at the other person, stand (or sit) upright and keep a calm tone of voice
- Do not apologize if you are in the right.
- Be polite but firm
- Try to relax, rather than become angry

I suggested to the students that they imagine a potential situation – during a board meeting, for example, - when they could put this technique into effect. I therefore set up a series of dry runs or rehearsals in class in which one student played the hostile councilor and the others had to respond to her aggressive views in an assertive manner. This proved a great success, and to reinforce this preparation, I also included in one lesson practice in the use of the "I statement" whereby students rehearsed using statements that began with the word "I" – for example, by offering, assertively, constructive criticism of a colleague's report by saying, "I had to read that part of your report three times before I understood it", rather than, "This section was rubbish and very confusing", or "You need to learn how to write clearly before attempting to write reports".

## Some sports psychology strategies

I had played a great deal of sport in my youth and, as a result, much appreciated the need for effective team effort, as well as assertiveness, in order to consistently win games. I also remembered that my sport psychologist colleagues had frequently told me that team building was essential to effective group work, and that I should not assume automatically that my students would instinctively be prepared to work together as a team. Indeed, after discussing with them the relevance of sports psychology to the improvement of teaching and learning in the classroom, I came to the conclusion that some theoretical approaches used in sport psychology were relevant to areas where optimum collective performance – including the work of classroom and community groupings - is crucial, and that I should endeavor to put these to use in my weekly classes.

My first step in this process was to take on board my colleagues' views that groups generally develop in a predictable and sequential way, and that students do not become teams without having dedicated time to "forming, storming, norming and performing" (Tuckman; 1965). In other words, my students should, first of all, have time to come together as a group and to get to know one another. They also needed time and space to brainstorm ("storm") and to assign individual roles, such as leader/organizer of the group and record keeper, to specific individuals. The third stage of group formation required that members "norm", or decide, how the group will work (by consensus or majority vote), while finally, in the last stage, the team actually got down to business and started to perform.

I regarded the model devised by Bruce Tuckman as pivotal, and spent a while explaining its simple yet complex process to the class. I pointed out that though all groups pass through the four development stages organically, not all groups go through the stages smoothly. Each stage was either positively or negatively affected by the previous stage's completion. If a group introduced one or more new members, then it had to revert to the forming stage - the same for a new task that it faced or attempted to implement. From my experience of working with community groups I had noted how easily groups could slip into acrimony due to ineffectual forming or incomplete storming. But I also noticed that those groups that spent more time evaluating their situation and carefully defining their objectives and actions - all initial forming tasks - were generally better equipped to achieve positive outcomes. Similarly, groups that explored new ways of tackling problems were significantly more successful in hitting their objectives. In brief, I found Tuckman's model extremely useful in identifying and understanding why some groups were successful, while others failed despite containing many committed individuals.

After explaining the Tuckman Group Development Model, I divided the class into three groups of four students and asked them to reflect on the workaday groups of which they were members (particularly the Partnership groups created by the Communities First programme in Wales), and to discuss which stage they thought their partnership had reached. The students considered this question for thirty minutes then reported back to the whole class. I then asked the class to consider each of the three reports, the stage of development of each partnership, and what they thought the next stage of partnership development should be, how long it was likely to take to reach this stage, the reasons for their decision, and the actions the partnership could take to benefit the community that it served, given the stage it was at. I also asked the students to study my own actions as a player of these roles, and to judge me as a role model as I endeavored to create a coherent, active learning group out of my own class; and to note, and comment upon, the effectiveness of my actions in a later feedback session (which they did with forensic glee).

While implementing this team building process, I discovered some additional effective strategies to help me in teaching effective group work. For example, I found it best to avoid cliques by assigning friends to separate groups. I discovered that I should allocate sufficient time for members of each group to get to know each other and to brainstorm on a specific issue. To function effectively as a team, I realized that student groups need tasks that can be delegated to members, and that individual accountability should be attached to these tasks. I discovered too that I should provide guidelines on how the groups are expected to work together, and how I would intervene to resolve conflicts, at the start of the course.

I also found that asking groups to allocate names to themselves was a great help when it came to asking them to implement a specific task. Shouting "Come on, Rhondda Boys and Girls, time to finish that survey," was far more effective than "Come on you five over there by the door". Also, by forming actual groups as part of class activities, I found it easier to explain how, by identifying the stage a group is in, or about to enter, a member could time interventions so that the group would be ready to move forward at the appropriate time. Also, when referring to its last activity, I could point out that by recognizing the current stage of group development, a group member is better able to diagnose problems, to bring out the human resources of the group, and so increase the group's options.

To achieve even greater levels of motivation in the classroom and in the community, I decided to introduce even more concepts that were frequently examined in sports psychology to my course. I knew that many of my students felt under great stress when arranging and participating in, and sometimes leading, community meetings, especially those where local councilors with strong personalities, and high ranking representatives of the local authority, were present. I pointed out that sports coaches often spent time with their teams talking about ways to cope with the "big game", helping them visualize their actions and their likely consequences; and that international athletes generally plan their performances and develop fall-back plans before events (Orlik, 1986). Such people understand there will be obstacles to their success, but that they can refocus their performances and produce, if necessary, more effective outcomes by having alternative plans. These proactive planning techniques were, I underlined, used to ease stress, and were based on knowledge of problem-centered and emotion-focused coping strategies – strategies which could also be applied to their own situations. To reinforce the need for such proactive thinking, I stressed the effectiveness of pre-meeting gatherings where community activists could combine to plan their meeting strategies – and decide who was taking responsibility for specific agenda items, who was going to argue for or against a particular item, deciding who to oppose, who to support, and which collective attitude should be adopted for the occasion.

I also used the concept of team captain when undertaking group development, because I saw this concept as having similarities with the peer-mentoring strategies used in many classrooms. I specifically used team captains, chosen by a vote of fellow group members, to help organize their groups – through planning projects and reporting back on group attitudes – and by helping fellow group members decide on the content of at least three projects (a PowerPoint presentation, a debate and an extended essay/paper) to be delivered during the academic year. This move proved highly popular, especially when I rotated the captaincy for each of the three projects, and its use helped to create a sense of course ownership in the groups while simultaneously reinforcing leadership skills that could be put to use in future community settings.

By using captains, and increasing the profile of their teams accordingly, I introduced the element of competition into the class. Although I believed that within groups co-operation should be the general rule, my sports psychology colleagues assured me that competition is not always a bad thing. In their eyes, competition across groups could actually enhance motivation and performance. The key to maintaining the balance between co-operation and competition, in their view, was to make competition fun and worth relatively small rewards (e.g., a round of toast or a cup of coffee at the community centre bar). I thus used small competitions for group assignments, and found that by doing this the natural competitive tendencies of the students kicked in, and that they wanted their group to perform better than the other teams – an attitude that had obvious implications for their future work with local community groups.

Wrapping up this section on group activity, I pointed out that in my experience of working with community groups the most effective method of relating to them was by playing the role of a demonstrator. By using this role the worker initially does much of the group's work, and the intent is to show the group how to work on a given project or community-problem solving activity - so that it can proceed on its own the next time. Group learning occurs as the worker involves one or more members of the group in the activity, explaining what is being done and why.

I stressed that as a demonstrator the worker will often focus on problem-solving functions more than group maintenance functions. Enlisting support and co-ordinating work should always be emphasized. Working again with at least one group member and explaining what is happening, the worker might obtain support from community leaders. The worker might also try to co-ordinate the group's activities with those of other community groups, while explaining the value of such co-operation. She could also obtain the human resources for the group so that its members learn how to obtain resources themselves. The worker should also obtain vital information for the group but would show group members how to obtain similar information in the future.

But group functions will also be implemented. The worker might actually organize a community-problem solving group but would involve potential group members in the process. Thus they would learn how to maintain the group's organization, as well as how to organize a future community group. Training might be carried out by involving a limited number of group members in many of the worker's activities, and the worker would explain the how and why of various leadership functions. When the worker withdraws from an active demonstrator or leadership role, these group members could then assume more responsibility. Likewise, if encouragement or conciliation was needed, the worker could take time to explain the importance of such activity.

Finally, I stressed that community workers should not forget the importance of emotion in community groups. Community activity can generally be seen as a rational, logical process, proceeding step-by-step through a problem-solving model. Such a method obviously has its advantages, but I pointed out that in my experience the trust developed between the worker and the group, the group's feelings about their community's problems, as well as the encouragement provided by the worker, all influence the growth and effectiveness of the community group. Emotion is part of each of these factors, so learning activity in the midst of group development and problem-solving should always take into account these emotional elements.

## A simulation exercise

To give my students experience of conflict in a consensual setting, I sometimes used a simulation exercise. The one I used most often was the *Lost On the Moon* exercise (Hall: 1971 in association with NASA). This posed a problem that individual students first had to solve privately. After doing this, small groups were turned loose on the problem after I gave them a simple set of conflict-consensus rules: "present your views clearly, but listen to reactions before pressing your point"; "don't change your mind just to achieve harmony"; "avoid conflict-reducing techniques such as majority vote, coin-flips, bargaining"; "when stalemate comes, don't assume that some must win while others lose; seek a solution acceptable to all members"; and "remember that consensus does not require that everyone love the solution, but only that no one be strongly opposed to it". By providing the groups with these rules I was recognizing that conflict would occur; but that by them using them I was helping to constructively authorize and guide the very conflict that the students wanted to avoid.

When the exercise was over, individual and group solutions were scored for accuracy. If a group had followed the rules, the group score was almost always better than the average of individual scores – and it was often better than the best individual score in the group. When these results were not achieved, I stressed that it was often because the group had failed to follow the rules; but that if they were adhered to properly, then by playing the exercise the students had learned that all of them together could transfer their learning from the simulated problem to the real life problems they were currently facing, or were likely to face, as community work activists.

## Role Playing

In using this technique, a problem is selected which depicts a community worker involved with one or more people in a situation which is described to the training group. Students are asked to volunteer to represent the worker and the other participants, and then each is briefed in the initial attitudes and purposes of the person whose role she is to play - but no one is told just what to say or how to react to the others. The role playing starts with the "worker" trying to achieve her objective, and with the other actors reacting naturally according to their initial briefing and to what the worker decides to do or say. The exercise is time limited, and at the end the tutor discusses what took place, by posing such questions as: has the worker done well or has she merely aggravated the initial problem? Did she set about the task in the best way? If not, where and how did she go wrong? All the participants can participate, and each member in the exercise is free to suggest how she thinks the worker could have done better, and to volunteer to replay the worker's role according to her own ideas.

## A role play exercise
### The Problem

*Lack of a suitable, efficient chairperson was hampering the meetings of a community regeneration group. The last chair had resigned because he felt he could not provide adequate leadership in committee meetings: "I couldn't choose the right words and say them in the right way when I needed to" he had commented. A new chair was appointed, but she confessed she was not very confident at holding meetings together, asserting her authority and guiding members so that everyone contributed equally. The exercise was focused on a student who had volunteered to play the role of the new chair, with other class members playing the roles of committee members. An agenda was circulated to the chair and members just before the meeting and, drawing on their experiences of their own committees, they were asked to simulate a 20 minute meeting to see how well the new chair conducted herself: she having been provided fifteen minutes before the meeting with a checklist, or template, of points to follow during the meeting in order to help her deal with potential pitfalls.*

## The Meeting

*The chair opened the meeting by outlining the reasons for it being called - by reference to the agenda - and formally welcomed everybody. She then moved to the first item on the agenda, and asked for members' views on the subject. After ten minutes, six committee members had expressed their views very forcibly. It became clear that there were two distinct groupings within the meeting, both of which expressed their views dogmatically. Two members did remain silent during this period - and for the rest of the meeting. All this time, the chair allowed the conversation to flow in order to bring out the views of all those who wished to speak. Twice she did intervene to cut-off discussion that had strayed from the subject being discussed. After twenty minutes the chair closed the meeting and thanked all members for their attendance and contributions.*

## Analysis

*As the group observer I reported back to the class. I thought the "hands off" approach adopted by the chair to encourage general participation was fine in principle, but dangerous in practice. Because of this, the meeting lacked control and direction from the chair (she did not even inform members of the order in which to speak), and it became chaotic, with two hostile camps scoring points off each other. Although intervening twice to redirect the discussion, all the participants pointed out that the chair had failed to turn facts into questions and suggestions for the committee, ignored the reticence of two members to contribute, and failed to help each member rise above their own immediate concerns and consider the collective good.*

*Like her predecessor, the new chair "failed to chose the right words in the right way" - and at the right time! The checklist I had provided had been forgotten in the heat of the discussion. As a result, she had failed to summarize and evaluate during the meeting, and at its close, and the members had left it in a confused state as to any future action - and who should take it. In summary, the situation had not improved under the new chair who had adopted a "hands off" approach that gave the committee members too much space to indulge in points scoring. She should have controlled the meeting far more strictly, and used the checklist provided, remembering, and acting upon, the following points:*

- *summarize and evaluate what you hear as the meeting progresses and at its close*
- *keep the discussion focused*
- *don't be defensive or aggressive - use a humorous approach*
- *indicate the order of speakers*
- *use open questions that require people to say more than "yes" or "no"*
- *note how members react - should the meeting be speeded up or slowed down?*
- *encourage participation by words of encouragement to each member*

## Evaluation

*This first role play session was not a success. The students felt it was too artificial to be effective, and not one volunteered to take on the role of chair in our next attempt. To counter these (understandable) objections, I delayed the next role play exercise for two months, and then repeated it. It went much more smoothly, but was still not a total success because most of the class still felt uncomfortable playing characters they had little sympathy with. I eventually decided that the exercise was generating too much pressure on the class, so it did not figure in the programme during the rest of the academic session. At the end of the academic year I sat down and began to consider how I could make this exercise far more meaningful without putting too much pressure on the class - and at the time of writing I am still considering the problem.*

*Although the role play exercise was not a total success it, and the other techniques I used, did provide relevant material from which the class gained a great deal. But there was one other source of valuable experience which I only gradually came to recognize and use. I knew the students were alike in the sense that they were all working in the same occupation, but I was also aware that they were different in many ways - in personality, leadership ability and the ability to learn. They differed too in their attitudes to local people, to local power holders, to the course, to me, and to each other. I needed to recognize and work with these differences in order to help the students work as an effective group - by helping each other and learning from each other - as well as relying exclusively on my direction. In fact, I realized that my work with the class was closely analogous to that of the students when they worked with their community groups: so the way I dealt with the class revealed to the students my own assessment of a community worker's role, as well as revealing how good I was at performing it. In effect, everything I did with the class was a demonstration of my attitude towards people, and a reflection of my skill in working with them: and in this kind of education, I saw it as vital that my example should support and strengthen, not weaken and undermine, the principles and values that I taught.*

## Some Problem Solving Models

Next, I returned to the consideration of the developmental stages that groups pass through. I emphasized that the class should recognize that it was important for a community group to build agreements at each step of the development process, as agreement at the end is based on agreement built all the way through. To further the smooth use of such a linear process, I introduced the class to Fischer and Ury's (1983) 4 Steps to Problem Solving model. This consists of the following sequence:

## Step 1 - PROBLEM
What's wrong?
What are current symptoms?
What are disliked facts contrasted with a preferred situation?

## Step 2 - ANALYSIS

Learn about the problem:

When did it arise?

Who is affected?

What factors are contributing to the problem?

What are barriers to resolving the problem?

## Step 3 - SOLUTIONS

Generate alternative solutions

Consider alternatives to address several related problems

Select criteria to evaluate alternatives

Evaluate and select strategies

## Step 4 - ACTION

What specific action is involved?

Who does what?

When? How?

Analyze the effects of the action on the problem.

After considering this model, I asked the class if the steps, and the questions they involved, were familiar to them in their community activities. All confirmed that they had used similar questions to help solve problems in work, and that the structure and sequence of the questions, as laid out by me, made them realize the need to use a linear (planned and sequenced) process if they were to maximize group effectiveness in problem-solving. I reinforced the everyday validity of this process by reading from a Tennessee Valley Authority paper, which I had acquired while visiting its headquarters in Knoxville in 1990, which confirmed that the basic steps outlined were not merely theoretical because, over the period of one year, twenty-five community leaders in Tennessee had been asked to keep a record of their problem-solving processes, and all their replies included the steps listed above.

In a later class, responding to a theme suggested by my

students - "community work and its resourcing problems" - I initiated the development process by splitting the class into six groups of two students, and introduced them to the Pyramid Decision Group technique. In this technique, I set a decision-making task about effective ways of fund-raising for community groups. Each student wrote his/her decision or solution to the problem at the top of a sheet of paper, and then listed below it first, his/her reasons for it, and second their reservations or reasons against it. After five minutes the student met with a partner and took a minute or two to read their partner's decision with its reasons and reservations. This group then wrote down a joint decision with reasons and reservations - a move that required constructive criticism of their own and their partner's work in some detail. The pair of students then joined another pair. Each pair then constructively criticized the other pair's decision. The purpose of the merger was to get a wider perspective and to let individual opinions be tested by two or more of their peers in a reciprocal relationship. It was also a strategy for students to gradually build confidence in their own opinions and their ability to express them and receive criticism.

The next stage in the problem-solving process was a brain-storming session for a class of ten persons, to demonstrate the technique's usefulness in defining problems, generating alternative solutions and deciding upon evaluation criteria. I agreed to act as the group facilitator to help stimulate ideas, serve as a "traffic cop" to direct and channel student views, and stop any individual dominating the session. A recorder was appointed to write ideas and suggestions on a chart at the front of the class, while a timekeeper had the essential role of reminding the group of the time constraint and the importance of moving from one idea to another.

As facilitator, I ensured that all the class understood the objectivity of the activity and the rules of the process. At the start, I stated the group objective: "In the next fifteen minutes I want us to generate twenty ideas for getting the case for local voluntary action across to local politicians and business leaders". I made it clear that there was a specific time limit, that the participation of all class members was desired, that building upon or combining others' ideas was encouraged and that criticism, praise or evaluation of others' comments was not allowed until the end of the session: the quantity rather than the quality of the ideas was emphasized. I emphasized too that the exercise was fun if everyone entered into the sprit of free association of ideas. When the group could no longer think of any more relevant ideas (two minutes before the fifteen minute deadline), the recorder had written down 21 ideas.

The second phase of prioritizing the ideas meant that the students had to be more selective and creative. My assumption was that by now the ideas proposed had become disassociated from the person who mentioned them, thus there was no stigma attached to rejected ideas. It was this fear of criticism that the brainstorming method was designed to eliminate. Once a selective list of potentially useful ideas had been formed, the group used it to work towards a solution to the problem. The third phase of the discussion was focused on the practicalities of the problem - and once a solution had been agreed, the group worked out how it could be implemented.

**Managing Conflict Creatively**

"What a meeting. It was a mess, chaotic. Nobody was listening to anybody else. People started shouting and getting personal. In the end I had to adjourn it and we'll meet again next week to see if we can agree in a way forward" This statement was familiar to many students who were members of community committees and groups. So much time seemed to be spent keeping the various factions that make up the group happy. The students realized that keeping such elements happy was only one aspect of an approach to getting groups to work effectively, and harmoniously, together and that some training in managing group conflict would give them a foundation on which to build a way forward.

Several classes were therefore focused on understanding conflict within groups, its patterns, to identifying methods for handling conflict and becoming familiar with techniques for creatively managing conflict situations. I pointed out that everyone develops a sense of their position in a conflict. Early on, they learn to stand firm, avoid confrontation, to try to settle the conflict between the parties. Ideals are held dear. They are real and important. Other people may look at these ideals as fantasy or useless, but individuals fight to prove their worth. I then introduced the class to the fact that conflict usually develops in stages - what has been described as the Conflict Cycle (Bolton, 1986). This cycle is made up of the following stages:

*Tension Development* - as the disagreement or threat begins to develop, the various parties start taking sides. The conflict can appear immediately or over time.

*Role Dilemma* - groups which are involved raise questions about what is happening, who is right, what should be done. They try to decide if they should take sides and, if so, which one. (Tension development and role dilemma often occur at the same time).

*Injustice Collecting* - each party begins to gather support. Each one categorizes the problems, justifies their position, and thinks of revenge or ways to win.

*Confrontation* - the parties meet head on and clash. If both parties hold fast to their side, the showdown may cause permanent barriers. Confrontation may be lessened or avoided by one or both parties making adjustments to their position.

*Adjustments* - if one party is weak and the other is strong, the strong party can win by domination, but the conflict may reappear. If parties have equal power, and neither party decides to change, they can wage a cold war, each party trying to weaken the other. The two parties may choose to compromise, each gaining a little and losing a little. The two parties can collaborate in an active participation which looks for a solution that takes care of both parties' needs.

I explained that my experience of working in the voluntary sector had taught me that only compromise or collaboration resolves conflict over time. Other adjustments were, at best, only short-term solutions. If domination, cold war, or isolation was chosen, the conflict cycle was likely to become on-going. I then got the group to complete a Conflict Management Style Survey (Bolton 1986) to ascertain how individual students would tackle group conflict. This survey consisted of fifteen multiple questions which culminated in a self assessment scoring exercise which broke down the students' responses to conflict management into four categories - Aggressive/Confrontational, Assertive/Persuasive, Observant/Introspective and Avoiding/Reactive. I then asked the students to reveal the results of the survey and to share with the rest of the class the style they would adopt in a group conflict situation.

This part of the exercise caused some significant soul searching: some students were surprised by the results of the survey and maintained that the outcomes were incorrect. They could not accept that, in some cases, their style was firmly based in the Aggressive/Confrontational mould, while others would not accept that they were really passive and avoiding in the face of aggression and conflict. I pointed out that these results showed how we are often dishonest with ourselves regarding our methods of dealing with conflict - and that effectively dealing with it means that we, as individuals, have to look at ourselves and our personal attitudes and actions before we can effectively mediate between other groups and parties.

After this piece of psychological discovery, the class undertook a Conflict Negotiation exercise (Bolton 1986). This was designed to help two parties resolve a particular disagreement of conflict. I pointed out at the start that for this exercise to work both individuals must wish to have some sort of resolution to the situation. I then outlined the exercise process as follows:

Person A completes a sequence of four statements from his or her point of view.

- Description of the current situation i.e.,
  "The conflict I'm having with you is…"
  "The problem as I se it is…"
- Description of the ideal situation i.e.,
  "What I'd like to see is…"
- Description of current feelings i.e.,
  "The way I feel about this situation is…"
- Description of self-intention i.e.,
  "What I'm willing to do to create what I want is…"

Person B then paraphrases what Person A has said. If the paraphrase is accepted as accurate by Person A, Person B then moves through the same sequence of statements and Person A paraphrases.

Person A then asks, "Do we have a resolution?" If the answer is "no", Person A begins the sequence again. If the answer is "yes" both parties review their agreements.

Several classes later I asked the students if they had used any of these exercises to tackle conflict in their groups. The great majority said they had not developed enough confidence to implement any of them as they felt their use would be unreal or artificial in an everyday setting peopled by busy individuals who did not have time for "academic" fripperies. They were though working towards implementing these exercises, but in specific training or "awareness days" sessions.

The small number who had actually used the Negotiation exercise thought its use had generated positive, anti-conflict attitudes, and subsequent collaborative actions, in their groups - but they too stressed that the exercise had been conducted within a "safe" environment of a training session and had not been introduced during a formal committee meeting where signs of conflict were apparent. Overall there appeared to be some distrust of what were seen as theoretical tools, useful perhaps for academics and professional workers in formal educational or business settings - but of little relevance in the perceived "real world" of community and personal antipathies. My response was to argue for the utility of such exercises, while accepting that their implementation was probably more effective in formal training sessions than in confrontational environments where appeals to reason often fell on deaf ears. I stressed the need to introduce such conflict reducing tools gradually to the parties concerned, and to try them out in controlled settings beforehand in order to prepare their users for future use in real life settings.

### Dialogue, music, poetry and Insight
But I recognized the students also had to deal with the problems of the larger entity within which the community group operated - society itself. This was a much more complex, fluctuating and fluid system which included the thoughts, relationships and actions of many participants and contexts. Logical thinking alone was not always sufficient to understand it let alone solve its problems - there was sometimes a need for linear thinking to be complemented by lateral thinking - and here I returned to my, and my students', earlier discussions and disputes about the use of intuitive thought and reflective thought. As my course developed, and the longer it progressed and the more the experiences of my students and myself were examined by us all, the more I realized that intuition had a vital role to play in helping people look at

society, and how to understand it and tackle its problems. I still believed that analytical thinking could help solve a significant number of community problems, but I came to recognize that its constant use and its focused, one topic at a time perspective, often resulted in logic-chopping abstraction, intense introversion and a great number of sad, preoccupied individuals with virtually no interest in the wider world. I had previously seen intuition as just a flash of information that had reached me without any conscious reasoning. But, more and more after one of those mental leaps, I learned to go back and trace the trajectory of the new idea - how this thought or observation, and even another idea, had somehow fused at the base of my brain to create the insight that had suddenly shot into view.

This approach was based on my belief that an individual's memory has a great deal of stored information. If group members can first purge what is in their working memories, they will then be able, often through group dialogue, to unlock the vast store of knowledge that is available, often unconsciously, to them. I realized I was in fact drawing on my own store of unconscious knowledge here, as my thoughts on this matter had, apparently spontaneously, "come out of nowhere". Unconsciously, I had drawn on what the scientist and social philosopher Michael Polanyi had termed "tacit knowledge". As he wrote in his 1967 book, *The Tacit Dimension*, with regards to knowledge "we can know more than we can tell"; and it was this pre-logical phase of knowing that he labeled "tacit knowledge". Furthermore, he believed that this phase comprised a range of conceptual and sensory information that could be brought to bear - via hunches, imaginings and informed guesses - to make sense of things, and to help form new approaches or theories to tackle current problems.

What reinforced my view that a more unconventional approach was needed to solve problems and provide new answers, was my recollection of a book I had read while studying at university – Robert Pirsig's 1974 novel *Zen and the Art of Motorcycle Maintenance*.

Pirsig eventually comes to the conclusion in this work that what is needed "to achieve a metaphysics of quality" is a combination of traditional Western knowledge that stresses formal, unambiguous, systematic and scientific thought, and a system of thinking that encompasses "irrational" bursts of creativity and intuition which seem to arise from nowhere and are apparently not rationally explainable. Given my experience of working with community groups and their problems over a twenty year timespan, I believed that there were times when a more Eastern approach to problem solving could generate results when more traditional Western approaches had failed. Furthermore, I was reinforced in this view after reading, much later, another book which highlighted the value of intuitive, ambiguous and non-linear – that is, tacit – methods of insight generation: Nonaka and Takeushi's *The Knowledge Creating Company.*

In this work, the authors examine how the best Japanese manufacturing companies convert the tacit knowledge held in the heads of their employees into explicit knowledge in the form of products and services. They do this by encouraging socialization, and Nonaka and Takeushi argue that socialization can help people to trust one another and share their ideas. By doing this, explicit knowledge becomes tacit, held in people's heads when rules and procedures are internalized, and tacit knowledge becomes explicit when it is externalized when, for example, the new idea of an employee becomes transformed into a new procedure. All these steps – socialization, combination, externalization and internal-ization – are linked in what Nonaka and Takeushi call a knowledge-creating spiral.

I was, and am, of the opinion that such a process is not limited to large manufacturing companies, and that it is relevant to much smaller groupings, such as community organizations and voluntary groups. My first move to familiarize the class with such a process, was by introducing them to the Reversal and Flower Techniques in order to move the detritus of conventional ideas from their minds, start their brains working, and help them make connections they would not usually think of when analyzing problems in a linear manner. In the Reversal Technique, I asked the students to reverse a problem, so a statement such as, "How do we help people become interested in community affairs?" ended up as "How can we prevent people from becoming interested in community affairs?" People are often much better at coming up with negatives so the students filled a flipchart full of ideas. We then reversed each idea in turn to see if any useful themes came out of this exercise.

In the Flower Technique, the question "owner" was asked to choose one of the words of the problem statement and this was written in the middle of a flipchart. Everyone in the class was asked to call out words which they associated with the chosen word. Each new word was written in a petal of the flower. After a couple of minutes a wild card was introduced - "partnerships" – and the group was asked "what word comes to mind?" The most unusual idea from the flower was then used as the basis for another round of idea generation via group discussion. In this way the class moved from ideas that were obviously associated with the initial idea to ideas that were distant or tangential and which would not normally be associated with the original idea.

Next, I asked the group to consider another practical technique to stimulate their imaginations. I used the Thesaurus Prompter exercise in which the students were asked to draw up a list of commonly used community work words, look these up in a thesaurus and note the range of the synonyms on offer for each one. By considering these new words and their respective meanings, I wanted the students to see the problems they faced from a slightly new angle, thereby generating in their minds new word associations - and new ideas to tackle the problems associated with them.

In reality, though, I was often aiming for more than merely non-linear thinking - I was really interested in generating a process that was unconventional, did not fit within existing educational schemas, and which could not easily be explained rationally. I was looking to generate "understanding", "awareness" or what Newman (2006:178) has labeled "insight" - "something outside everything already known...a new and shocking understanding of the whole". This experience of "a new and shocking under-standing" - perhaps "revelation" would be an appropriate description - is well known to artists who often find the process of insight extremely difficult and yet pursue it with passionate intensity. I tried to explain this striving with illustrations from literature and chose, as an example of the novelist's struggle, a quote from MarcelProust's masterpiece *In Search of Lost Time*:

> *"It is often simply from want of the creative spirit that we do not go to the full extent of suffering. And the most terrible reality brings us, with our suffering, the joy of a great discovery, because it merely gives a new and clear form to what we have long been ruminating without suspecting it".*

I pointed out that not all experiences of "awareness", "under-standing" or "insight" are as extreme as Proust's though. They can occur in a wide range of intensities, from small sharp insights - the poet Paul Valery said that the first stage of artistic composition assumes itself as a dazzling light - to agonized and extended metamorphoses - such as St. Ignatius Loyola's "long dark night of the soul" (Noddings and Shore 1984). However they occur, they all contain bewilderment and loss of control that generate a sense of uncertainty. Artists and other creative people know how to embrace this uncertainty and loss of control. Novelists often report how their characters take on lives of their own in the process of creation, as the story seems to write itself; while jazz musicians who improvise and so create sublime music often cannot explain the process which is intangible (one I recently heard talking about just this type of experience on BBC Radio 3 referred to it as "the Zen moment" – "there is no today, no tomorrow, only now, when you realize that you are not just you, but part of an infinite universe made up of a multitude of others of which we are a small, but interlocking, part") - a combination of intuition, imagination and hard work.

After a great deal of confusion and doubt, the sudden arrival of insight is easily experienced as a mystical moment. Artists and scientists have often described these moments of awe and wonder when an often depressing and chaotic situation coalesces suddenly to reveal a novel idea or a solution to a previously impenetrable problem. Since the process of awareness or insight is often non - linear, it cannot be fully analyzed via conventional ways of reasoning, and so we tend to understand it with a sense of mystery. But I had to consider how, if the arrival of insight is commonly perceived to be an unconventional process, could I help my class experience these mind-altering mystical moments? I realized that such a process might be impossible to teach, but I thought that outlining some of my experiences of trying to induce insight might be of interest to the class. I stressed that though insight often strikes at unexpected moments, and is not to be relied upon to arrive when it is being consciously sought after, by relaxing, by listening to music and reading poetry, my unconscious mind was set free to wander, to ruminate and to make connections with areas of my imagination that seemingly lacked any positive linkage – and that this process had occasionally prepared the way for a precious eureka moment.

I then introduced the class to a range of music and poetry. In one session we discussed the works of Beethoven, Schubert, Mozart and Bob Dylan, composers whose music helped me summon up a store of feelings - melancholy, anger, tenderness and joy - distilled to their most intense, almost absolute form, and which emotionally transported me into spheres where I could imagine, for short periods, images and ideas that ranged from the mystically beautiful to the frighteningly grim and macabre. I pointed out that music of this intensity had the power to shape, through its structured motion, the patterns and dynamics of our mental lives and so become both a beginning and an end. It could be the entrance to other realities, different from those realities we can immediately perceive with our senses. And, I stressed, it was not always the music of the masters that provided an entrance to another world. I read a quotation from W B Yeats' essay "The Golden Age", found in his book *The Celtic Twilight* (2004) which, in beautiful prose, illustrates the impact of a tune played upon a simple fiddle had on him during a train journey to Sligo:

> "I seemed to hear a voice of lamentation out of the Golden Age. It told me that we are imperfect, incomplete, and no more like a beautiful woven web, but like a bundle of cords knotted together and flung into a corner...It said that with us the beautiful are not clever and the clever are not beautiful, and that the best of our moments are marred by a little vulgarity, or by a needle-prick out of sad recollection, and that the fiddle must ever lament about it all. It said that if only they who live in the Golden Age could die we might be happy, for the sad voices would be still; but they must sing and we must weep until the eternal gates swing open".

This passage had a great impact on the class. Yeats's sublime use of words to create an atmosphere of a lost time, and the way this other place is compared with the current situation, made the students realize that music can defy all physical boundaries, and open up vistas of alternative worlds and possibilities. Perhaps, I thus suggested, it is in music, more than in any other medium, that the path to other realities, of different ways of knowing about ourselves and the world we live in, of knowing about how alternatives to our current situation can be achieved, and of knowing how to get things done by confronting our devils and exorcising them by adopting high moral values and a belief in the triumph of virtue over evil, which most of us are looking for, is possible.

I also introduced the class to poetry that had a similar impact (but softer images), in particular the work of William Blake. I especially focused on a selection of lines from the poem "Auguries of Innocence":

*"To see a world in a grain of sand*
*And heaven in a wild flower,*
*Hold infinity in the palm of your hand,*
*And eternity in an hour.*

*A robin in a cage*
*Puts all heaven in a rage...*
*A dog starv'd at his master's gate*
*Predicts the ruin of the state...*
*The whore and gambler by the state*
*Licenc'd, build that nation's fate..."*

What Blake was saying in these lines is that a person can find vast truths in the smallest of things, and most mundane matters, and see the microcosmic as representative of the universal. In my view, the lines said that knowledge of the world can be gained from examining its smallest constituent part, and that even such a small thing as a caged robin is an affront to both God and man: in many ways tiny things can be symptomatic, and absolutely representative, of the whole. As I thought about these lines, everything fell into place in a burst of incandescence that illuminated my thoughts and my world. I saw the problem of poverty within the context of the spread of capitalism. The scales dropped from my eyes: this ruthless system, I realized, stays alive and grows by fostering competition, greed and the oppression of the mass of the people by the rapacious pursuit of profit. I had linked Blake's lines with the larger world, and its current complex economic and political state. I saw them as illuminating the fact that as individuals we feel increasingly powerless not just before the immensity and unknowableness of the universe, but also before the vast economic and political forces confronting us, and that we are losing the capacity to think critically about our world. As a result, we are increasingly unable to see the big picture, and are unable to realize that we are part of a system that operates intentionally to diminish our critical faculties. In the words of Erich Fromm (1941: 276) life is seen as "composed of many little pieces, each separate from the other and lacking any sense as a whole".

The acquisition of an insight stimulated by classical music, Bob Dylan and Blake's poem, gave me a new view of the world in which I realized that individual decisions are framed by much broader social and economic structures. It opened my mind to the potential of community action and community education as critical instruments of change: and it also generated in me an action-orientated view of the world, as I started to see situations in my own private and working lives as manifestations of broader social and political contradictions - and realized that these situations could not be changed without my own individual commitment and a broader engagement with collective educational and political action.

Blake's poetry had jolted me into seeing society not as an immutable system, but rather as a set of identifiable processes of realpolitik and economic influence, of identifiable centers of power and capital, disinformation and distraction. But what the acquisition of insight also taught me was that the identification of these obstacles was not enough, and that committed individuals and communities had to acquire the confidence to provide an effective counterbalance to them. In the words of the cultural historian, Raymond Williams (1983), I came to believe that "the task is to establish the lines of development for an alternative. It is only in a shared belief and insistence that there are practical alternatives that the balance of forces and chances begin to alter. Once the inevitabilities are challenged, we begin gathering our resources for a journey of hope. If there are no easy answers, there are still available and discoverable hard

Empowering Education

*answers, and it is these that we can learn to make and share".*

I was not entirely sure that my emphasis on poetry and classical music had convinced my students of their power to generate insight. Some students recognized what I was saying, but held out little hope that acquiring a taste for classical music and "old fashioned" poetry would give them the appropriate stimulus. Others thought they might obtain some new thinking patterns about the world by listening to their current popular music favorites, while a third grouping stoutly maintained that music and poetry were solely for enjoyment and not concerned with spiritual or political matters. Despite this mixed reaction to my efforts, I consoled myself with the thought that by encouraging my students to think imaginatively, to acquire insight through the use of literature and music, I was genuinely seeking to offer a critique of the present by invoking thoughts of an alternative future providing, simultaneously, a corrective to depressive inaction and a stimulus to creative thinking about, and acting for the better upon, communities in particular and the world in general.

## Contrary conversations
Throughout all these conversations I constantly stressed the importance and centrality of focused discussion as a tool to generate collective learning about community development. Experience had taught me that the members of small community groups came to know their minds, and recognize their strengths and weaknesses, best by explaining themselves to other group members - a view endorsed by Bruner (1996) who believes:

*'We do not learn a way of life and ways of deploying mind unassisted, unscaffolded, naked before the world. Rather, it is through the give and take of talk, the active discourse with other minds, that we come to know about the world and about ourselves'.*

248

But I knew from experience that genuine "give and take" was often difficult to achieve. Frequently, in small classes, students who were not familiar with group learning techniques spoke a great deal but ignored the views of other students in the group: convinced of their own righteousness, they disregarded any alternative point of view. Additionally, in declaiming their own views, they frequently diverged from their main theme into a plethora of verbal and mental tangents, thereby making the whole discussion chaotic and unfocussed. To encourage my students to listen respectfully, talk succinctly, and hear others accurately, I determined to set an example by treating all my students' contributions seriously, by replying crisply to all their points, and by modifying the existing pedagogical process of the class. To do this, once a gap for dialogue appeared, I grabbed the moment and consciously co-ordinated the dialogue - I tackled the problems of talkers who liked the sound of their own voices, and students who were unable to link their experiences with the current academic subject matter by interrupting and saying, "That's interesting, but how does it relate to the topic we're discussing" or "A good point, but I think John's point is more relevant and we should follow his example. What do the rest of the class think of John's point of view?"

I also attempted to modify the class process by introducing it to Freire's (1972b) distinction between authentic and inauthentic language. He believed that if the words used by people had been put into their mouths by other people, if they merely regurgitated the thoughts and ideas of other people, then their language was inauthentic. I pointed out the frequency of such talk in pubs where acquaintances, and sometimes strangers, argue by referring to the opinions of the ubiquitous "they" - "they said that..." (on enquiring, usually a view derived from a friend who acquired the view from another friend, a newspaper headline or "the news"). If, on the other hand, people spoke about ideas and thoughts they had generated themselves, then their language was authentic. In

Feire's view, while people use inauthentic language they will remain docile social entities. They will be relying on, and being spoken for, by someone else. They will remain passive observers unable to transform reality. But if people use their own words, they will become controllers of their own destiny – and active players in creating their own reality. I therefore saw my role as helping my students abandon inauthentic language, and start using their own authentic language and words, by asking each other, during discussion, where and how they obtained their views and language

To help implement Freire's method, I also insisted on the students staying silent while their colleagues in the class were speaking. I stressed the importance of listening, because I believed that by listening intently the students gained new insights into a learning process, and that by mentally filling the conversation vacuum they would find themselves thinking about, and reflecting on, matters they had not fully understood or even effectively accepted the existence of beforehand. To stress the importance of listening I quoted a well known saying frequently used to highlight the communication process:

*"We hear only half of what is said to us, understand only half of that, believe only half of that, and remember only half of that".*

Good listening, I pointed out, takes a lot of serious practice. One way to practice is to concentrate for one minute out of every hour on something specific that one person is saying. At the beginning, most of the students will only be able to concentrate totally for a few seconds. It will take practice to hold complete concentration for just one minute, and doing this will be much harder than anticipated, but it can improve listening proficiency. Concentration practice may not make perfect listeners, but it can make good listeners. The result of all this hard work is better understanding, increased efficiency and close working relationships.

I followed up this advice with a snap exercise to see how well the students listened to instructions, and to demonstrate that hearing and listening were not the same thing. I gave every student a sheet of paper and pencil. I told them they would receive some simple instructions from me that they should follow by using the sheet of paper. They would be stated only once, and in a quick and clear manner. The students should follow directions without any questions and not repeat any directions. I then read out the instructions once, loudly and clearly, but quickly:

a) On top of the left hand side write the country's name where you live

b) Along the right hand side write the name of the county you live in

c) Draw a line from the top right corner to the bottom left hand corner

d) Draw a line from the centre of the top to the centre of the bottom

e) Fold your paper along the centre line with the left side over the right

f) Now draw a diagonal line from the top left corner to the bottom right corner and write your first name three times on the diagonal line

g) Fold your paper into thirds and hand it to the person on your right

After I read the instructions to the group, I had everyone open the sheet they ended up with and asked them to raise their hands if they thought it was correct. I told them that usually at least 25 per cent of the participants did everything correctly. I then started a discussion (but one usually took place spontaneously anyway) by posing some questions: Why do you think so many people didn't do the exercise correctly? Would anyone have done better if this were an important group task or item of business? What would have happened if it had been? I then used the results of the exercise to lead into a discussion about listening versus hearing, and what it means to the effective working of community groups.

To reinforce the centrality of listening in the work of community groups I instituted a KIVA Exercise (Bolton, 1986; Middlebrooks 2008). The Kiva was the circular room which evolved from a religious site to a chamber of governance among the Pueblo tribe of the south western USA. It was a unique space offering opportunities for listening, reflecting, learning and discussion. Building on this history, my exercise was designed to help students listen to diverse opinions in their group and consider their implications. I highlighted that the structure of the exercise provided time and conditions for discussion so that many points of view could be expressed, thereby helping to build a collaborative spirit and clarify the significant points of agreement and disagreement. I then asked the students to arrange their chairs in circles (three circles, one within the other) with each circle representing a different role (e.g. one circle representing paid community workers, one volunteers and one committee members). Next, I announced the amount of time to be allocated to each group. I then presented a clear statement of the issue to be discussed, but stressed that the group in the centre circle should use its time to talk without interruption from opposing points of view, or the members of the other two circles, about their opinions, experiences and wishes. Each group then rotated into the centre and I gave it the same amount of time to explore the issue. Finally, after all groups had talked, I allowed additional time for questions, clarification and interaction among all participants - and then created a full discussion around such questions as:

- Did the exercise help you to listen to opposing opinions more objectively?
- Was there a more co-operative feeling after doing this exercise?

- Did the significant points of disagreement become clearer?
- Did significant points of agreement become clearer?
- What did you learn about the issue?
- What questions do you have about the issue now?

What became clear from this exercise was that it really did encourage all the participants, by listening attentively to all the contributions, to reflect on the connection between what they knew and what they had to learn, and by connecting the knowledge of the other speakers with their own knowledge and concepts. Also, in a strategic sense, the participants in the Kiva connected where they were, both as individuals and group members, to where they wanted to go, and made it clear how, by using their silences, they had started to develop their ideas in order to make progress in the desired direction.

In a following class I took the opportunity to point out that as well as effective listening and using silence as a learning tool, questions can also be used in order to learn. I encouraged the students to ask pertinent questions of the speaker they had been listening to (not questions that "take off" on tangents or are related to peripheral matters), and then consider the reply. The reply is usually expressed in the form of a statement. Sometimes statements impose finality on the learning process, but more often focused questions generate uncertainty into the process - and a need for more thought and reflection on the part of both speaker and listener. The speaker's answers thus become prompts for another question - the finality of the answers is decided by the questioner. If the students as a whole go on asking questions, they move the focus of both the questioner and the respondent from certainty to challenge and from the expression of solutions to the formulation of problems. Freire (1972b) calls this "problema-tising" - a process of continually defining community action and life in general - in terms of problems to be acted upon.

The attempt to bring other members around to an individual's point of view by using this methodology carried the risk, of course, that the individual concerned might adopt the others' point of view instead. But I believed that individual members had to enter imaginatively into their colleagues' arguments, if only for the purpose of refuting them - and that they might well end up being persuaded by those they sought to persuade. My belief was that discussion was always unpredictable but was the heart of collective learning and knowledge: a belief reinforced by my familiarity with the effectiveness of opinion forming and knowledge creation via experience of group discussion sessions I attended while visiting community projects in Arizona, North Carolina, Pennsylvania and Tennessee in 1990, and my first hand knowledge of working with numerous community action and regeneration projects across Wales for the Wales Council of Voluntary Action in the 1980s and early 1990s (Hopkins, 1995).

An illustration of this process in action was when a group member adopted a strongly held specific viewpoint on collective action that generated heated discussion and argument. I, playing agent provocateur, posed the question: "is it realistic for communities to even begin to develop grassroots action to take more control of the local economy within a global power system where capital and industry can hop, skip and jump to any part of the world?" I then withdrew from the conversation, which continued with one group member thinking that collective action was doomed to failure within such a global economy: and she quoted examples of local initiatives that had failed to make any impact in their localities after traditional industries had left ("I believe the evidence for lack of sustainability is overwhelming..."). Other group members produced evidence of the validity of an alternative viewpoint: one that stressed the positive long term changes implemented by local collective actions through initiatives such as local exchange trading schemes, food co-operatives, credit unions, development trusts, community businesses, regeneration groups and neighbourhood crèches ("Are you sure, because if you look closely at the sustainability record of local community initiatives such as...").

This contribution proved so persuasive that the original group member modified her stance and took up the alternative point of view. Later in the dialogue, she reflected on the examples offered by the tutor in previous classes, and her reading of Wainwright (2003), on the positive impact of successful collective initiatives in Brazil, the Basque country of Spain, the Appalachian Mountains in Tennessee, in Newcastle and adjacent areas of Wales. So, because she saw more possibilities in the adopted stance than the original holders of that stance, and by absorbing these new possibilities into a new action viewpoint, the original sceptic pushed the whole group mindset on the topic forward to a markedly new degree. This type of intra-group "give and take" took place many times during the class. By using this method, as Schoenfeld (1989) has observed, the outcome of group interaction extended far beyond the original inputs that could have been made by the individual students involved: the class thus made significantly more progress towards understanding collective action, so vital in community work, than any of the individuals involved could have made by acting on their own. This is a process that has been confirmed as vital for knowledge generation by the research of Nonaka and Takeuchi (1995), while Young (1997:59) has argued that:

*"Through such dialogue that recognizes the asymmetry of others, moreover, people can enlarge their thinking in at least two ways. Their own assumptions and point of view become relativised for them as they are set in relation to those of others. By learning from others how the world and the collective relations they have forged through interaction look to them, moreover, everyone can develop an enlarged understanding of that world and those relations that are unavailable to any of them from their own perspective alone".*

# PART FIVE:

# TALKING ABOUT POWER

# Chapter Nine

## Different types of power

To site the group work techniques and discussions within a social setting, I made a conscious effort to introduce generative themes, for example, "power" and "community action", into regular class discussions. In addition, I used exercises to highlight the power relations within a community. In one, I drew a line on a chart labeled the "community power boundary", and invited students to name people and organizations that had power in their community and place them above the line. Then, for every person or organization that had power, I asked the students to name one that did not have power, and write this below the line. In another, I asked the class to list the major institutions, businesses and local government services in their community - and to relate these institutions in terms of influence and power to their own organizations and their work in the community.

In the discussion that followed, the students illustrated how they saw their organizations being influenced, even sometimes coerced, into accepting a subsidiary role when working in partnership with major institutions - especially the local authority. By swapping anecdotes of their experiences in committee meetings, planning meetings and networking groups, the students vividly highlighted the unequal power structures they had to operate within and how often they felt powerless, and unable to act effectively on behalf of their communities. Taking my cue from these personal anecdotes, and using my knowledge of the power sources listed by Mayer (1987 quoted in Newman 2006: 124), I pointed out how organizations used different types of power to influence local conditions in their favor. I observed that *institutional power* is generated by many public and private sector organizations through their use of internal authority structures; and that employees use the powers and attitudes created by these structures, and their managerial procedures, to create a corporate mindset that regards external voluntary groupings as amateur and inferior systems. The prestige conferred by the managerial and hierarchical structures is then utilized by their employees to browbeat community opposition and distort communication between the two sectors.

A very fine example of this type of asymmetrical power system was highlighted by the experience of some of my students. They reflected that while attending a previous course at a neighboring higher education institution they had discovered, very late on in their studies, that several modules they had already passed were now invalid and would not count towards their final accreditation. It appeared that the original validation document for their course had approved delivery of the constituent modules in a specific, chronological order – but this condition had not been conveyed to the course tutor, who had therefore not been able to implement the correct course procedures.

When this error was finally discovered (by accident and without the permission of the institution's management), the students wanted to know from the institution's management why they had not been informed of the correct procedure at the start of their course, when their employers had already paid their fees and allocated time for their attendance on the course – or later, after they themselves had committed a great deal of effort to passing the modules concerned. The authorities then adopted delaying tactics by refusing to reply to student 'phone calls, letters or even request for personal meetings. The attitude adopted by the authorities implied that the complaints of the students carried little weight (they were only adult part-timers after all!), and that community-based students from the voluntary sector were not really of equal status with full-time, campus-based, "professional" students. At the time of delivery of my own course, some eight months later, the matter had still not been resolved, and all the students involved were still awaiting clear, concise and specific reasons from the institution's management for its secretive and retrograde actions – and what it proposed to do about them.

(As a postscript to this episode, I was subsequently told after I had finished teaching the course, that instead of letting the tactics of the authorities grind down their determination to obtain justice in their struggle, the students had taken their protests to a more direct and personal level: they picketed the offices of the professor and staff involved in the dispute, verbally confronted them in public and private, and made it cleat that, as a group, they would remain collectively determined in their efforts to achieve a just outcome and, if necessary, publicize their grievances further afield by initiating contacts with the local press and media. As a result, the management agreed that they should keep the credits they had already acquired in their studies (in whatever timeframe these had been accumulated) and that they could continue their course on a part time basis by attendance one day a month on campus as a supplement to some part time community classes).

Again drawing on Mayer and Newman (2006: 124-126), I stressed that institutional power is very closely allied to *instrumental power*. This is based on direct strength and influence, as when an organization uses its superior funding resources, specialized knowledge and skills to intimidate partnership colleagues into accepting a specific course of action, or exercises its influence on the allocation of financial resources such as grant applications. Next, I highlighted how *hegemonic power* - colonization of the mind through the use of ideas - is used. I pointed out that some organizations, including local councils and government departments, often chant the mantra "we have always done it this way" to frustrate any new ideas and practices being generated by community groups to tackle social problems. The "big guns", as one student referred to them, use arguments that stress their established customs, and tried and tested traditions, to emphasize their effectiveness and, by doing this, they imply that their practices are superior, while the practices of the community sector are unprofessional, lightweight and of unproven quality.

## Some practical strategies

Then, to encourage immediate participation and questioning, I asked students what they thought they had gained from the "power" exercise. I justified its use by arguing that analyzing power is a necessary preparation to any action, whether that action is oppositional or collaborative. In my eyes, it helped students understand themselves and their opponents - while it also encouraged community groups to choose suitable, appropriate action in an oppositional or supportive role. The students stated that receiving information about the various types of power structures was illuminating and helped to put local situations in a wider perspective. However, they thought they also needed a more focused, local approach to tackling power structures - so, after agreeing that the local authority was indeed the main structure to influence, we explored how, as workers and citizens, they could put such an approach into effect.

Our starting point was an acceptance that community workers and volunteers had to get involved in local public affairs if they wanted to stand a chance of making changes in local society. But, I asked, playing Devil's Advocate, "what do you workers in the community currently know of your local or national political scene?" To help them answer this question I asked them eight questions:

1. Did you vote in the last local government election?
2. Did you vote in the last general election?
3. Name your current Member of Parliament
4. Name your Welsh Assembly Government member
5. Name your European Assembly member
6. Have you been active as a private citizen on a local issue in the last year?
7. List three issues of prime concern to citizens in your area

8. Have you written to or contacted the local authority supporting or arguing against legislation in the last six months?

I allocated points to each of the questions and scored the answers on the basis of:

80 to 100   Very good. Almost a pro! Keep up the good work.
60 to 80    Keep looking and listening. Must become more informed.
Under 60    Get out more, read more, watch more current affairs programmes!

Although done in a light-hearted manner, the exercise showed that almost three-quarters of the class failed to answer two or more questions. They were particularly weak on the identity of the European Assembly representative and their activities as private citizens concerning local issues during the past twelve months. They accepted that they were not perhaps quite as involved in local affairs as they should be, and that this situation would have to change if they were to function as effective citizens and community workers. What they also accepted was that they must get used to dealing with a variety of power structures as illustrated in our previous exercise on above/below the power line. One of the most vital tasks, they agreed, is to identify power clusters or organizations which are all interested in the same thing. Their own organization, I pointed out, was part of such a cluster, and co-ordination with other agencies or groups interested in similar issues could strengthen their organization. Also, power clusters communicate with each other and form power networks, while individual members can also form networks, thereby expanding their sources of advice and expertise. Finding and joining networks appropriate to their organization should therefore be a priority for community workers in their struggles to influence local power structures, while identifying and utilizing the gatekeepers and information brokers within and among networks will provide community groups with even more resources and influence. After a lengthy discussion we listed six points for community workers to bear in mind when dealing with power structures:

## Actively acquire power

It is up to workers to acquire the power to do the job. No one will give power to a worker freely.

## Take responsibility

Workers should be prepared to take responsibility for management and for doing the real work. They should identify how much work needs to be done and who is available to help. People must be organized and given tasks appropriate to their individual skills and interests. Individuals who want attention and glory, but who do not want to work must be weeded out.

## Get organized

People who are committed and willing to work must be brought together. Workers must get community support from those who may not be able to work on the project, but who will stand up and speak for it.

## Do your homework

Community workers must get the facts and figures to back up their positions. They must check out other communities' activities related to their own development programmes. They must know which laws and regulations apply to their programme, make presentations to elected officials where necessary, rehearse such presentations, think of any questions that officials might ask and have answers ready.

## Do not surprise public officials
Lobby with officials and members of the informal power structure ahead of any presentation or meeting. Give them time to think over new ideas and evaluate them in relation to other issues they must consider

## Compromise, but set a bottom line
Workers must not accept a compromise that will cause their group to fail - it will damage its reputation for future projects and action.

I followed this listing by stressing the important role of community meetings in combating local organizational power structures and the attitudes of their representatives. I suggested that community activists should always assume that their opponents have agendas of their own, and remember that meetings are not always the genial, respectful gatherings they pretend to be; that to manipulate them to their own agendas, activists should encourage as many of their supporters to attend the meeting as possible; lobby support for their point of view before the meeting; hold a pre-meeting with supporters to plan an action strategy; and get supporters to make encouraging noises while the meeting is taking place.

I also stressed the need for community activists to be effective speakers and be willing to prepare what they are going to say before a meeting starts. We held a session on making a presentation or speech at a meeting, and came up with the following pointers:

A. You must give your speech purpose and form when communicating your ideas. Direct it to your audience's interests.

B. Organization is vital.
1. Get your audience's attention and tell them what you are going to tell them.
2. Tell them.

3. Tell them what you told them.

C. Finally, practice, practice, practice. Enjoy giving your presentation with high confidence. Always remember, you do have something important to say.

I highlighted other factors that could influence positive community outcomes: the siting of a meeting (is it accessible for other friendly community activists?); the timing of meetings (can supporters get there on time?); and the internal environment (how the layout of seats and tables can be used to site community supporters near the front and "in the faces" of rival attendees). I then asked if these suggestions were morally acceptable to the students. By adopting such a "political" approach to community work were we undercutting our personal values and lowering ourselves, and our moral foundations, to the same level as our opponents, thereby loosing the moral high ground?

The group accepted that sometimes some readjustment of practical strategies was needed if workers were to win their battles on behalf of their communities. In short, they accepted the explicitly oppositional role of community workers and adult educators as stated by Baptiste (2000:43), and the methods suggested by him, to combat local power structures and their representatives (and which they subsequently put into very effective practice - see postscript above on page 147). Such was the intensity of the discussion on this subject that I used the students' responses to launch a wider debate on morality, values, community groups, and their relationships with power systems, as starting points for even more discussion: the debate thus developed from the students' own ideas which I then recycled to them as further themes and problems for debate, discussion and reflective analysis.

## Luke's three dimensions

Later, after listening to the students' experiences, using stories and anecdotes, I outlined my own experiences with local power holders such as the local authority, banks, the higher education sector, various central government agencies and even some community organizations. As an illustration of the pervasiveness of power, and to highlight that its influence is not confined to local structures and personalities, I drew on the ideas of Stephen Lukes who, in his 1974 essay, *Power: A Radical View,* postulates that there are three dimensions of power, each of an increasing level of sophistication, which he analyses as follows:

In the **one dimensional view**, power is related to "the study of concrete, observable behavior" (page 17), and focuses on behavior in the making of decisions on issues over which there is an observable conflict of interests. As far as community workers are concerned, if they are involved with matters involving political decisions in which the preferences of the ruling elite run counter to those of any other grouping, the preference of the elite will regularly prevail.

The **second dimensional view** of power examines the forces that prevent potentially controversial issues from generating "observable conflicts"; so, in order to understand this second dimension, "it is crucially important to identify potential issues which non decision-making prevents from being actual" (page 23). A non-decision is thus a decision that results in the suppression or thwarting of a latent or manifest challenge to the values or interests of decision makers. In Lukes' view therefore the two dimensional view incorporates into the analysis of power relations the control over the agenda of politics, and of the ways in which potential issues are kept out of the political and decision taking process.

The **three dimensional view** of power is concerned with getting people and communities to do what they do not want to do, by exercising power over them by controlling their thoughts and desires. In Lukes' view, "is it not the supreme and most insidious exercise of power to prevent people, to whatever degree, from having grievances by shaping their perceptions, cognitions and preferences in such a way that they accept their role in the existing order of things, either because they can see or imagine no alternative to it, or because they see it as natural and unchangeable, or because they value it as divinely ordained and beneficial?" (page 28). In this dimension of power, actual conflict is not necessary because power has been used insidiously and effectively to prevent a conflict from arising in the first place.

The students thought that Lukes' ideas were genuinely thought provoking, and relevant to the actions of community groups vis-à-vis local power holders, but they considered his use of phrases such as "hidden forces" and "non-decision making" as too vague, too sociological and too academic to explain the reality of power. So, to further reinforce the idea of the pervasiveness of power, and the workings of the three dimensional process, but in more mundane terms, I explored the personal educational experiences of my class students. All the class had sat, and failed, written examinations while at school (as had I also). They had taken their failure as evidence of their own innate incompetence and lack of dedication to learning and, as a consequence, saw their subsequent low employment status and feelings of intellectual inadequacy, as their own fault. They had never thought of the role of the examination, how it had evolved from an inter–personal exercise to an impersonal assessment, and the subsequent consequences of such a process.

### Foucault's ideas

Here I introduced the view of the French philosopher and sociologist, Michel Foucault, who pointed out in his book *Discipline and Punish* (1979), that early academic tests had used the oral system and so left room for a dialogue between the teacher and the student: the student had the chance to ask questions, to query what he had learned, to demand clarification and elaborate on his views. The written test, on the other hand, introduced a form of discourse which altered the act of communication from a dialogue to a one way channel of communication, focusing on what the teacher had taught, without considering the student's spoken views and interpretations. So, while the oral method was characterized by negotiation, expansion of ideas, elaboration, use of contextual clues, argument, correction, revision and debate, the written system was one-sided: information flowed in one direction as the student wrote what he knew in response to his interpretations of a written stimulus.

I discovered too that the students, as well as not recognizing the evolution of the examination as a mechanism for exercising power over the pupil, had never considered it as a tool of subservience and discipline either, until I drew their attention to another passage from Foucault's writings (1979:184):

> The examination combines the techniques of an observing hierarchy and those of a normalizing judgment. It is a normalizing gaze, a surveillance that makes it possible to qualify, to classify and to punish. It establishes over individuals a visibility through which one differentiates them and judges them. That is why, in all the mechanisms of discipline, the examination is highly ritualized. In it are combined the ceremony of power and the form of the experiment, the deployment of force and the establishment of truth. At the heart of the procedures of discipline, it manifests the subjection of those who are perceived as objects and the objectification of those who are subjected".

Before reading and analyzing this passage, examinations to the class seemed to be part of the natural educational order - while the educational system itself appeared the natural way of imparting knowledge to learners. What Foucault was suggesting, I pointed out, was the degree to which our educational institutions, along with other social institutions, curtail our freedom and limit severely our potentialities as human beings. Not passing examinations, not being successful, feeling different from those who were successful - such feelings are so familiar that we generally consider them as natural. Could it be though, I postulated, that they could also be the internalized values of a society which depends for its smooth functioning on the willing obedience of the individual? Examination failure therefore generates individual guilt and, by associating misfortune with moral blame, it becomes an instrument of social control inside the heads of the very individuals who are to be controlled. Such a strategy was not new either, I revealed, as Jean Servan had very perspicaciously written, in late eighteenth century France, (quoted in Foucault, 1979) of the necessity of linking the ideas of crime and punishment in the minds of people such that they:

*"follow one another without interruption...When you have thus formed the chain of ideas in the heads of your citizens, you will then be able to pride yourselves on guiding them and being their masters. A stupid despot may constrain his slaves with iron chains; but a true politician binds them even more strongly by the chain of their own ideas; it is at the stable point of reason that he secures the end of the chain; this link is all the stronger in that we do not know of what it is made and we believe it to be our own work; despair and time eat away the bonds of iron and steel, but they are powerless against the habitual union of ideas, they can only tighten it still more; and on the soft fibers of the brain is founded the unshakeable base of the soundest of Empires".*

As well as influencing individual and collective thoughts, the examination also, in Foucault's view, installs its users in a swamp of documentation. Writing in the on-line Stanford Encyclopedia of Philosophy, Gary Gutting (2010:6) points out that Foucault notes that the results of examinations are recorded in documents that provide detailed information about the individuals examined, so allowing power-systems to control them via the allocation of grades and prestigious certificates or the notification of poor grades and failures. On the basis of these records, those in control can formulate categories, averages and norms that are in turn a basis for more knowledge compilation and documentation. The examination therefore turns the individual into a "case" and acts as a technique of surveillance and control of the individual in a disciplinary bureaucracy of power.

The examination system, I pointed out, also had a significant impact on individuals in a wider sense - and could do so in regard to the future of my students, too. Even though they might successfully pass all their examinations (those linked to the current course, and any they might undertake in the future), such success often came at a heavy cost. To illustrate this point, I quoted from what I regarded as a seminal work of the late 1950s which had had a great impact on adult education thinkers and practitioners - Richard Hoggart's *The Uses of Literacy* (1957). In this book Hoggart drew extensively on his own experiences as a "scholarship boy" who had successfully made the transition from the working class to the middle class, thanks in part to his passing of examinations - but who realized that such success instilled in him (and he believed in a great many of his fellow scholars) an outlook or mindset which greatly affected the way he subsequently viewed society and his place in it. It is worth quoting Hoggart at some length on this subject in the following two passages found in the chapter headed "Unbent Springs: A note on the Uprooted and the Anxious":

*"He (the scholarship boy) begins to see life as a ladder, as a permanent examination with some praise and some further exhortations at each stage. He becomes an expert imbiber and doler-out; his competence will vary, but will rarely be accompanied by genuine enthusiasms. He rarely feels the reality of knowledge, of other men's thoughts and imaginings, on his own pulses; he rarely discovers an author for himself and on his own. In this half of his life he can respond only if*

there is a direct connection with the system of training. He has something of the blinkered pony about him; sometimes he is trained by those who have been through the same regimen, who are hardly unblinkered themselves, and who praise him in the degree to which he takes comfortably to their blinkers. Though there is a powerful, unidealistic, unwarmed realism about his attitude at bottom, that is his chief form of initiative; of other forms - the freely ranging mind, the bold flying of mental kites, the courage to reject some "lines" even though they are officially as important as all the rest - of these he probably has little, and his training does not often encourage them" (p 297).

"...when he is at last put out to raise his eyes to a world of tangible and unaccommodating things, of elusive and disconcerting human beings, he finds himself with little inner momentum. The driving-belt hangs loosely, disconnected from the only machine it has so far served, the examination-passing machine. He finds difficulty in choosing a direction in a world where there is no longer a master to please, a toffee-apple at the end of each stage, a certificate, a place in the upper half of the assessable world. He is unhappy in a society which presents largely a picture of disorder, which is huge and sprawling, not limited, ordered, and centrally heated; in which the toffee-apples are not accurately given to those who work hardest nor even to the most intelligent; but in which disturbing imponderables like "character", "pure luck", "ability to mix", and "boldness" have a way of tipping the scales" (p 299).

## A personal example

Hoggart's description of what examination success can do to the intelligent person came as a surprise to my students. They had taken up my course and its examinations with the hope that they would become better community workers, volunteers and activists - and also benefit from a new, more positive view of their place in society as a result. They found Hoggart's thoughts disturbing, but they accepted with reluctance that by entering, and hopefully exploiting, the academic system they could be open to influences and ideas that affected their personal and social philosophies in new and unexpected ways. Despite accepting the potential modification of their personal views, they all pointed out that they came to examinations as mature adults and not as "cloistered teenagers" or even as "successful callow youths". They felt that they had seen enough of life to maintain a mental and philosophical equilibrium, "keep their feel on the ground" and deal practically and realistically with any examination success they gained. They would not loose their roots and take examination or academic fortune as their yardstick for living. Most of the students had been affected in their personal and working lives by "luck", "boldness" (or the lack of it) and other vicarious factors - and would not let academic garlands knock "common-sense" out of them.

In addition to the implications of successfully passing examination suggested by Hoggart, I then highlighted how the experience of examination failure could also affect a person's life and outlook by drawing on my own experiences. I narrated how my failure of the 11 plus examination had left me in an undisciplined, leaderless, inferior school with feelings of personal inadequacy and educational trauma. I then stressed that I managed eventually to convince myself that I was not unintelligent and that my failure to qualify for entry to a grammar school had more to do with my poor educational background than with my innate intelligence. Evidently someone in my secondary modern school agreed with this assessment, and I was eventually transferred (on recommendation) to the county grammar school. But the period at the modern school had left its mental scars, and it took another psychological effort to convince myself that I could compete academically with the mass of middle class students who made up the majority of my new school's intake. Examination success became the criterion for educational and social advancement, and the fear of experiencing a relapse into my former uncertainty spurred me to achieve entry to university – again to face a struggle to survive academically against well educated middle class entrants.

I realized though that I was engaged not just in a struggle to compete academically, but also to exist in a foreign culture, one that stressed learning as an individual experience and not a collective one. I had been brought up in a working class family and community where shared learning was the norm. However, in my grammar school, and later in university, it was quickly made clear to me that the collective sharing of ideas and knowledge was not acceptable, and that individual academic effort was what was expected. This put me at a disadvantage against the sons of accountants, solicitors, chemists and doctors, who had traveled abroad, knew how to pronounce foreign languages, and who could fall back on the knowledge (and funds) of their professional parents when learning mathematical formulae and scientific theories. I realized quickly that my working-class, shared experience, had been educationally disenfranchised, and that the educational establishment (both secondary and higher) of which I was a member was part of a class structure with different values that prized isolated individual learning and the prestige of examination success – a structure that I had to either join or reject. I decided to join it, but on my own critical terms which would keep alive my commitment to my class origins and a determination to continue to value collective action as a means of improving society.

I believed that despite my lengthy involvement with higher education curricula and personnel I still maintained a critical view of the larger and more focused worlds within which I lived and worked. I was profoundly aware that the university system which I experienced as a student differed sharply from the system that currently employed me as a tutor. Whether the same was true for my colleagues I was not so sure, as their attitudes towards recent developments in higher education seemed to indicate that they saw the shift in focus from teaching to learning, from teaching to practical research, and to making students employable rather than thinking members of society, as entirely natural and organic. To me, on the other hand, these apparently natural developments were nothing of the sort - rather they were "top-down" strategies, part of a neo-liberal political movement which had imposed its view of society on academia. By applying Foucault's reasoning, I believed that the new regime had not been merely imposed from above by politicians and managers, but was applied and maintained by the practices of the individual tutors and students involved. Every time a lecturer followed the dominant practices, he helped to reinforce them and, in turn, became disciplined by them through what Foucault had termed "technologies of the self" - specific habits by which individuals accommodate themselves within and towards systems of power which are often accepted at face value and appear to be natural.

## Some contrary views on power

Foucault saw the examination and its debilitating influence as a society-wide insidious social control mechanism – part of a stream of power flowing through all aspects of society, its influence regulating the behavior of individuals, the systems of knowledge and every interaction between people. He, furthermore, saw individuals as having very little chance of escaping from the system. I underlined the importance of Foucault's view by quoting from a novel, *Border Country*, by a local author, Raymond Williams, which describes how a character in it felt about the defeat of the workers during the 1926 General Strike, how the faith he had invested in collective action had been destroyed, and how his optimistic view of society had changed as a result:

*"For Morgan, really, there was no satisfaction. A struggle had been lost; a common effort had failed. And it was not only the failure that*

*broke him, but the insight this gave, or seemed to give, into the real*
*nature of society. His life had been centered on an idea of common*
*improvement. The strike had raised this to an extraordinary practical*
*vividness. Then, suddenly, a different reality had closed in. The brave*
*show was displaced, in an hour, by a grey, solid world of power and*
*compromise. It was not only that the compromise angered him; not*
*only that he was sickened by the collapse into mutual blame. It was*
*that suddenly the world of power and compromise seemed real, the*
*world of hope and ideas no more than a gloss, a mark in the margin.*
*He had lived on his ideas of the future, while these had seemed in any*
*way probable, and they had seemed probable until now. And a man*
*could bear to lose, but the sudden conviction that there was nothing*
*to win - that the talk of winning was no more than talk, and collapsed*
*when the real world asserted itself - this, deeply, was a loss of his*
*bearings, a change in the whole structure of his life... You could talk*
*about creating the future, but in practice, look, people ran for shelter,*
*maneuvered for personal convenience, accepted the facts of existing*
*power. To see this happening was a deep loss of faith, a slow and*
*shocking cancellation of the future. You could live only by what you*
*could find now"* (190).

Some of my students saw the power of this diagnosis, and began
talking of never being able to influence alternative strategies that
would effectively oppose this situation, because the system
appeared to be spreading throughout society. Several students
quoted from a paper they had discovered on the Internet (A
Report on the Surveillance Society for the Information
Commissioner by the Surveillance Studies Network, September
2006) which formed the basis of class discussion for several subsequent lessons:

*"We live in a surveillance society. It is pointless to talk about surveil-*
*lance society in the future tense. In all rich countries of the world*
*everyday life is suffused with surveillance encounters, not merely*

*from dawn to dusk but 24/7. Some encounters obtrude into the routine, like when we get a ticket for running a red light when no one was around but the camera. But the majority are now just part of the fabric of daily life. Unremarkable...It is not just that CCTV may capture our image several hundred times a day, that check-out clerks want to see our loyalty cards in the supermarket or that we need a coded access card to get into the office in the morning. It is as if these systems represent a basic, complex infrastructure which assumes that gathering and processing personal data is vital to contemporary living."*

Our discussion brought out the fact that some forms of surveillance had always existed as people watched over each other for mutual care, for moral caution and to discover information covertly. But it was the link between bureaucracies and the power of information technology which made government and business demand for efficiency, speed, co-ordination and, above all, control, so potent and threatening a force in society. It was agreed that surveillance is two-sided, and its benefits should be acknowledged. However, at the same time, risks and dangers should be recognized too, as should the fact that in a large-scale surveillance system power does corrupt or at least skews the vision of those who wield it. Recent experience, the students believed, proved that we do not have to imagine some wicked tyrant getting access keys to social security or medical databases to see the problem. Rather, the corruptions of power include leaders who appeal to some supposed greater good (such as victory in a war on terror) to justify unusual or extraordinary tactics.

The majority of class students thought that though caution about surveillance was justified, Foucault's views were far too pessimistic, and that his belief that power permeated society at all levels, for repressive purposes, was greatly exaggerated. They were more inclined to see power, and its influence, as much more limited, as emanating from specific sites - the more obvious coercive institutions such as the army, the police, the civil service, the local town hall and prisons - thereby leaving areas untouched and therefore capable of being developed as sites of resistance. In the view of this grouping, the disciplinary society could be countered by such simple acts as meeting with friends, by listening to, or making, music, by walking in the countryside, by thinking and talking about an alternative society, by painting, writing and particularly by leaning about society and how it could be improved through collective community action and adult education. As a result, they all enthusiastically endorsed the view of writer and journalist A L Kennedy who, during the protest march on Gleneagles in November 2005 at the G8 summit, reminded her fellow marchers that despite the influence of capitalists and governments: "We have the choice to try for a new world every day, to tell what we know of the truth every day, to take small actions every day". (Quoted in Rankin, I. *The Naming of the Dead*. London: Orion Publishing. 2006).

In taking this view the majority were thinking along similar lines to James Scott who, in his 1990 book *Domination and the Arts of Resistance*, claims that hegemony scarcely ever happens. In Scott's view, people keep silent because they are weighing up when it is opportune to resist, not because they necessarily embrace their masters' beliefs. To Scott, hegemony is a myth that is accepted by Marxists and their followers – in reality, he believes it only really happens in very rare conditions such as in the brain-washing regimes of southern Asia. In his view, "in public, those who are oppressed accept their domination, but they always question their domination offstage". And not always offstage either, according to Hall (1996: 234), who points out: *"far from there being no resistance to the system, there has been a proliferation of new points of antagonism, new social movements of resistance organized around them - and consequently, a generalization of "politics" to spheres which hitherto the left assumed to be apolitical: a politics of the family, of health, of food, of sexuality, of the body...Perhaps there isn't...one "power game" at all, more a network of strategies and powers and their articulations - and thus a politics which is always positional".*

Hall posits an on-going, constantly evolving situation which, if as fluid as he implies, suggests that it is vital that community workers – and adult educators – embrace the on-going practice of critical thinking in a wide variety of areas, and follow the call of Edward Said (2001: 502/3) to consistently question power rather than merely consolidate it, enter into the public sphere in order to alleviate human suffering, make the connections of power visible, and work collectively and individually to create the social and educational conditions necessary for what Pierre Bourdieu (2000: 42) has labeled "realist utopias".

In this context, I pointed out how relevant the views of Raymond Williams remained in the struggle against the determinism of the status quo. I stressed that Williams recognized that inside any political and cultural structure, "sites of resistance" are always available. The dominant system contains elements of the past, and these elements can act as catalysts for new cultural, social and political forces which can be used to undermine the existing order. Human thinking and acting, in Williams' view, always stalk the dominant power. As he wrote in his 1977 book *Marxism and Literature*: "no mode of production and therefore no dominant social order and therefore no dominant culture ever in reality includes or exhausts all human practice, human energy, and human intention" (p125).

One of the female students then made a very valid point: we have been discussing politics and power but, in her view, had omitted to mention or discuss what she called "the politics of patriarchy". She pointed out that in her work in the community she met a large number of "grassroots" groups concerned with childcare, nursery education, community regeneration, mental health and community transport and that all of them were overwhelmingly run by women. Male involvement in community action at this level, particularly in the Valleys, was extremely low - but when it came to the formal decision-making processes of local government, she highlighted how the picture changed, and how it was men who always seemed to be in control of executive committees and panels.

I agreed with this analysis having discovered it myself during my development officer days. Men it seemed were loath to get involved at ground level but were intensely involved in the corridors of power. For greater female participation we all proposed that women should take their commitment and energy to this higher level by putting themselves forward for election to local councils, but while doing so recognizing that they are struggling against a cultural inheritance that has historically stressed systems of power where men dominate. I stressed that in south Wales it seemed to me that the old "macho" image of men working in heavy industry, and politicking in smoky rooms, was an enduring one, but that it was reinforced in its durability by our western heritage where the three main systems of classical empires, the ecclesiastical establishment, the nation state and the modern corporation were all male dominated and gave women very little scope for action or influence. Altering the mindset generated by such systems was a formidable task, but by building on the gains achieved by the feminist movements of the twentieth century it was one that should be pursued widely and forcibly within our local communities and in contemporary society as a whole.

# Chapter Ten

## More Conversations About Power

By becoming an integral part of a collective learning group and fully utilizing my own, and my students', life and work experiences, my class analyzed communities in relation to their potential for community decision-making and developing the opportunities for collective action to combat local power structures. To underpin these class analyses with written investigations of power, I introduced the class to an overview of the literature of community development, capacity building and collective action and, in particular, a study of power and powerlessness in a very unequal, external community. I drew on my readings of John Gaventa's book *Power and Powerlessness: Quiescence and Rebellion in an Appalachian Valley* (1980) which discussed the "hidden faces of power" and their ability to shape actions and consciousness in communities in ways that are not immediately apparent in the formal political process.

After considering this foreign example, I asked the students: "do these situations demonstrate that for someone to have power, someone else must be without it?" I then told them to consider the question in silence for a few minutes. After such consideration, the ensuing discussion lasted for 10 minutes or more. I consciously remained detached from the conversation during this period to let the students develop and clarify their ideas, but after 10 minutes, when I saw an opportunity, I intervened and suggested a way forward - by giving a synopsis of the previous student responses, discussing those which appeared to me to be based on misconception, reviewing generalizations, analyzing comparisons, providing alternative analyses and giving his own interpretation of the subject. I had stated before the synopsis that students could intervene if they want to, and if a discussion developed in this way out of any point I made, it was followed through. This process,

merging into general group dialogue again, completed the introduction, and the class moved on to develop further the theme of
power and its relationship to community action.

To do this, in subsequent classes I posed a further series of
questions: "can local, individual communities achieve their own,
unique type of regeneration strategy within current funding initiatives - such as Objective 1 and Communities First - directed by
local power élites? How do collective efforts to achieve
community participation that come up against established
political obstacles plan arguments and strategies to counter these
obstacles? Can shifts in power towards local people over local
management of public finances generate pressure for a more
general redistribution of wealth and power? Is the local political
system sufficiently democratic for local communal pressure to
work its way through to the real centers of power?" All this
questioning was designed by the tutor to provoke responses,
initiate debate and trigger refutation. As the students spoke, I
made probing replies in order to draw out more responses. I
learned from the students the importance of specific themes – the
intransigence of local politicians, the apathy of local people, the
increasing professionalisation of the community sector, the short
term horizons of funders - in their work, and I recycled these as
problems for reflecting on in class.

## Integrating near and distant concepts
As this process unfolded, I integrated and contextualized the
expanding volume of information, because I saw my role as
helping members of the class to develop more general thinking, to
see the local as part of the whole; to help individuals see
themselves in a wider perspective, to reflect on their situation and
make connections between the local and the general. In thinking
about how to do this, I found the distinction used by *Geertz
(1983:57)* between experience-near and experience-distant
concepts helpful:

*"An experience-near concept is, roughly, one that someone – a patient, a subject in our case, an informant – might himself naturally and effortlessly use to define what he or his followers see, feel, think, imagine and so on, and which he would readily understand when similarly applied by others. An experience-distant concept is one that specialists of some sort or another – an analyst, an experimenter, an ethnographer, even a priest or an ideologist – employ to forward their scientific, philosophical or practical aims".*

Keeping a distance between the immediacy of experience-near concepts and the abstractions of experience-distant concepts, but allowing one to inform the other, was difficult, yet I saw it as a vital part of my role in generating critical thought. To reinforce the potential of these two concepts, I pointed out to the class that in his works, particularly in relation to the often expressed view that community workers should empathize with the inhabitants of the communities they served, Geertz (1983:58) was not a supporter of this approach. To him, the belief that anyone could perceive what other persons perceive by empathetically "imagining themselves someone else...and then seeing what they thought" was false. He believed that instead of trying to perceive as others perceive, we should try to discover "what people perceive "with", or "by means of" or "through". The aim of community workers should thus be to "re-describe": to construct accounts of how other people make sense to themselves by discovering "the symbolic forms - words, images, institutions, behaviors - in terms of which people actually represent themselves to themselves and to one another".

But, if we do take up this phenomenological method, Geertz (1983:59) believes that rather than attempting to place the experience-near concepts of others within the framework of the development worker's experience-distant conception, which is what the extolled "empathy" in fact usually comes down to, understanding these other experiences demands setting the worker's experience-distant conception aside, and seeing the experiences within the framework of other people's idea of what selfhood is. But how to do this exactly? Geertz's answer is "by hopping back and forth between the whole conceived through the parts that actualize it, and the parts conceived through the whole that motivates them" (p69). If workers do this, he believes they can come to a sense of what uses their experience-near concepts can be put to by gaining a sense of the general form of their life as a whole, and by "placing" the parts such uses play (in relation to each other) within that whole.

Not surprisingly, many of the students found Geertz's methodological pronouncements and use of models too esoteric for their taste. Rather than clarifying the link between local and universal perspectives, and that between the common-sense daily world and the cultural world through which we try to understand it, his approach often confused the students' perceptions. As a result, while grasping the general thrust of his message, many found his analyses, theories and language complex and perplexing. Some indeed saw Geertz's approach as being representative of many of the authorities and experts they had studied on the programme. Rather than communicating clearly and unambiguously with them, they felt that these authorities, through their complex ideas and language, were acting as inaccessible, privileged elites to the very people to whom they wished to convey liberating messages of hope and support. I had to confess that I too sometimes found it difficult to follow Geertz's language and thought, but I also stressed that with patience, and a few re-readings of the passages, his ideas became more transparent and more obviously relevant to what we were studying. Nevertheless, I took the hint about the perceived complexity of thought and language, and decided to introduce a more accessible thinker into the programme, one who spoke in basic, even earthy, language and who made his points unequivocally and forcibly - Dr. Morris Massey.

## Dr Massey's Value Programming

I showed the class two videos I had acquired while on a German Marshall Fellowship in the USA. I pointed out that Morris Massey was then a sociologist at the University of Colorado who had compiled and synthesized several different models of value systems to try to teach a basic understanding of why people act the way they do. With this understanding I believed we could learn to be more effective community activists and leaders, for by understanding Massey's concept of how our own value system is created - and altered - we can hopefully better understand others' value systems and learn better interpersonal communication and relationships.

But what is a value system? In the first video "What You Are Is What You Were When", Massey maintains that people think, respond and behave the way they do based on the way they value things: they usually value things and people according to the way they were raised, so different things have different importance to different people. Massey then divides what he calls the "Value programming" period of individuals into three main time frames:

the **IMPRINTING** period (0 - 7 years); a developing child learns to behave like an adult through observation

the **MODELLING** period (7 - 14 years): modeling oneself on "heroes" - what do you want to be when you grow up?

the **SOCIALISATION** period (14 - 20 years): peer group, friends, "significant others" in an adolescent's life become very important

At about 20, the value system thus programmed in locks in, and from that point on, we filter everything through this system unless it is altered by a significant emotional event. Massey then talks about the major influences in our lives: family, friends, school, religion, geography, income, electronic media and how these affect our value system. He then develops one of his basic concepts: "At approximately 10 years of age, 90 per cent of our gut level values have been programmed in". Consequently, his premise is: look at groups of people when they were 10 years old and determine where they were at that time - when they were gut-level programmed. He proceeds to highlight the main events on the timeline of social change, namely:

- Economic Depressions
- Wars
- The Electronic Media revolution
- Music and popular entertainment innovations
- The rise of consumerism

His discussion during this part of the presentation is leading the audience toward an acceptance of his statement that *"If you truly want to be effective in today's world, if you sincerely want to understand other people, it seems absolutely critical that we accept the reality that all these other people out there who are different from the way we are, are just as right, correct and normal as we are. We're all right. We're all normal. But we're all very different because what we are now is directly rooted to where we were, when we were gut level value programmed".*

I pointed out that Massey used some "four letter words" in his presentation, language that neither I nor the students would use in everyday conversation, and that their reaction to the appropriateness of this language to the message Massey was delivering was a fine, candid test of their own value systems at work. In order to stimulate further discussion, I then asked:

- What do you think of Massey's style and content?
- What do you think of his model?
- Is there much truth to it for you?
- Do you have a better understanding of why people behave

the way they do as a result of watching the video?

- Can some of the values in others be explained through this model?

A very exciting discussion ensued. Individual students seemed eager to share a significant difference in values they had discovered between themselves and someone that they had recently met (including myself). The listing and sharing of non-private, significant emotional events that had influenced their own view of the world was also surprisingly open, and out of all this talk came a general consensus that Massey's ideas and concepts had value, and provided a chronological and value-orientated template, a frame of reference, that they could put to positive use in their work as community activists.

In our next class I played the second video - "What You Are Is Not What You Have To Be". In this video, Massey focuses on the differences between people based on their espoused values. He says there are four basic generation groups functioning simultaneously in his society. These are people born before 1945 who he labels Traditionalists; people born between 1946 and 1965, the Baby Boomers; those born between 1966 and 1977, Generation Xers; and the group born since 1978 often termed the Generation Yers. Massey maintains that to understand the similarities within each generation group and, more importantly, the differences between groups, a values analysis needs to be performed, because if we examine the value system shared by generation groups then we can better understand their diverse beliefs and behaviors. In his view, we do not have to agree with the values of different generations but we can strive to understand the mind-sets of different generations and how each group sees the world based on its experiences. Massey then outlines the values he associates with each generation group:

### Traditionalist Values (age: older than 55)
- acceptance of authority
- patriotism and trust
- belief in social order and economic stability
- formality in personal and professional behavior
- a "puritanical" outlook and the acceptance of traditional religious values
- the acceptance of the work ethic
- the belief in the command and control approach to problem-solving

### Boomer Values (age: 37-55)
- hard work necessary for success not because it is the right thing to do
- belief in the team approach to work not the command and control system
- anti rules and regulations
- acceptance of people on an equal basis as long as they are deemed worthy of respect
- acceptance of competition

### Generation X Values (age: 25-36)
- belief in independence and creativity
- belief in the entrepreneurial ethos
- belief in the right to challenge the social order and affect economic change
- informality and flexibility in personal and professional behavior
- great reliance on constant access to information networks
- abandonment of the traditional work ethic in favor of leisure time
- the belief in individual initiative rather than a group/team approach to problem-solving
- value easy access to as much information as possible

### Generation Y Values (age: 12-24)
- stress need for greater personal autonomy
- belief in a positive approach to life
- believes in making and spending money
- see cultural diversity as a way of life
- believe the need for systematic and frequent feedback

I pointed out that Massey's conclusions are generalities about groups of people, and that they do not apply to all members of a particular generation - but they can help us to understand the gut level programming of individuals within those groups. Conflicts arise from the different perceptions and behaviors of individuals rooted in different value systems so, as community workers, we must learn to understand the differences, learn to deal with them, and move towards suitable communication techniques and decision-making procedures when dealing with people from other generations. In other words, if we take the time to understand the values that drive people's behavior, we will be better equipped to work with them. I followed these observations with a discussion on what we had just viewed on the second video, and we considered such questions as: "What role does each group play in today's society?" and "What are the strengths and weaknesses of each group?"

In considering these questions, I started by asking the students to consider their own values in comparison with those of their grandparents, parents and brothers and sisters. Was there still a definite generational difference in attitudes and values within their families? Who were the Traditionalists, the Generation Xers, the Baby Boomers and the Generation Yers? Did their values relate to their age and generation group? We then extended the comparison to local organizations and their personnel which the students had dealt with, and were still in contact with, in their working lives - local authorities, the Welsh Assembly Government and the community and voluntary sectors, and came up with some interesting observations on how community workers should behave and communicate with specific people such as Council Leaders, Chief Executive Officers, Departmental Heads, and local development staff who impacted regularly on their work and its development. The suggestions put forward included:

## With Traditionalists
- Because they are "private" people, development workers should not expect members of this generation to share their thoughts immediately with strangers
- Because they believe in keeping their word, workers should focus on words rather than the inference of body gestures
- Remember that face to face or written communication is the preferred option
- Don't let them feel workers are being frivolous and wasting their precious time

## With Baby Boomers
- Because they are the "show me" generation, body language is important when communicating with this group
- workers must remember to speak to Boomers in a direct, open style
- Workers must answer questions thoroughly and expect to be pressed for details
- They must present options to demonstrate flexibility in their thinking

## With Generation Xers
- Remember to use e-mail as a primary communication tool
- Talk in short sound bites to keep Xers' attention
- Provide them with regular feedback and ask regularly for their views
- Share information with them regularly and keep them "in the loop"

- Use an informal communication style with them

**With Generation Yers**
- Workers must use action words and challenge Yers regularly
- Do not talk down to this group as it will cause resentment
- They too like to receive e mail information
- Use humor and create an open learning environment with them
- Encourage them to take risks so that they can explore new ways of working

One of the students then drew our attention to the fact that what we had learned from Dr Massey's videos was not too distant from our original focus of study in the last few classes - the ideas of Clifford Geertz, and particularly his experience-near and experience-distant concepts. The student gave as his evidence for this belief a quote he had discovered on the Internet from a lecture given by Geertz in 1999 and printed as an occasional paper for the American Council of Learned Societies (page 13) in which he stated:

*"To discover who people think they are, what they think they are doing, and to what end they think they are doing it, it is necessary to gain a working familiarity with the frames of meaning within which they enact their lives. This does not involve feeling anyone else's feelings, or thinking anyone else's thoughts, simple impossibilities. Nor does it involve going native, an impractical idea, inevitably bogus. It involves learning how, as a being from elsewhere with a world of one's own, to live with them".*

Although this quote was aimed at dealings with people from other cultures, the class thought it extremely pertinent to their work, especially the reference for the need to gain a working familiarity with "the frames of meaning within which they enact their lives".

They all agreed that Massey's value action programme gave them one of the best techniques for attempting to place their working colleagues, community allies and opponents within such frames (in fact, they observed, were not Massey's concepts in effect generation as opposed to culture-based "frames of meaning"?) and, as a consequence, help them, as community leaders, communicate, motivate and interact with other community participants more effectively than they had previously done.

## Uses of a sociological imagination

After consideration of the ideas of Dr Morris Massey, I turned to another American who wrote in vigorous, accessible language, and advocated relevance and critical engagement over academic detachment when challenging the policies of the ruling elites in society – the American academic and critic, C Wright Mills. Mills studied the structure of power in the USA. In his book *The New Men of Power: America's Labor Leaders* (1948) he concluded that the workers were appeased by "bread and butter" policies, they had become comfortable within the system and, as a result, had given up any challenge to it. In *White Collar: the American Middle Classes* (1951) he contended that bureaucracies had overwhelmed the individual city worker, depriving him/her of all independent thought and transforming him/her into a cheerful automaton. The worker accepted a salary, but became alienated from the world because of his/her inability to alter it. *The Power Elite* (1956) described the relationship between the political, military and economic elite, noting that the individuals who made up their membership shared a common world view based on:

- The military mindset – a military definition of reality
- Common class identity: recognizing themselves as separate and superior to the rest of society
- Interchangeability: they move within and between the three institutional structures and hold interlocking directorates

- Co-optation/socialization: of new members is based on how well they have "cloned" themselves on the existing elites and their culture.

The elite maintains its power, purpose and personnel, according to Mills, by basing its unity "upon the corresponding developments and coincidence of interests among economic, political and military organizations" (1956:292). Mills though was not only concerned with describing and analyzing these power structures, but also dedicated to changing them. In his book *The Sociological Imagination* (1959) he describes a mindset – the sociological imagination – that can be utilized to combat the influence of these structures by encouraging people to grasp what is going on in the world by understanding what is happening in their private lives as expressions of broader social, political and economic developments: in other words, by getting people to connect their personal concerns to impersonal public issues. Mills maintains that government often presents public issues as private troubles with, for example, the blame for unemployment being laid at the door of lazy, feckless individuals rather than the result of incompetent political or economic arrangements. To achieve the necessary knowledge to combat this situation, Mills stresses that individuals must be able to mentally shift from one intellectual perspective to another when considering society and its power structures – from the political to the psychological; from the social to the economic, from the cultural to the scientific , from the financial to the recreational. In short, it is the capacity to range from the most impersonal and remote transformations to the most intimate features of the human self, and to see the relations between the two, that must be generated in individuals for the good of society (1959:229. 1954:12 quoted in Brookfield 2005:174).

What Mills is saying is that we cannot see what is happening in society just by looking at everyday life. To see what is really happening we must look in a different way, then we will see things that are currently invisible to us. To do this, Mills proposes we adopt the sociological imagination so that we will then see secret structures that influence our social and economic lives, recognize that reality has hidden dynamics and that there are visible and invisible, open and secretive social systems at work. By adopting such a mindset, Mills believes the individual enters a much larger world. His involvement in the public issues of contemporary society gives him the opportunity to try and alleviate the structural troubles which affect him, as well as helping to shape and reshape the institutional framework of his society. With this insight, the individual sees that others also share these troubles, and that the solution is not to struggle individually, but to join forces with those who also share his experiences. (Wikipedia entry, *C Wright Mills*).

I then explained how Mills's concept of the sociological imagination had affected my own view of society, growing up as I had during the socially conservative 1950s. To me, this was a bolt out of the blue, a radically new way of seeing society and the world - a way that excited my imagination and made me question contemporary social structures, actions and attitudes. Ultimately it reshaped my attitude towards politics and its role in remodeling society, and I enthusiastically endorsed Mills's view that people should be involved in the political processes of their society. This call to political arms is inherent throughout his argument, in that the logical outcome of having a sociological imagination leads ultimately to an increased political involvement. In fact, it could even be said that the basic purpose underlying the sociological imagination is to create a wider level of public involvement in the political questions of society. When seen from this perspective, the sociological imagination is as much a political argument as it is a sociological one – a view that could also be slightly modified in the name of education rather than sociology, and applied to my course.

## A messy outcome

My teaching strategy in class concerning power and its influence and distribution, was thus based on generating local/global, personal/impersonal, individual/communal connections and reflective thinking. Such effort was far from easy and provided all those involved with often complex and intellectually "messy" discussions and thinking processes. This was due to the fact that the students, most of whom had left formal education at the earliest possible opportunity, had received little training in writing, had seldom read a book and had minimal exposure to history, philosophy, psychology or literature. Their only acquaintance with the world's culture came through a cursory reading of daily "red top" newspapers. As a result, their stock of general knowledge was limited and seemed to become more celebrity orientated every day. They could not recognize allusions to Shakespeare or the classics or the Bible, or their country's own history, and they were almost totally oblivious to what was happening on the world stage (Iraq being the one notable exception). My introduction of concepts of local/global and individual/communal interconnections, with reinforcing anecdotes and illustrations from history and politics in particular, proved a lengthy and sometimes frustrating process; so much so that on times I felt that my classes were being transformed into Liberal Studies discussion sessions wherein the students received a crash introduction course to sociological and historical trends in western civilization.

I was particularly concerned about the students' lack of historical perspective. A great many of them saw the past, in L P Hartley's terms, as "a foreign country: they do things differently there". There was little understanding of continuity: enduring concepts such as values, beliefs, power, violence, co-operation and collective action were ignored. The past was cut off, compartmentalized and offered nothing to the present. Apart from an obsession with the Second World War, which was constantly replayed in television documentaries and celebrity-focused Hollywood films, the past held no interest or lessons for my students. As one remarked to me, "Why should we study history when all the facts we need can be retrieved from Google?" The students therefore had vague ideas that "some old stuff" had happened in the past and was now stored on the Internet. Any inkling that the study of the past could provide us, in the present, with lessons for current and future actions, did not exist.

My counter argument was that a great deal of what we know about the past is often unsubstantiated rumor, unverified prejudice and unexplored tradition; while much of what we retain about the past is a confused collection of facts, received opinions and accumulated moral judgments. I made it plain that I agreed with the words and belief of the 2009 Mann Booker prize winner, Hilary Mantel, when she wrote:

> "To try to engage with the present without engaging with the past is to live like a dog or cat rather than a human being: it is to bob along on the waters of egotism, solipsism and ignorance...History offers us vicarious experience. It allows the youngest student to possess the ground equally with his elders; without a knowledge of history to give him a context for present events, he is at the mercy of every social misdiagnosis handed to him". (The Guardian, 17 October 2009).

"According to you, then, learning history should act as a guarantee against tyranny and form part of an education in citizenship", one of the class observed. I said that I believed this to be the case unequivocally, and so we entered into a lively, spirited, and on-going, debate as to the need for history to be a central element of the modern curriculum. This development maintained my belief that my class had became an active, thought provoking, emanci-patory learning site for many of its participants – a site where students were encouraged and given the space to speak with their own voices, examine their experiences, explore their histories, their values, and the relevance of all these factors to local society: and how such values were often distorted in the interests of the powerful. The more thoroughly the classes examined local issues and values, and investigated outside examples, the more students wanted to discover about structural and ideological forces and how these influenced and restricted their lives. Indeed, the whole concept of power and its role in shaping individuals and communities was highlighted, and used as a discussion topic to demonstrate just how pervasive the concept of power is in shaping society and communities. Moreover, I pointed out that even learning and reflection in a community group are, in the words of Said, (1985):

*"shaped to a degree by the exchange with the power political (as with a colonial or imperial establishment), power intellectual (as with reigning sciences like comparative linguistics or anatomy, or any of the modern policy sciences), power cultural (as with orthodoxies and canons of taste, texts, rules), power moral (as with ideas about what "we do" and what "they" cannot do or understand as "we" do)".*

**A three-dimensional model**

To get the class to look at the concept from another angle, I outlined Ledwith's (2001) proposal that to counter the complex interweavings and intertwinings of power and "oppressors" in a community, activists should consider a three-dimensional model: one that has a power strand moving through difference – age, race, gender, ability, ethnicity - on one axis; another through contexts – economic, cultural, intellectual, physical, environmental, historical, spiritual - on a second axis; and a third between levels – local, regional, national, continental and global - on a third to form a complex set of interrelationships which interweave between axes but which also intertwine on any one axis. Ledwith uses this model to help her pose the complex interrelatedness of a range of questions, and to locate this "locus of oppression" within a work context and on a community level. She points out that these elements are not fixed: they are interchangeable on each face of the model. The purpose of the model is to stretch the thinking of tutor and students in a multi-dimensional way by locating the interface of different dimensions of "oppressions" and, in doing so, pose further questions.

## The midwife method

I did not, though, consciously launch into a monologue when presenting these new questions and concepts. Students' replies did not get lost in a tutor-orientated commentary: instead I drew on my academic knowledge, not just in community work but in history, politics, economics and sociology, to highlight how I arrived at my beliefs - but only after the students had established a foundation for the discussion in their own words. I therefore adjusted my expertise to fit the shape of a dialogue the students had evolved in response to my problem-posing and questioning. I resisted reverting to the hierarchical authority of traditional classes in which students believe that when the tutor begins talking he is going to tell them what the answer really is. By doing this I was implementing what Belenky (1986: 217/8) had labeled the "midwife" approach to teaching, in that:

> "Midwife teachers are the opposite of banker teachers. While the bankers deposit knowledge in the learner's head, the midwives draw it out. They assist the students in giving birth to their own ideas, in making their own tacit knowledge explicit and elaborating it. They support their students' thinking, but they do not do the students' thinking for them or expect them to think as they do"

I therefore made the students' views and ideas, rather than my own, the starting point for developing discussions, and I utilized this method to communicate respect for the students and their ideas - to me their ideas, thoughts, values and views were of great importance and formed the foundation of all my classes. I was well aware too that my own views were not infallible, and so my questions were also produced to explore new avenues of thinking and generate new ideas. Indeed, like Foucault (1980:193) commenting on his own writing, my talk often:

> *'does not have the function of a proof. It exists as a sort of prelude, to explore the keyboard, sketch out themes and see how people react, what will be criticized, what will be misunderstood, and what will cause resentment'.*

# Chapter Eleven

## Collective Knowledge and Action

The effectiveness of this method reinforced my belief that knowledge is a social product which, in the words of Wainwright (2003: 18), "can be transformed by people who take action - co-operating, sharing, combining different kinds of knowledge - to overcome the limits on the knowledge they individually possess". This view of knowledge as a social product, and its development via collective discussion, heightens the possibility of people gauging, through exchange with others, the possible consequences of their intended actions and therefore being able purposefully to influence community relations and conditions. By using this participative method the students were encouraged to go beyond merely repeating what they already knew and had already been taught - as was I. I, too, accepted that I must be open to argument and challenge and that, if necessary, be willing to change my perspectives, to modify them, and to admit errors in my thinking. The class as a whole, therefore, reflected on the realities of community life and on their own values, words and interpretations in ways that illustrated meanings they had not perceived before. Their discussions transformed their thoughts and, ultimately, their actions in the communities in which they worked and lived.

This co-operative group discussion, and its basic process of questioning and problem solving, challenged passive methods of teaching where students learn that education is generally something done to them rather than something they can do for themselves. It invited students to become active learners who questioned received wisdom. I motivated the critical potential in my students by posing knowledge and history as on-going, and as processes which they could transform through their thoughts and actions stimulated by an oral sharing of information in class. It was this connection between democratic group dialogue, active learning and community action that I continually highlighted. My objective was that my students should learn by developing meaning and knowledge from consideration of their own experience of community work, and from the similar experiences of other students in the group. Their work activity was the foundation of the students' experience and the precursor of new knowledge. By sharing their experiences of past work-actions, and the meaning of these actions with each other - and by projecting further actions on the basis of what had been learnt from one another - the students' reflected knowledge became the basis of considered and effective action.

We all agreed that this effective action should involve the students making the case for more collective working, by organising community responses, especially economic and social initiatives, in response to debilitating conditions, by arguing the case for greater employee and community involvement in the workplace and in campaigning, even participating in, local political life. We all agreed too that one of the most vital actions was to work to change the prevailing attitude towards the perceived irrelevance of collective responses to the current capitalist model. One of the first actions undertaken by community workers, I suggested, should be to alert communities and their inhabitants to the fact that there are currently business alternatives operating outside the mainstream capitalist model, many of which are already part of everyday life and which are thriving in our society.

In their recent book based on extensive research into unequal societies, The *Spirit Level*, Wilkinson and Pickett (2009: 246) outline the vital role still played by building societies in the United Kingdom (there are 63 with over 2,000 branches and 38,000 employees), 650 credit unions, 70 mutual insurance companies as well as 250 friendly societies which provide a range of financial services to their members. There are almost 170,000 charities with a combined annual income of over £44 billion. In 2007 the Co-operative Bank, with £40 billion of assets, was recognised as the most corporately responsible company in the UK according to the charity, Business in the Community. There was also the example of employee co-operatives such as the Tower Colliery in Hirwaun where the miners, facing redundancy in 1995, used their redundancy payments to buy the pit from the Coal Board and run it successfully for another thirteen years, an event which to someone as myself, keen to preach the virtues of collective action, was a seminal local event. The John Lewis Partnership, a retailing company with 68,000 employee stakeholders and annual sales of £6.4 billion, is one of the country's most successful firms, while other examples of successful employee-owned companies include the Polaroid Corporation, Carl Zeiss and the London Symphony Orchestra. It is also worth noting in this context that those two beacons of British academic excellence - the Oxford and Cambridge colleges - are governed democratically by all their fellows.

Even in that bastion of market fundamentalism, the United States, Gar Alperovitz in his book *America Beyond Capitalism: Reclaiming our Wealth, our Liberty and our Democracy*, (quoted in Wilkinson and Pickett: 245), points out that there are also successful alternatives to the capitalist model. Some 4,600 Community Development Corporations (CDCs) have become a major component of social and economic regeneration: in a free-enterprise nation they are finding ways to open doors to classes, communities and individuals otherwise excluded from the American dream. CDCs, controlled by boards of directors - primarily community residents who contribute to fund-raising, lobbying, policy setting and credibility building - have become the principal suppliers of low-income housing in the United States. They finance and operate shopping malls, industrial parks, business "incubators" and retail franchises. An industry survey published in 2006 found that the CDCs promoted community economic stability by developing over 86,000 units of affordable housing and 8.75 million square feet of commercial and industrial space a year (www.community-wealth.org/). They also start their own businesses; increasingly they provide venture capital, loans, and technical assistance to other job-producing enterprises. Their social service arms, from health to child care to drug counselling to care of the elderly and homeless, mediate between individuals in need and a society that provides cold and bureaucratic services, if any.

Alperovitz stresses the importance of the alternative, collective contribution to the country. As well as highlighting the role of the CDCs, he notes that there are 48,000 co-operatives in the US, with a membership of 120 million people; 10,000 credit unions with assets totalling $600 billion, providing services for 83 million Americans; some 1,000 mutual insurance companies, owned by their policy holders; that 30 per cent of US farm products are marketed through co-operatives; and that there are 2,000 municipal electric utilities which supply 40 million people with electricity. As for employee-owned companies in the United States, the National Center for Employee Ownership lists companies that include Hy-vee Supermarkets which has 51,000 employees, Publix Supermarkets with 142,000, the engineering and construction company CH2M Hill with just over 19,000 and Tribune which, among other media operations, publishes the Los Angeles Times and Chicago Tribune, with 19,000 employees (www.nceo.org/library/eo100.html).

In mainland Europe, the Mondragon Co-operative Corporation, based in the Basque country in Spain, is one of the most admired examples of workers' self-management. Established by local communities to combat high unemployment after the fascist defeat of the Republican government in 1939, the co-operative built on the strong tradition of collective and self-help organisations in the region. The Mondragon Corporation, with 40,000 worker-owners, over 150 co-operatives including manufacturing and engineering interests as well as retail, financial, and educational arms, is now the Basque country's largest corporation, and the seventh largest in Spain. In 12006 it contributed 3.8% towards the total GDP of the Basque Country, has the highest labour productivity in Spain, and is generally considered to be the largest worker co-operative in the world (Oakeshott: 2000).

The scale and diversity of all this organizational experience, based on a collective philosophy, leaves no doubt that profit-making business is not the only effective way people can work to create jobs and provide vital services. I recalled the impact that visiting the Chicanos Por La Causa CDC in Phoenix, Arizona - established in the 1970s by a group of community and student activists of Mexican descent - had had on my view of how effec-tively the community-based sector can serve both its workers and its community, when I witnessed its work in the fields of housing development, job training, counseling services, mental health and drug rehabilitation programmes, day care centers, shelter for the victims of domestic violence and services for the elderly. "The advantages are that you bring services down to the local level, you get the community involved in the project", Pete Garcia the CDC director had told me in April 1990. "Rather than the bureaucracy, it's the community saying we're going to do what we think our community needs". In other words, the idea is not only to provide an efficient service, but to get more compassion and more commitment from those people delivering the service (the service had previously been provided by a profit making business). It is also the intention, according to Pete Garcia, "to promote compe-tition, to use small units of workers capable of more flexibility and humanity than large bureaucracies or profit generating businesses, and to take advantage of the diversity of community organizations to serve populations that are often beyond the reach of state and federal government welfare systems".

I thus saw the type of critical education I was delivering as a way of preparing students to engage in, or to initiate, a challenge to the current individualistic, market orientated status quo by promulgating an alternative way of working and thinking. I realized that by doing this, and arguing for greater use of community knowledge and involvement, I would be increasing the likelihood of division in the community by conflict with those individuals and groups holding power. To underline this point, I quoted my students some lines that had caught my attention when studying the American Civil War as an undergraduate. The words are those of the black abolitionist Frederick Douglass and, though he was specifically taking about freedom, I thought his words could with equal validly be applied to community:

> "Those who profess to favor freedom, and yet deprecate agitation are men who want crops without plowing the ground. They want rain without thunder and lightening. They want the ocean without the awful roar of its waters."

## Raising Political Awareness

Such a commitment to social change had been instilled into the students early on in the course by encouraging a collective emancipatory approach to learning, and had been reinforced by a new, more critically focused understanding of power and community reality: from initially assuming, for example, that the value of their community work was self-evident, class members discovered that it was in fact something they had to struggle to validate. As one student commented, regarding his local councilors' attitude, "they used us as a potter uses clay: in public pretending to be sympathetic, helpful and conciliatory. In private though they were wheeling and dealing and pursuing their own agendas". The students' early belief in "authority", particularly its local manifestation - the local council, its representatives and their views - and its assumed support for local struggles for social improvements, was soon replaced by disappointment, and an understanding that authority was not neutral, was often embedded in social, economic and political interests, and that community action could be prone to indifference, sidelining or even take over by paternalistic, tradition dominated authorities.

Such understanding stimulated more critical thinking - which in turn brought into question the pronouncements and policies of local political power holders. As a result, the students raised such questions as: "Why has the need for community action come to prominence, and been promoted by politicians, so late in the day? Why hasn't it been encouraged earlier, on an on-going basis? Is it only being implemented now due to the availability of significant European Union funding?" Class discussion of these questions lead to a close examination of European funding programmes, especially the eagerly anticipated Objective 1 and Communities First elements. This examination encouraged the students to pose even more questions - "Why are these programmes being lauded as wonderful opportunities for the Valleys when their award indicates that the area is on the same economic and social level as the poorest parts of the European Union? Why have the Valley communities and the region as a whole been allowed to fall into such a state? Who is to blame for all this? Is the current deprived and excluded state of the Valley communities anything to do with a historical lack of grassroots democratic activity and popular pressure and the repeated encouragement to the "brightest and best" to leave and venture further afield? Was it all the fault of capitalism and its recent codification as a global system without the counterbalancing influence of an effective socialist movement?"

By reflecting on these questions throughout the course, the group came to the conclusion that Valley communities had indeed been "let down" by the obsequiousness of their politicians, a docile population, and the mobility and ruthlessness of capital: and this finding was reflected in the group's view of the untrust-worthiness of the political world in general. The initial response of the class to this situation was the use of strong emotional language. Blame was allocated to the parties involved in angry, sometimes crude and negative, terminology typical of what Hobsbawn has characterized as "pre-political thought", which is incoherent, immediately focused and lacking in long-range goals or actions. Not until later, after a period of discussion and reflection in further classes, did the students produce a more considered critical position which fell into what Hobsbawn has characterized as a "coherent viewpoint providing an interpretative framework for the understanding of relations between society, culture and political economy" (quoted in Perlman, 1980).

What the students expressed in these classes was moral indignation, and I used their sense of grievance to insert another discussion into a lesson on whether their sense of morality was born with them, or whether they had developed it as they lived their lives. Some students thought they had acquired a moral sense at birth, genetically and intuitively: it was a natural part of their "make-up". Others (the majority) thought this was too simple an explanation, and believed that their moral sense had been acquired by their interpersonal and social experiences while growing up. They thought that through working, living, reading, observing and conversing with other people they had acquired the habit of allocating value to their conduct and their thoughts. They agreed with the view of Habermas (1988:170) too, that they had not fully realized the existence of their moral sense until well into adulthood. They appreciated his idea that until adult life granted them enough diverse experiences to provide them with comparative information to judge their current experiences against, they could not truly indulge in critical reflection and form a critical consciousness or value system.

In fact, though this discussion generated a great deal of interest, and stimulated ideas, the students felt that however they obtained their moral values (innately or experientially), it was still undeniably "wrong" that their views and activities were now regarded with disdain by local vested interests. They also felt a sense of powerlessness, in that they believed they were on their own and had no critical public support to reinforce their attitude towards politicians, business networks and "the system" in general. I replied that current anti status quo attitudes had become purely private concerns largely unsupported by any public institution. With the exception of some committed vicars, even the Church had now practically abandoned moral teaching about the accumulation of wealth and its distribution in society. Our present society, in my view, appeared to have dismantled the moral systems through which the operation of power interests could be countered and, by the acceptance of neo-liberal economics as somehow inevitable, we had reduced to a minimum the degree to which political opposition can expose and oppose the operation of government and business interests. In such a situation, I stressed, it becomes vital for community workers to increase awareness of the degree to which we are all under the influence of vested interests - and to learn to implement collective actions to combat them.

I then emphasized that if class members made judgments about the morality of the attitudes of local powerholders, this would not of itself change the situation - but it would certainly be a first step of the kind of moral and political action by which the structures and institutions of local communities could be altered. I underlined that the ills communities suffered were not consequent upon local peoples' personal imperfections or moral faults: rather they were the inevitable result of publicly endorsed and communally practiced forms of indifference, greed and exploitation, and it required a moral reconstruction of our collective way of life to contest them. To reinforce this point I quoted the view of Smail (1998: 152) that:

*"Instead of abusing power, we need to use whatever power we have to increase the power of others, to take care rather than treat, to enlighten rather than mystify, to love rather than exploit, and, in general, to think seriously about what are the obligations as opposed*

*to the advantages of power. Ideally, the foremost obligation on power is to "deconstruct" itself".*

After reflecting on this view, and discussing in detail the whole question of community work, politics and morality, the class agreed that if we, as citizens and activists, accepted that we were currently inflicting incalculable, but avoidable, damage on each other, rather than working together to improve ourselves and our communities, we had to force open around ourselves and our communities, a moral space which would give us room for collective action. This, we all agreed, could only be achieved through the reinsertion into that space of committed public activity.

To achieve this, we agreed that there was a need for a new kind of democracy - one where links could be forged between community participation and political democracy. Such links, the class felt, would radically change the character of politics for the better, requiring local and national politicians to face the demands of the organized poor and their communities. In the eyes of the class, collective action had a transformative role to play, one that could create experiments of a truly equal and democratic nature which other communities would then be inspired to reproduce. The students had observed the way political parties imitate traditional relationships of power and reproduce them when they gained power themselves. They believed that the goal of collective community action should therefore be to break this power pattern and so obstruct the reproduction of established power structures and attitudes.

### Taking action - the majority view
The majority view in the class was that local power holders, particularly local authorities, should open their structures and involve all citizens in deciding how these structures should work, thereby generating a collective process that was both personally and

socially transformative. This was especially true of the local authority's budget. The majority felt it should become a genuinely participatory budget and be directly influenced by representatives chosen, through a series of public meetings, from the communities sited in the local authority area - and that these individuals should take to the local authority the spending priorities in the field of public works, community services and the social economy decided by local people.

I pointed out that this open, conversational method of financial decision-making had been enshrined in the constitutions of some countries: the Philippines adopted this approach in the early 1990s, as did Indonesia - both following the process initiated in Porto Alegre, Brazil in the late 1980s. Here, some 100,000 people, about a tenth of the adult population, attended participatory meetings during the course of the initiative in the 1990s and 2000s to open up the budget-setting process. This approach has been graphically described by Wainwright (2003:48-9), and was discussed in great detail by the class, where it was seen by the majority as an effective antidote to an historical tradition of secrecy and paternalism. Furthermore, its supporters stressed that such action could initiate a cycle which ran counter to those processes which always put the poor and their communities in last place. Such a cycle they believed could set in motion a realization of individual and collective capabilities inconceivable in a culture of individual action, and that collective community action could effectively oppose the apathy characteristic of local patron-client politics. This cycle of action, they accepted, did not guarantee total success, but it could effectively put into play different dynamics from those traditionally linked with the exercise and challenging of power.

The majority also believed it was very much more difficult for patronage to gain the upper hand in so transparent a participative democracy. Its view was that a new administrative behavior was imposed on the local bureaucracy by such an open system -

bureaucrats were not left to their own deliberations, but were forced to leave their offices and explain in comprehensible language what they consider possible or impossible - and that this process formed part of an invaluable educational process for all concerned.

The crucial point made by the bulk of the class about the relationship between participative and representative democracy was that the activity of the first guarantees the quality of the second. They believed that if it worked well, participative democracy could generate transparency, constantly question financial choices, build wider circles of decision-making, and play a crucial role in the formation of a small but expanding group of experienced, educated and active citizens who had an ethic of public service. The majority also felt that in Wales, a small step in this process of greater democratic input had been made by the creation of the Communities First programme, and the community representation on the programme's Community Partnership Boards, but that this step was only the first stage in a lengthy operation that had to be consolidated and developed even further.

## Taking action - the minority view

The minority view was that this process was still open to local authority manipulation and influence, that local authority representatives would never willingly release their grip on power, and that the views of the community could never be adequately or consistently represented this way. This group saw the Communities First programme as an attempt by the Welsh Assembly government to manage conflict and to gain knowledge of, and better control over, local conditions: it believed Communities First to be a "top down" approach to community development that attempted to ensure that the target communities conformed to external and official expectations, and pointed out that though each designated community could compile its own action plan for social regeneration, its subsequent actions were always implemented within the "guidance notes" issued by the programme's funder - the Welsh Assembly Government.

In the eyes of the minority, all that the Communities First programme did was create the illusion of democracy and popular participation while, in reality, imposing a strong central control from Cardiff. The establishment of local partnership boards was a considered attempt to create the appearance of meaningful participation by citizens but was, really, through the imposition of placemen and political puppets, no more than a cynical ploy to lull the local citizenry into compliance with government policy. So, despite Assembly claims to devolve democracy, empower people and delegate decision-making, what local communities in Wales have experienced is the creation and maintenance of an illusion whereby central government control is tightened and central government policy imposed by stealth.

Because of this, the minority favored a dual strategy approach, the first strand of which was focused on developing grass-roots social action and was designed to generate commitment in place of the prevailing apathy. The minority recognized that individuals are generally only willing to get directly involved with people who need help and who live in the immediate vicinity. It also recognized that individuals find it hard to conceive of action and ideas on a grand scale – they may be aware of a large social problem, but they have very little idea of how to acquire the skills necessary to deal with, and act on, such a "big issue".

The minority grouping's approach was therefore based on the belief that the mass of people only act on matters when they see the situation as one they can personally identify with, or which they feel is directly oppressing them in some form or other. So, although it saw the sense in this quote which I put to them from Tom Paine's *The Rights of Man*:

> "It appears in general observation, that revolutions create genius and talent; but those events do no more than bring them forward. There is

*existing in man, a mass of sense lying in a dormant state, and which unless something excites it to action, will descend with him, in that condition, to the grave. As it is to the advantage of society that the whole of its facilities should be employed, the construction of government ought to be such as to bring forward, by quiet and regular operation, all that capacity which never fails to appear in revolution"* (page 277),

the group recognized that such a revolution was extremely unlikely, but that by encouraging local social action in place of revolution, it was bringing forward, in its own small way, "a mass of sense" currently lying dormant in the local population. By acting as allies with particular skill and expertise, this group wanted to listen to the community and so work to get people to participate in public life around important issues: to encourage them to become social actors, buttressed by a profound desire to overcome injustice. This approach they saw as not consolidating authority but questioning it and holding it responsible for its actions. Indeed, they were very much in sympathy with the view of the American historian Howard Zinn when he observed in 2009:

*"Where progress has been made...wherever any kind of injustice has been overturned, it's been because people acted as citizens, and not as politicians. They didn't just moan. They worked, they acted, they organized, they rioted if necessary to bring their situation to the attention of people in power. And that's what we have to do today".*
(Quoted in The Guardian 30 January 2010).

The majority realized that to make the approach effective it also had to undertake political action at the local level, and to further this we undertook an exercise based on the old saying "The secret of walking on water is knowing where the stones are" - that is, identifying those individuals, and the levels they operate at, in the local authority who can influence policy-making decisions that are best suited to a community's purpose.

The exercise involved the students discussing a community problem - the building of a miniature golf course in the locality - and was presented as follows:

**SCENE:** A member of the community who owns a parcel of land in a residential area, wants to build a "pitch and putt" miniature golf course on his land. Besides the outdoor game, there will be electronic games in the golf clubhouse. Since it is a residential area, the planning committee of the local authority must give permission to build a commercial business on a lot currently allocated to residential use.

This is an informal meeting being held by local residents. It is a chance for people to discuss how they feel about the application and to talk with the land owner before it comes to a formal hearing before the planning committee.

Some people think the development will be a benefit to the community; children will learn skills playing these games, and they will be closer to home and better supervised. Others are concerned that it will change the character of the neighborhood, create parking problems and hazards for young children. They worry too about noise and lighted signs at night.

We discussed this problem for 40 minutes and took another 15 minutes to summarize our findings. We then listed a range of levels - and the expertise of the people working in them - which we thought the residents should be aware of in their attempt to influence the decision-making process about the land development. The list had six levels and some rules that we thought useful for political activists:

**Staff** (administrative support to executive level of local government): A source of information, advice and opinion. They can make small decisions within the scope of their procedures but, as a rule, they have no authority for short term changes.

**Remember** - you must determine who has the authority for the subject you are interested in. You have to identify the appropriate department, division, section - and then the right person within it. Patience and lots of telephoning and questioning will eventually pay off.

**Elected Officials**: A source of information, advocates for policy changes, intermediaries for community groups and citizens.
**Remember** - get to know them individually. Establish your credibility. You can do this by writing a letter, phoning them, asking for a meeting, using a letter-to-the -editor space and e mailing them. Why not be a candidate yourself?

**Committee** (standing, ad hoc, sub committees): Typically an advisory level of government. Recommendations for higher levels of government are prepared here. This is the level where the work leading up to a decision is conducted. Committees are characterized by the airing of positions of all interested parties, and the brokering or negotiating of trade-offs between interest blocks.
**Remember** - ask which committee deals with the subject of your concern?; who are its members?; who is chair?; which staff members are assigned to the committee for support?; how often and where are the meetings?; who prepares the agenda for them, and can you get on it?

**Councils**: The final decision making and action level for communities. Frequently council decisions are ratifications of committee recommendations. They are characterized by more formal procedures and presentations. The likelihood of action without prior committee recommendation or referral is remote. It is the least likely arena for compromise or conflict resolution. It is the most public area of the policymaking process, therefore the PR value of confrontation is the greatest.
**Remember** - you must acquire information on the members of the

council; who is the chair?; who wields the influence?; who prepares the agenda? A courtesy call to the chair introducing yourself and your concern represents time well spent.

**Voters:** Ones who have direct access to legislative power through the initiative or referendum process. Voter influence applies to legislative action only - it can either propose grass roots legislation or challenge a decision made by policymakers in referring their action to popular vote.

**Remember** - gather support for your aims via letter writing to papers, Internet contact, leaflet drops and public meetings will help you to reach as many voters as possible.

**Media:** Relevant to any discussion of the political process, although it is not a bona fide category of political action. Letters to the editor, feature stories, radio talk shows and, increasingly, use of the Internet on current events are desirable, no-cost strategies for influencing public officials and contributing to the public debate.

**Remember** - to raise your organization's profile, and its objectives, letters to the editor are vital as are human interest stories in the press, on radio programmes and on the Internet. Remember the influence of senator Obama's Internet usage in his successful presidential campaign of 2008.

But to supplement this process, the minority also thought it should publicly proclaim its beliefs, and subsequently act on them. It did this by "getting its hands dirty", by "entering the corridors of power" and attempting to deal with the core issues facing excluded communities by addressing them at the centre of the local power structure - the local authority. It did this by implementing the second element of its strategy - by actually creating a political party.

The minority group had listened closely to our discussions

about the participatory planning and budgeting process developed in the Brazilian city of Porto Alegre (based on Wainwright 2003), had done its own additional research into the subject and, from this, had concluded that the success of this process lay not only in its participatory element but also in its political support. It remembered that the foundations of the process were put down in the early 1980s when the Workers Party campaigned at local and state level to challenge the status quo. It distanced itself from the centralism of previous socialist parties by organizing itself around "nuclei" – small community groups, schools and workplaces, which all elect delegates to zonal, municipal and regional party seminars. The objective of this pyramidal system was to ensure bottom-up decision-making. A political party thus developed a culture of participation and was ready to take decentralization and participation seriously when it came to power in 1989.

This approach, which allowed for inputs from the grass-roots, was much admired by the minority. It believed that the lesson to be drawn from Porto Alegre was that people must get power first, they must officially connect local government structures, and the people who control them, to local initiatives that are struggling to combat social injustice. The best way to achieve this, in the minority's view, was by forming an official political party that could contest power and, when achieving it, could direct resources on a regular basis to community initiatives, alter the political culture, and open up the machinery of local government to the community. I had put forward a similar view in 1995 when I wrote in the *Community Development Journal* (p52): *"because economic redistribution in a free market system nearly always works against poor communities and their inhabitants there is a need for political intervention, especially when this intervention is defined as an act designed to affect the collective consciousness, change policy at all government levels, or alter the way some groups of people or organizations view an issue"* - an opinion that I believed would have been sympathetically received by Antonio Gramsci who thought that:

> *"democracy requires a certain kind of citizen...citizens who feel responsible for something more than their own well-feathered little corner; citizens who want to participate in society's affairs, who insist on it; citizens with backbones; citizens who hold their ideas about democracy at the deepest level"*. (Quoted in Berman 1997: 37).

An alert citizenry is therefore essential as it is the ultimate bulwark against the nefarious activities of politicians and commercial and financial institutions. Effective governance depends on individuals exerting their responsibilities and rights, monitoring the actions of governments and applying pressure to ensure that the rule of law is not violated or usurped. My belief therefore was that politics should be closely linked to the active engagement and participation of citizens in community affairs in order to improve the community of which they are a part. In my eyes, every citizen must learn how to be a activist - or a good candidate or councilor. Such a move will involve making hard choices, like less television watching or computer game playing, but that is how a democracy works. If we apathetically allow the political playing field to fall into the hands and control of the other side, they will win the power battle by default.

## A locally focused regeneration strategy

Using the intention of some of the students to form a political party and make a bid to acquire power - and assuming this bid to be successful - I posed a problem for the class as an end of year discussion session:

### The Problem

*"What should an intelligent development strategy in a poor community look like, now that those individuals who had successfully completed the programme are local authority councilors who sit on the powerful*

*economic regeneration committee?"*

## The Discussion

*I then distributed copies of my paper on "Community Development: A Question of Scale" in the Community Development Journal (1995) to each student to see if they could take any suggestions and ideas from it, and use it as a catalyst for new thinking. I asked the students, who had a fortnight to collect their thoughts on the subject, to remember that though they should put themselves in the shoes of new councilors who had real power, and bear in mind that the local authority had far greater powers than individual voluntary agencies and their workers, they should, in compiling a regeneration strategy, always remember the role of community development and its impact on local people and their actions and feelings. The class then adjourned to consider the problem. It reassembled fifteen days later, and after a detailed discussion, the students, before listing its recommendations, started by pointing out that: the goal of any intelligent strategy should be similar to that of a community development process - the creation of an action process, a process that is generated from within and that can at some point become self-sustaining. The local strategy should also follow the same method-ological principles as a development strategy for the broader society, and should contain the following elements:*

## The Diagnosis

*The local authority should ask a community group in each administrative area to carry out a study of the local community – a study that included economic as well as social factors. Such surveys would give the authority a comprehensive overview of the condition of the communities that make up its region, and would help it identify those neighborhoods that still retain enough social cohesion and common identity to help an effective development strategy lift them out of poverty. The surveys would also identify which neighborhoods lack social cohesion but still have the potential for significant improvement. Communities like these operate as transmission belts: they provide an inexpensive place to live while new arrivals find jobs and save enough money to seek greener pastures. Here the impact of a strategy is likely to be patchy, for even as it succeeds the successful beneficiaries would leave to be replaced by poor newcomers.*

*In such a precarious situation an effective approach would require large-scale investment. Such investment would be necessary to attract capital through the use of public-private-community partnerships. Partnerships are concerted activities undertaken jointly by public authorities, private companies and community organizations where a genuine sharing of planning and decision-making among citizens and officials is possible. Partnerships are also forums where citizens begin to have some degree of real power, and where they can help solve community and economic problems in a way that yields benefit to all the parties that co-operate. Partnerships can be seen as arrangement systems for community development, and can be used for planning, initiating, organizing and monitoring policies, programmes or projects – and their use must be genuinely encouraged if any long-lasting impact is to be made on the local economy and the attitudes of local people.*

*The council, in partnership with the community and its groupings, should then adopt a strategic development role. The council in particular is in a prime position to develop an effective response to poverty by drawing on the skills, knowledge and commitment of all those groups and organizations with an interest in, and commitment to, the community. This means it ensuring the mechanisms for attacking poverty are in place rather than running all the initiatives itself: it can provide seed money, training and technical assistance, and move the resources necessary to deal with problems into the control of community organizations. The local authority should then adopt a targeted approach to geographical neighborhoods or specific groups of people, especially those on low pay, female workers, ethnic minorities and those with special needs.*

*At its core, the regeneration strategy must contain an element which is vital to its success, but which is generally still only given lip service - the involvement of the whole community in the operation. This means as many of the inhabitants as possible, as well as the great variety of community organizations based in the locality. Individuals and* community organizations often have their own agendas but feel alienated because nobody listens to them. It may sometimes be the case that these agendas would coalesce well with the plans of the local council. Until now, very few councils possessed either the enthusiasm or the mechanisms to consult and compare agendas with individuals and voluntary groups. Every effort should be made for all sides to get together on a regular basis to exchange ideas and plans – a process that should be co-ordinated by the local Council of Voluntary Service that plays a strategic role in community affairs in each local authority administrative area in Wales.

It is essential that the local authority give the inhabitants of disadvantaged communities a say in planning the solutions. Techniques and mechanisms for achieving this are available and tested. The simplest method of seeking the views of residents is through a series of regular meetings held within the targeted communities. More complex responses include processes through which the community can act itself to develop its own agenda for change, modelled on the budget allocation process undertaken in Porto Alegre. Democratic forums based on statutory electoral wards could be allocated the product of a 5p to 10p council tax, depending on local deprivation levels, and the power to spend the income in partnership with the local councilors. This is the vital democratic contribution community development can make to a regenerative strategy, and there is now significant evidence to support the view that urban regeneration does not succeed, nor is sustainable in the long run, unless the people themselves, and their community initiatives, are centrally involved in the process.

The council must also bear in mind that the integration of economic and social programmes is particularly important in any regeneration strategy for deprived communities. A study of the work of the Community Development Foundation in Newport, Gwent (Hopkins 1989) revealed that such integration is essential if development is to have any significant impact - a finding confirmed by an in-depth study of revitalization strategies undertaken for the American Enterprise Institute (1984) which found that efforts which lacked this dual focus usually *failed. In healthy communities social structures such as the family, churches, informal community networks and voluntary organizations reinforce stability. They also encourage marriage, work and education and discourage crime. In many poor communities, however, these structures have largely been eroded.*

*Next, local authorities must remember that genuine development occurs not only because buildings are erected or houses renovated but also because people begin creating something of value. Councils must bear in mind that investments in the capacities of poor people - to hold jobs, to create businesses, to improve the housing stock and to build neighborhood organizations - can also be extremely effective. In short, effective development efforts must focus on building the capacity of local individuals and institutions. The use of local authority support workers to help council tenant groups acquire and adopt community development techniques to reinvigorate their neighborhoods should be a priority: the principal actors in the development process must therefore come from within the targeted community and must be encouraged to contribute their time, talent and treasure to this process.*

*While it must be local, an effective regeneration strategy must also be comprehensive. In a community that is spiraling downwards, a development strategy that attacks only one or two problems will generally be overwhelmed by a mass of other problems. So a strategy implemented piecemeal will lack synergy. Appropriate scale is also critical, so once viable local organizations are in place, the public sector must be prepared to make significant investments - in a disadvantaged community it must create the minimal market conditions necessary to give enterprising local people and groups a chance to make an impact.*

*Again, an effective regeneration strategy must possess regular monitoring functions, good market feedback mechanisms and operate with long-term perspectives. The strategy is responsive to changing economic conditions: if one strategy fails another one must be tried. The council must have enough capital and sufficient commitment to try a series of approaches until it finds those that work. If the council demands results within a short period such as three years, and pulls the financial plug when that does not happen, no development strategy will ever succeed.*

*In brief, therefore, the most effective community-based development strategy would, in the eyes of the students, create comprehensive development organizations, such as cross-sector partnerships. These institutions would possess enough resources to implement their work, and would target both social and economic problems. Their aim would be to generate investment rather than merely spend money, and they would try to attract as much of this as possible from the private sector. They would seek to build the capacity of local people and community organizations and involve them in policy and decision making. They would also contain in-built feedback mechanisms, and they would have enough political and financial support to stay in place for the long term.*

This strategy was compiled out of a recognition by the students that though collective action to improve the community's social and economic structures forms the core of a local development strategy, any current strategy must also take into consideration the scope of, and resource capacities of, local authority action. In a time of change, they all recognized that community-based solutions must be supplemented by the impact of local municipal strategies and funds, as well as whatever amount of private resources were available. What they were calling for was a new understanding of the problems facing communities in south Wales - and they were also offering some new ideas for action to which, they hoped, elected officials would respond positively sooner rather than later. As luck would have it, I was asked to implement a survey of voluntary activity in Cardiff a few months later, and a great deal of the thinking that went into the class exercise formed the basis of this survey and the subsequent report for Cardiff City Council . And, indeed, soon after presenting the report, we all began to notice the appearance of new phrases in official documents. Welsh Assembly Government and local government publications now contained phrases such as "public/private/

voluntary partnerships", "community empowerment", "partici-patory planning and action" and even, "community devel-opment" (which was often confused with "community regener-ation"). Whether the students from the programme who had entered local politics had been instrumental in the making of this verbal, and policy, paradigm shift was not clear - but we all felt that we had anticipated the new official Zeitgeist and had done our bit to mould official opinion.

## Taking local action – an update

Since the intense discussions held on the course, the actions favored by the majority and minority groupings have moved significantly forward. The majority has worked tirelessly throughout south east Wales, using the Communities First programme (which they saw as reflecting many of the elements contained in the local regeneration strategy they had complied) as an educational vehicle, to encourage the inhabitants of disadvan-taged communities to form groups to tackle local social and economic injustices and encourage a more critical view of local society and its power structures. The members of this group report that though the Communities First programme is spread thinly, and has suffered from bureaucratic rigidity in many areas it has, overall, helped regenerate a spirit of collective awareness and energy which is beginning to produce new action strategies in several areas.

But it is the action of the minority group that gives local communities most hope for future sustainable development, in that the desire, expressed during course discussions, to establish a political party and push for influence at the centre of local power, has come to fruition. Several group members joined with other community activists to form two new parties – the People's Voice and the People before Politics. Both these groupings put forward candidates in the 2004 and 2008 municipal elections and had representatives voted on to several local councils. Although the numbers are still relatively small, a start has been made, the mental barrier to participation breached, and real power acquired where the new representatives hold the balance between the established political groupings (although none, as yet, have been appointed to positions on influential council committees). In south east Wales the old battalions of monolithic politics have lost control of authorities such as Blaenau Gwent, Merthyr Tydfil and Torfaen to more independently minded, participatively focused, groupings which have promised to consult widely, and regularly take into account the wishes of their constituents – but the latter are still awaiting details of exactly how this new openness will function and how the voices and actions of local people will be heard and supported.

### Remember the planet, too

The election also revealed a growing concern among the communities of south east Wales about the precarious future of the planet and what should be done to ensure its survival. The increased vote of the Green Party reflected this concern, which had also become increasingly apparent among my students the longer the course progressed. Indeed, by the time of its conclusion there was a sizeable environmental lobby within the class which insisted that the course curriculum should, in future, contain more teaching about environmental matters, and that the teaching should start with input that stressed a wider role for the concept of community and a sense of place. The programme, the lobby suggested, should include studies of the "bio-community" which would encompass studies of the land, the history of the community as part of an ecoregion, and a study of the history of the people of that ecoregion. When challenged by the rest of the group as to the purpose of this education, the "greens" argued that cultivating a sense of history of a community enabled people to develop loyalties and commitment to that community. In a future when it is likely that the global economy will shrink due to shortage and exhaustion of resources, the cultivation of a sense of locality and place could, they believed, act as a corrective to the uncertainties of globalization by stressing the potential for developing an independent local economic network capable of providing goods and services for the inhabitants of that locality.

The "greens" also thought that the curriculum should stress that we all live our lives in a larger cosmological context that is far more relevant in the long term than our current market vision of our communities and the world. One student in particular pointed out that Brian Swimme, Director of the California Institute of Integrated Studies, writing in the Pacific Sun Magazine (2008), deprecated the current attitude towards our planet when he observed that "the current common sense understanding of the Earth is as a gravel pit or a hardware store...The modern period has been organized around the theory that Earth is just stuff we can use". Rather, Swimme stresses, we must articulate a planetary context for learning that is communicated in such a way that it will effectively challenge the hegemonic culture of the market, consumer orientated, vision and so help people and communities work towards the creation of an environmentally viable world.

The group thus linked the industrial exploitation of their own communities with the global exploitation of the planet as a whole due to the globalization of capitalism. It then advocated that the institute recommend to local education authorities that they develop a system of education for sustainability focused on ecological literacy, at the primary and secondary school levels. This would involve: a pedagogy that placed the understanding of life at the centre of the education process; an experience of learning in the real world (growing food, harnessing energy and restoring waste land) that overcomes our alienation from nature and reignites a sense of community; and a curriculum that teaches pupils the fundamental facts of life - that matter cycles continually through the mesh of life; that diversity assures resilience; and that life from its start did not take over the planet by conflict but by networking.

The students also suggested that in the future my curriculum should stress the transformative potential of adapting the collective and sympathetic community development process that the current course applied to local communities to consideration of a planetary development strategy. This view generated a great deal of argument and discussion. A few students thought that for this approach to be successful people would have to adopt an almost spiritual mindset towards the planet and its uniqueness, and two students in particular, to reinforce this view, quoted from a book by the cosmologist and cultural historian Thomas Berry who, in 1989, wrote:

*"The universe in its full extension in space and its sequence of transformations in time is best understood as Story; a story in the $20^{th}$ century based for the first time with scientific precision through empirical observation. The difficulty is that scientists have until recently given us the story only in its physical aspect not in the full depth of its realty or in the full richness of its meaning. The greatest single need for the survival of the earth or of the human community in this late $20^{th}$ century is for an integral telling of the Great Story of the Universe. This story must provide in our times what the great mythic stories of earlier times provided as the guiding and energizing sources of the human venture".*

They also quoted approvingly the view expressed by Noel Keough in the following lines, discovered by one of them in a Community Development Journal article written in July 1998:

*Newton and Descartes were wrong*
*we and our world, our universe*
*are not one big machine which piece by piece we take apart*
*to understand the essence of the whole*
*for who, when things are torn apart*
*can point to me, the soul?*

The other students thought that such spiritual attitudes and stories would be extremely difficult to implement given the current rationalist and materialistic mindset of much of western society. They argued that the adoption of a more locality-based, collective, democratic and citizen-orientated development strategy focused on networking (via personal contact and technological contact), local exchange trading schemes, timebanking and other social enterprise initiatives was more likely to be heeded by the populace if it stressed, along with spiritual values, the need for sustainability based on Enlightenment values and scientific evidence. This group recognized that any acceptance of such values would have to rely on political action, and that the great challenge of our time would be to change the value system currently underpinning the global economy, in order to make it compatible with the demands of human dignity and environmental sustainability.

# PART SIX:

# EVALUATING THE PROGRAMME

# Chapter Twelve

## Methodology

At the end of each of the two years of the programme I invited the students to reflect on it and suggest some improvements. I handed out prepared forms on which I invited the students to write their thoughts, comments and suggestions - but not to sign them. During the summer break I studied the replies, and categorized the comments and suggestions under appropriate headings. As the prime objective of each evaluation was to improve the existing programme, I requested class members to limit their comments to points with which they were dissatisfied, and to specific suggestions for dealing with them. I did not make a request for positive comments as I knew I would be informed of the students' views on this topic in face-to-face encounters at coffee breaks and post class refreshment taking at a local pub.

This was an extremely informal assessment system, but I was happy with it because I could not think of a more succinct method of measuring changes in attitude and the creation of new mental strategies on the students' part. I made it clear throughout the course that the core value of the course was respect for people – as it is the core value of community work. I felt the best way to assess if such changes had taken place was by mixing with the students on an informal basis and listening to their views and ideas throughout the course and noting how they had evolved, or not, during this period. Furthermore, I believed that if a formal assessment had taken place, it would have destroyed the trust, enjoyment and equality of relationships that we had built up over the period of course delivery.

This system worked well for the first four years, and the suggestions put forward concerning improvements helped me to modify the programme where and when necessary. However, in the mid 1990s, with the acceleration of accreditation, my informal system was changed. Now my administrative department insisted I had to distribute pre-printed and prepared forms with set questions and tick boxes. The students' did not think much of this "mechanical" process, primarily because it turned an evolving learning process into a "set" job with pre-arranged outcomes and targets which contradicted the whole ethos of the learning they had undertaken. As one student remarked: "how can they assess our increased confidence to think clearly and critically, and so make considered judgments for ourselves?"

In their written comments in the informal system, the students used words such as "applied", "practical", "functional", "effective", "efficient" and "sensible" to describe the course. Such vocabulary surprised me because the course had been held in a variety of meeting rooms, in a series of community centers, and not "in the field". When I asked the students exactly what they meant by "practical" and "functional", they replied that it was the discussion element of the course that made it so. Through the use of focused discussion they could see the relevance of each component of the course to their everyday work - and they also had had sufficient time when attending the course to learn from their own experiences and those of the other students - and to decide more effective ways of carrying out their work. The general view was that having attended the course they knew why what they had been doing everyday at work was correct - or not. As a result, they had become far more confident of their methods, and were now increasingly able to see how to apply these methods in a variety of circumstances.

## Student perspectives

Even using the unpopular, formal system, it became clear that the course had had a positive influence on student attitudes. The most marked influence was on their attitude towards the people they worked with on a daily basis: they quickly realized that all genuine "authority" in community work resided with the people however much their employer organizations had urged them to believe that authority rested with themselves, and that by using directive methods, or carrying out work on behalf of the people rather than helping them implement it themselves, they were continually storing up problems for themselves in the future. The students continued to express their views to me about how their attitudes, perspectives and thoughts had been influenced by the course, utilizing word-of-mouth conversations in our traditional venues and haunts. Typical views included:

*"I thought the course was challenging and stimulating. It was also very useful because it got me thinking about all sorts of issues, gave me a wide spread of knowledge and understanding, and trained me to think highly analytically"*

*"The value of the course was that it gave me powers of critical thought, which I can put to use in any situation. In my book, the essence of being an effective community worker and good citizen is that you have a mind that can move around".*

*"I'm convinced that the need to analyze and assess information and develop lines of argument helped me to develop a maturity in my thinking processes, and also a certain rigor in the way I go about doing things now. I also learned that creativity isn't something that just happens on a whim, it's something that can only really take off if you bring a bit of discipline to the process of tapping into it".*

Other responses focused on the theme of "new ways of seeing the world" and "seeing things - people and events - differently", realizing for the first time that "behind the day to day reality of life there is another, often hidden reality - one that contains power, influence, corruption, greed and also a great deal of good". Other conversations stressed the importance of links and connections: "it's about connecting things I never realized could be connected before", "about linking up my own life with the lives of people far away", and "it's a type of lateral thinking where I can now play with ideas and think eccentric thoughts". For the majority of students, it was about transcending cultural and political values to form links between everyday experiences and new ways of looking at society: a central response theme was the "eye opening" way of looking at one's community and ways of improving it - and how this new perspective had changed, even in some cases undermined, previously held moral certainties.

## New thinking or old thinking?

The great majority of the students revealed in their conversations with me just how much of a paradigm shift the programme had generated in the class. A paradigm, in the words of Capra (1997:6), is "a constellation of concepts, values, perceptions and practices shared by a community, which forms a particular vision of reality," and by this definition the intellectual community that the students inhabited after studying on the programme was "a world away from the one we inhabited before we attended it". "It was not just a world away, but a completely different world" was the opinion of another respondent. Ironically, it was the view of a significant number of respondents that the new mental paradigm was the result of the tutor creating his own learning paradigm, one in which he created the conditions for collective discussion and active participation; conditions that differed from the previous learning paradigm encountered by many of the course students - the individual-orientated, passive, lecture dominated, environment.

Indeed, the strategy I used to stimulate new ways of thinking, by increasing student self-expression and group imagination, was overwhelmingly seen by the students as part of a process of freedom from "the dead hand" of formal academic tradition. As one respondent put it: "amazing - a higher education class where I was allowed, even encouraged, to argue with the tutor and the other students", while another commented: "My previous experience of higher education was with lectures. There I was expected to listen, record and stay awake. There was no verbal contact with the lecturer. I was very pleasantly surprised, because on this course I could express my own views and challenge those of others", and went on to say: "it was so exciting that I started to enjoy it, and think for myself. I began to express my personality and beliefs through class conversation".

Despite acknowledging the high level of teaching received, a minority of students insisted on their innate ability to think critically: when asked how critically aware they had become while studying on the programme, practically all replied either "more aware" or "much more aware". But their strongly held belief was that though they significantly increased their critical judgments facilities, they had all innately possessed the critical facility anyway - the course and the teaching had helped sharpen it and extend its depth, focus and range of operations - as is shown clearly by the following quotes: "same thinking - but developed, sustained and applied to a far greater range of events"; "thinking applied to world-wide events and organizations, not just local and personal ones" and "group discussion and high quality teaching made me see the connection to things on a constant basis. Previously I had glimpsed the links between situations only haphazardly: the course taught me to be "on guard" and maintain criticality all the time" - an opinion that bears out the view of Gramsci (1971) that, "it is not a question of introducing from scratch a scientific form of thought into everyone's individual life, but of renovating and making "critical" an already existing activity".

However, the majority of students thought that the courses had initiated their transformative experiences, and the specific contribution to this transformation that they highlighted again and again was class discussion: "If my ideas or beliefs had never been questioned with other classmates or the tutor, then I would never have changed or thought about changing my views or beliefs", and "participating in class discussions has opened my eyes to different opinions about politics and society, and helped to broaden my mind and help me gain objectivity". Several students specifically commented on how critical reflection is part of the process of perspective transformation: "I started to think more critically and independently, and this process was reinforced by class dialogue that caused me to reconsider my values, beliefs and assumptions".

**Viewing oneself**
From the replies there also came evidence of the close link between the development of critical thinking about community and society and the journey to self-actualization. Many students saw the generation of critical thinking as a creative, liberating process, a form of release from old-fashioned modes of thinking not just about community and society - but also about themselves. Perhaps it is not surprising to note that this process stimulated the following observations from one of the female members of the class after following two modules of the programme:

*"It took me almost my entire life for me to realize that I had learned things that should not have been learned at all because those very things kept me down in life. In the course of my first two and a bit decades, I was led to believe that I was not bright enough and that almost certainly I would not amount to anything of worth. I was just a manual worker: I was no more than a pair of hands. Deliberately or not, I was taught by my own family, school and society generally, that I was going to be a failure in life. Unknowingly, to ensure the validity of such a prophecy, I learned to believe what I had been taught".*

*"As an unknowing victim of such a learning, I became a failure in much of the work that I did or tried to do. Then, one day I started reflecting about these things and the more I reflected, the more some*

*of them did not make sense anymore. I had been taught to be my worst enemy, and only now, nearly thirty years later, has it become clear to me, thanks to the adult education course, that I have to unlearn a great deal of things about myself that have cost me so much time, and so many years of effort, hard graft and unreflecting routine to learn".*

A view repeated by another student in her reply who said:

*"About three years ago I was a shadow of myself, a single parent under the influence of my parents, doctors, environment, government and a society rigid with expectations of how I should live my life. Today, my 35th birthday, after three years of enjoyment, exploration, confidence building and realizing I was somebody on the course, my life has just begun".*

Such increased self-confidence affected the belief systems of many of the students. By joining a learning culture, sharing a new paradigm, belonging to a new community through an active process of "dissenting from the outside", and by being confronted by a choice about which community to belong to, many chose the one offered by the classes, thereby modifying their "worldviews" and their attitudes towards their work and its associated action. The information I collected after the completion of the course from letters, e mails and personal conversations, clearly demonstrated that the great majority of those who attended the classes were committed, even reinforced in their belief, to take action in a variety of ways, and the following quote from a letter by one participant from Blaenllechau in the Rhondda Valley can be seen as representative of the views of a majority of the class:

*"I'm so confident now, that I'm convinced I can act positively in my community by setting an example of self-confidence, self-assurance and on-going endurance. I can use my new powers of persuasion through increased verbal fluency, my knowledge of relevant infor-*

*mation, and a capacity to discover solutions through logical thought and intuitive thinking. I can stimulate development in non-threatening ways and help to resist change for positive reasons. I can also help the community gain power through the expression of traditional values, the utilization of appropriate strategies, and the generation of action based on solid working class beliefs and a healthy dose of critical thinking."*

This personal view exemplified the attitudes of a high percentage of the students who attended the course for, as their verbal and written responses clearly showed, the students chose to define success, and the acquisition of critical thinking, not in terms of increased wealth or social mobility, but rather in terms of increased capacity to render service. In this sense, the students came to embody an almost Jeffersonian ideal for the committed commonality, using their talents and education to become social change agents and practical advocates for the socially excluded and their disadvantaged communities.

### Tutor Teaching Methods

I believed totally in the statement that I made during one of my classes: "It's about the relationship between me and you (the class). Both of us must be willing for things to go wrong...for anything to happen. My job is not to impose how I see the world on you - rather it's to facilitate you to have the confidence to say what you as individuals want to say...to genuinely feel that you have something to contribute". The students overwhelmingly saw this non-hierarchical, collaborative, flexible and sometimes risky, teaching method as vital to their success as students, and to the generation of their critical thinking. One compared my approach with that of a campus-based colleague, with the former "actually having the audacity to talk with you, not at you". Another student stated: "the tutor's attitude encouraged me to open all the doors of my thinking: it really inspired me to believe I could really achieve something and not hold back". In the study, a majority of the students considered that their critical thinking and course success had been positively affected by the collaborative teaching style employed on the course, and the ability of the tutor to get his students to explore ideas and concepts, view the world from different perspectives, connect, combine and synthesize, develop new knowledge and - most importantly - generate new meanings from all these links "without being dogmatic, boring and pompous". As one student summed it up: "I didn't worry about the pressure (to conform) inflicted by the academics. I believed in the course, I lived the theory and I had a great teacher".

The ability of the tutor to generate enjoyment and enthusiasm was another vital ingredient of course success stressed by the responses. "It was a pleasure to go to lectures. I felt valued, my ideas were discussed and all I did was carried out within a circle of enjoyment in a non-threatening environment", according to a second year student. "But the sense of enjoyment that was there was triggered by the tutor - it started with him and spread throughout the class" was another typical comment. The tutor's encouragement of student independence of thought - within a collective and supportive situation - was also much appreciated. The tutor's conscious attempt to get his students to "learn how to learn - to get them to switch from the idea of information being delivered to them to gathering information for themselves - and then making up their minds" was much appreciated, with student responses suggesting that nearly two-thirds of those who contacted me rated the importance of independence of thought as a significant factor in student creativity, critical thinking generation and course success.

The students also highlighted the tutor's willingness to listen to what they said respectfully. "It was great having a lecturer who gave serious consideration to what we said - and to what we didn't say" was one observation. The tutor in their eyes treated their views with the respect he treated the views of the academics and political scientists that he quoted. "My views and ideas were discussed and analyzed as seriously as the ideas and theories of Habermas, Foucault and the rest of those highflyers. As a result I saw the ideas of these pre-eminent academics, not as some Olympian diktats handed down from above, but as the considered, sometimes fallible and challengeable, ideas of ordinary human beings who faced the same daily pressures as we all do".

My ability to see in front of me in class not just students but people with private, family and work-based lives - and to allow these individuals to draw on their experiences from these sources and help them see the link between their worlds and the wider world generally: "We were encouraged to link our personal concerns with issues of public and social concern, just like C Wright Mills had said a good teacher should do" was one heartfelt student observation; while another commented "the tutor's approach got us all to see ourselves in a wider and deeper context, thereby strengthening our characters and stimulating us to see our lives more clearly".

### Tutor-Student Relationships

A high proportion of students indicated clearly how much they valued the empathy between themselves and the tutor. "He was very approachable and helpful. You were never refused a chat or discussion about your work (or even your domestic situation) and how it was progressing" was one reply, while other retrospective views included: "the tutor was enthusiastic about our progress. He was concerned with our academic and personal well being - and you always felt welcome in his class". "His enthusiasm was infectious, and besides using his considerable knowledge to make the lessons interesting, he also used it to make us aware that we too could go as far academically as we wanted if we put our minds to it". "In his class there was a sense of genuinely belonging and of being valued", was another viewpoint expressed by a sizeable number of respondents - a viewpoint which seemed to indicate that high levels of teaching skills depended as much on the tutor-student relationship as it did on the tutor's academic ability and his expertise in delivering that ability to his class.

Indeed, the intellectual ability of the tutor and his command of his subject, although highly regarded by the students, did not score as high (67 per cent) as the state of the physical and intellectual environment within which the tutor expressed his ideas. The sense of security, together with safety from mockery and academic points scoring, were prime factors in the students' favorable assessment of the course. In addition, the tutor's interest in his students' academic and vocational progress, his patience with their queries – however apparently bizarre and tangential to the topic under discussion – plus his general approachability, seemed to count more than his ability to communicate his subject matter. In fact, these attributes appear to bear out the recent research findings of Moore and Knol (2007:139) who explored teaching excellence through the retrospective views of former students, and came to a broadly similar conclusion as myself in that the responses' dominant message "relates excellent teaching more to something that you are rather than to what you do, and more to an interest in and focus on the student than to a command of the subject." Furthermore, having read and analyzed the questionnaires, I was reinforced in my conviction that good teaching is more than technique: it comes essentially from the identity and integrity of the teacher and that, in the words of Parker J Palmer (1998: 2):

*"Teaching, like any truly human activity, emerges from one's inwardness, for better or worse. As I teach, I project the condition of my soul onto my students, my subject, and our way of being together...When I do not know myself, I cannot know who my students are. I will see them through a glass darkly, in the shadows of my unexamined life – and when I cannot see them clearly, I cannot*

*teach them well. When I do not know myself, I cannot know my subject – not at the deepest levels of embodied, personal meaning. I will know it only abstractly, from a distance, a congeries of concepts as far removed from the world as I am from personal truth".*

I would not have used such spiritual  language myself when describing the art of teaching, but I appreciated what Palmer was saying from his religious perspective; and his view, plus the questionnaire findings, reinforced my belief in the personal, collective and more informal attitude that I had adopted towards my work. In addition, they also highlighted that classroom interventions that focus on developing interpersonal skills between tutors and students, generating more learner-focused cultures, and rewarding accessibility generally between staff and students, might provide significant indicators about the importance of learners' relationship with their teachers, and the perceived characteristics with which positive teacher-student interactions are associated.

PART SEVEN:

TUTOR'S OVERVIEW

# Chapter Thirteen

## The programme - the pedagogy

I realized long before the end of the course that the type of teaching I had utilized was not a "set" method but rather an on-going process based on self-learning and continual modification. It was a method that improved with practice and experience, and the heightened criticality and understanding that this method and experience fostered. Most importantly, I realized that it was an approach in which my authority depended on the degree to which I demonstrated the democratic principles of my teaching, adopted a genuine enjoyment and displayed a continuing willingness to question my own knowledge and current understandings - in concert with the self-questionings of each of the students on the course.

The enjoyment and learning that the course generated convinced me that the often unpredictable, collective questioning method that I had adopted was the correct one. I realized that some of my colleagues looked askance at what they saw as its in-built unpredictability, where the core of learning could not always be controlled. I argued that if I adopted their ideas and methods I would be working to undermine my belief that students, class-rooms and learning groups were complex systems: and that by removing what they classified as "undesirable behavior" I would in fact be removing the interactive activities that I was most wanting to promote. To put this another way, learning arises, according to Vygotsky, in a situation where there are multiple possible feed-back loops, where students can reflect upon their own motivation, substitute alternative conditioned responses, and alter their own behavior at will. Systems with non-linear responses and multiple feedback loops are complex and so tend towards behavior that we describe as chaotic.

Of course, I knew how to prevent or reduce any chaotic

behavior: I simply removed or reduced the non-linear responses and multiple feedback loops. The more I could control those characteristics the less likely that the class would contain chaotic behavior. I realized therefore that I could "system out" the chaos by reducing the complexity of the system itself but, at the same time, I saw that by doing this I was squeezing out the learning element - because the mechanisms that generated complex behavior were the same mechanisms that resulted in learning. I accepted therefore that the view of my teaching as "eccentric" was a view I could live with, and be proud of, in an adult focused, community-based context.

As a result of pursuing this type of partially directed Chaotic method, I identified a list of core activities that generated what I referred to as "enabling circumstances" for critical thinking and consciousness raising to succeed. These included:

- putting the students, and not my own performance, at the centre of my teaching activities;
- focusing on what the students, rather than myself, were doing;
- encouraging group action to generate self-directed learning;
- allocating time during classes for students to interact and to discuss the problems they and I had posed;
- evaluating class activities to reveal conceptual change;
- provoking debate;
- using class time to question students' ideas, and developing conversations with them during lectures.

By implementing these activities, I believed I generated a durable and genuine, as opposed to short-term and superficial, approach to learning in my students. This methodology utilized their own experiences to foster strategies for effective action, developed their imaginations by searching for links between local patterns and universal principles, encouraged research and theorizing, made links between individual efforts and current social and historical developments, generated suppositions to stimulate creativity, and nurtured understanding by comparisons with other subjects and divergent opinions.

But this type of teaching was undoubtedly more directive than I had anticipated. I had to use, more often than I originally calculated, the authority granted by my own experience of "reading the world" in order to point the students in the right direction and so engage them in genuine critical thinking. I did this though in a spirit of openness and mutuality that I would have found very difficult to do had I not previously committed myself to adopting an open, informal teaching system based on the student-focused methods of Paulo Freire and Myles Horton, the psychological ideas of Lev Vygotsky, the anthropological views of Clifford Geertz, the philosophical writings of Jurgen Habermas and Antonio Gramsci, and the systems processes of Complexity Theory. So, when I directed and prescribed, I did so from the basis of an alternative educational position, while telling myself that what I was doing could not be equated with the more formal and traditional academic modes of control and classroom management. Indeed, the combination of general informality and occasional prescription, aimed at those students who were genuinely seeking to engage in this type of emancipatory learning, acted as a catalyst to critical thought, thus raising the level of enthusiasm, energy and overall commitment of the whole class.

### The programme - a wider view

I also saw the programme as a constructive alternative to the current absorption of education into the market system - it was my heartfelt riposte to the general standardization and commodification of education, and the resulting reduction of pedagogy to a mechanistic compilation of credits and academic credentials. Rather, alongside Henry Giroux (2004: 8), I saw pedagogy as a critical practice that *"should provide the knowledge, skills and culture of questioning necessary for students to engage in critical dialogue with the past, questioning authority and its effects, struggle with ongoing relations of power, and prepare themselves for what it means to be critically active citizens"*, and I deliberately intended my courses to reinforce this practice.

Taking a wider view of the potential influence of the course, I also saw it as making a positive contribution to a political manifesto for the twenty-first century. I saw the course as providing a small element in the wider struggle against the emergence of a Darwinian world (highlighted by Pierre Bourdieu in 1998) which was destroying collective structures capable of counteracting the widespread imposition of commercial values imposed by the free market; creating a global army of the unemployed; and subordinating nation states to the real masters of the economy. I remembered, too, what T S Eliot had written in 1944 about the rise of a new type of provincialism:

*"it is a provincialism not of space, but of time: one for which history is merely the chronicle of human devices which have served their turn and been scrapped, one for which the world is the property solely of the living, a property in which the dead hold no shares. The menace of this kind of provincialism is that we can all, all the people on the globe, be provincials together; and those who are not content to be provincials, can only become hermits"* (Quoted in The Guardian, 9 June 2007).

My teaching was designed to counter the current trend towards universal provincialism - my students, I hoped, would remember the lessons of history, especially in regards to their communities and their historic, collective struggles for justice and, far from becoming hermits wailing and wandering in the wilderness, would become active citizens who would agitate for a better expression of community than the emasculated welfare state, act to limit the population's increasing dependency on the self-interest of the market, dispute the platitudes of free-market politicians, and combat the growing profit-orientated power of global corporations.

The role of the programme in a socially and economically disadvantaged environment was to further community knowledge, learning and change through collective learning relationships, thereby reinforcing rather than undermining people's identification with their local community and its culture. Such a role was part of my recognition that though the programme could rarely solve important social problems, it could promote learning about how these problems might be solved through collective action. It was also my recognition that new forms of scholarship, to reflect what Schon (1995) has labelled "knowing-in-action", were required to complement the more traditional ways of academic knowing. The most common ways of knowing in the higher education sector - those based on the assumptions that theory-based knowledge is a purer form of truth than practice-based knowledge, and that practice is an extension of theory - appeared inadequate to understanding so many of the social problems and issues of south Wales communities. I therefore considered the local sector's s adjacent communities as sources of energy and accepted that these sources contained what Bender (1996) has called "wonderfully complex intellectual problems, and non-academic intellectuals who have much to offer". Furthermore, I accepted that the traditional academic model had to be adapted, and be complemented by an educational approach that facilitated two-way conversations between myself and the many intellectually hungry groupings within communities in south east Wales.

The success of the programme rested to a large degree on the foundation of group solidarity that had emerged from the creation of a range of community-based initiatives to counter social and economic deprivation during the previous decades. Students attended my courses already familiar with local conditions and problems – and each other. They shared a common bond and identity, and by pooling their knowledge and experience they enhanced their commitment to, and identification with, a local way of life – and the struggle for its improvement. I therefore delivered, with the students' help, an on-going educational partnership that forged links between the classroom and the community, that grew out of peoples' direct relationship to their community, their desire to work together towards its survival, and my intention to create a curriculum to support an explosion of new adult learning needs and desires that could not be met in conventional academic ways.

# Postscript

The programme attracted over eight hundred enrolments during its existence, and proved to be very popular and successful. However, my involvement with it came to an end earlier than I anticipated. The reasons for my departure were varied, but I list below some of those that I believe were most pertinent and which hold lessons for higher education institutions which operate adult focused programmes in deprived community environments in the present political and economic climate.

When I started the programme the prevailing teaching scenario was a traditional one - a lecturer speaking or reading to a class of young students who adopted an approach based around the mantra, "I talk, you listen and you learn". The lecturer was seen as an expert who was qualified to deliver knowledge (even truth) to neophytes who were qualified only to passively receive this knowledge and truth. In this scenario, according to Parker Palmer (1998: 101), *"truth is a set of propositions about objects; education is a system for delivering those propositions to students; and an educated person is one who can remember and repeat the experts' propositions. The image is hierarchical, linear, and compulsive-hygienic, as if truth came down an antiseptic conveyer belt to be deposited as pure product at the end"*.

A high proportion of my students though were part-time attendees, working in local voluntary and statutory organizations, with an average age of 27 , who found this type of teaching inherently condescending and frustrating. They were far more open to a collective, interactive, expressive and "messy" form of teaching. But group-focused teaching of this type still struggled to be accepted within the institution as a genuine learning activity, - - and progress in this field is still alarmingly slow, with the emphasis on departmental publication profiles remaining dominant, and likely to continue so in the foreseeable future.

The institutional structures within which the delivery of community-based courses was set were also often incoherent. For example, the department in which my programme was embedded was not an academic department, so it delivered courses compiled and provided by neighboring academic departments. Because of this, the quality of the services provided to my students was not the delivery department's main concern - this responsibility, in its eyes, lay with the academic departments within which the delivered courses and modules were set. Unfortunately, there appeared to be little co-operation or co-ordination between the course delivery section and the departments that provided their programmes for dissemination. Furthermore, the delivery section utilized funding from the Welsh Assembly Government to extend student participation, and was often therefore driven by the need to attract student numbers to generate future funding rather than by delivering an on-going commitment to student support systems.

An additional hindrance to coherent course delivery in community development, and adult education generally, was the learning culture within the institution. A culture that recognized informal, non-formal and formal community-based learning was not allocated a high priority. As a result, the relevance of the curriculum to meet real life community problems, and the support systems that are required to maintain adult student commitment, were conspicuously lacking, as was any political will at organizational level to push through the appropriate support structures for part time, community-focused learners. Full-time students remained very much the focus of attention and, because of this, in-depth, internal questioning of what student development and support should be provided for part-time, older learners was noticeably absent. However, this climate may be shifting as concerns with quality provision for part-time adult students are currently being raised by the students themselves, and this situation may force departments to start to posing questions about what exactly quality support for adult learners is all about.

There are also examples of organizational policies being contradicted by regulations or daily practices in the institution. Indeed, within academia generally there are many practices and procedures that seem designed, and are often interpreted, to conserve the institution and its traditional culture - and frustrate non traditional approaches to educational delivery. In order to make headway against the prevailing status quo, by transforming internal systems and attitudes, the institution's executive leaders need to be fully committed to change. A co-ordinating agency, working across the institution, with its leadership and faculties, also needs to be introduced if progress is to be made. Finally, there needs to be the political will to drive changes at both the institutional and the organizational level. At this level, some progress has been made within micro-organizational practices to align them with the institution's community-focused mission, but the institution can only respond to pressures that it can effectively measure – therefore it must have in place methods for detecting important information.

It is here that the ideas of Argyris and Schon (1996) again have particular relevance, for in the process of creating community relationships, the institution and the community have become closely connected. But loops of learning specifically refer to the collection and use of information emerging from that connection. In the case of a single learning loop, which the institution is operating at present, the gathered information is used to make adjustments to keep the organisation functioning: there are no changes in organisational values or the theory-in-use. Double-loop learning involves an additional step in this process, and occurs when an issue is given a "double look" and adjustments are not just made automatically. This double loop allows for the questioning of whether operating norms are still relevant and effective. Argyris and Schon (1996) point out that double-loop learning requires that organisations be willing to question their own assumptions and behaviours. If they are unwilling to honestly assess their theories-in-use by adopting the double-loop learning system, they will be largely blind to understanding how a fundamental shift in organisational behaviour and structures might be necessary - and so continue to operate in one-dimensional and uncoordinated ways.

# Acknowledgements

The actual writing of this book had taken three years, but its gestation period has been much longer. Since I started teaching adult students in the 1970s a great many friends, colleagues and students have contributed to the ideas that have formed my view of education and the world within which it is being delivered. Prime place in any acknowledgement list must go though, to my wife Ruth who first got me interested in community work and whose knowledge of the subject is far superior to mine, and whose support and encouragement was vital in the creation and continuation of my writing.

Mention must be made of Hywel Griffiths who, when Director of the Wales Council for Voluntary Action, sparked my interest in community development, while special thanks are due to my work colleague Michael Nightingale who provided me with evidence of voluntary sector training schemes, their successes and failures, strengths and weaknesses, whilst we worked together in Brynmawr. Grateful mention must also be made of colleagues who supported my work in the community, especially those based at the local councils of voluntary service (particularly Katherine Rowles) and at the further and higher education institutions in south Wales where I taught. My gratitude must also go to Professor David Turner whose ideas on education made me think seriously about setting in print my experiences of teaching in the community. Without the enthusiasm and ability of these individuals to persuade community workers and volunteers that my classes were worth attending, then the belief in the effectiveness of community work training would still remain the preserve of a very small number of people.

Finally, but by no means last, I must thank all the students who attended my classes. In community centres and village halls, in the depths of freezing Welsh winters and humid summers, from

Glynneath in the west to Brynmawr and Abergavenny in the east, from Barry and Newport in the south to Maerdy and Merthyr Tydfil in the north, the ideas, thoughts, enthusiasm and straight talking of all who attended taught me a great deal about community work, the condition of communities during a time of economic stress, and about the collective responses, often heroic, of ordinary individuals to an increasingly market-orientated, individual-focused society.

# References

Adams, F. (1975). *Unearthing Seeds of Fire: the Idea of Highlander.* Winston-Salem. North Carolina: John F Blair Publishers.

Alinsky, S. D. (1989). *Rules for Radicals: A Programmatic Primer for Realistic Radicals.* Revised edition. New York: Vantage Books.

Allman, P. (1987). "Paulo Freire's Education Approach: A Struggle for Meaning". In G. Allen, J. Bastiani. I. Martin, and J.K. Richards (eds.), *Community Education,* Milton Keynes, England: Open University Press.

Allman, P. (2001). *Critical Education against Global Capitalism: Karl Marx and Critical Revolutionary Education.* London: Bergin and Garvey.

Alperovitz, G. (2004). *America Beyond Capitalism: Reclaiming our Wealth, our Liberty and our Democracy.* Hoboken, NJ: Wiley.

Andrews, D. (2007). *Living Community.* Australia: Tafina Press and Community Praxis Coop.

Argyris, C. (1982*). Reasoning, learning and action: Individual and organizational.* San Francisco: Jossey-Bass.

Argyris, C. (1991). "Teaching Smart People How to Learn". *Reflections.* 4(2), 4-15.

Argyris, C. and Schoen, D. (1974). *Theory in Practice: Increasing Professional Effectiveness.* San Francisco: Jossey-Bass.

Argyris, C. and Schon, D. (1996). *Organizational Learning II: Theory, Method and Practice.* Reading, Mass: Addison-Wesley.

Asimov, I. (1973). *Second Foundation.* Panther Science Fiction.

Atkins, S. and Murphy, K. (1993). "Reflection: a review of the literature". *Journal Adv. Nursing.* 18. pp. 1188-1192.

Badiou, A. (1998). *Ethics: An Essay on the Understanding of Evil.* London: Verso.

Baptiste, I. (2000). "Beyond Reason and Personal Integrity: Toward a Pedagogy of Coercive Restraint". *Canadian Journal for the Study of Adult Education.* 14 (1). 27-50.

Barber, B. R. (2007). *Consumed: How Markets Corrupt Children, Infantilize Adults, and Swallow Citizens Whole.* New York: W W Norton.

Batten, T. R. (1957, fifth edition 1965). *Communities and Their Development: An Introductory Study with Special Reference to the Tropics,* Oxford University Press.

Bauman, Z. (1999*). In Search of Politics.* Stanford: Stanford University Press.

Bauman, Z. and Tester, K. (2001). *Conversations with Zygmunt Bauman.* (Malden, Mass: Polity Press).

Belenky, M. Clinchy, B. Goldberger, N and Tarule, J. (1986). *Women's Ways of Knowing: The development of self, voice and mind.* New York: Basic Books.

Benney, M. (1946). *Charity Main: A Coalfield Chronicle.* London: George Allen and Unwin.

Berlin, I. (1969). *Four Essays on Liberty.* London: Oxford University Press.

Berman, P. (1997, May 11). Havel's Burden: "The Philosopher King is Mortal." *The New York Times,* sec. 6, pp. 32-37.

Bernstein, R. J. (1991). *The New Constellation: The Ethical-Political Horizons of Modernity/Postmodernity.* Cambridge: Polity Press.

Berry, T. (1989). "The Twelve Principles for Understanding the Universe and the Role of the Human in the Universe". *Teihard Perspective* 22, no. 1

Biggs, J. (1999). *Teaching for Quality Learning at University.* Buckingham: Open University Press.

Bligh, D. (2000). *What's the Point in Discussion?* Exeter: Intellect Books.

Bloom, B. S., ed. (1953). "Thought processes in lectures and discussions". *Journal of General Education,* vol. 7, pp. 160-169.

Boehm, C. (1999). *Hierarchy in the Forest: the evolution of egalitarian behavior.* Cambridge, MA: Harvard University Press.

Bolton, E. (1986). *Leadership Development.* Florida: Institute of Food and Agricultural Sciences, University of Florida.

Bourdieu, P. (1998). "The Essence of Neoliberalism". *Le Monde Diplomatique*.

Bourdieu, P, (2000). "For a Scholarship with Commitment". *Profession*.

Braudel, F. (1982*). Civilization and Capitalism, 15^{th}-18^{th} century. Vol.II: The Wheels of Commerce*, London: Collins.

Brenner, R. (1998). "The economics of global turbulence". *New Left Review*, 229, 1-265.

Brookfield, S. D. (1983). *Adult Learners, Adult Education and the Community*. Milton Keynes: Open University Press.

Brookfield, S. D. (2005). *The Power of Critical Theory for Adult Learning and Teaching*. Maidenhead: Open University Press.

Bruffee, K. A. (1999). *Collaborative Learning: Higher Education, Interdependence, and the Authority of Knowledge*. 2^{nd}. Edition. Baltimore: the Johns Hopkins University Press.

Bruner, J. S. (1996). *The Culture of Education*. London: Harvard University Press.

Bryson, J. M. (1988). *Strategic Planning for Public and Non-Profit Organizations*. San Francisco: Jossey-Bass.

Buber, M. (1947). *Between Man and Man*. London: Routledge and Kegan Paul.

Camus, A. (1991). *Notebooks, 1935-1942*. New York: Marlowe.

Capra, F. (2002). *The Hidden Connections. A Science for Sustainable Living*. London: HarperCollins.

Checkoway, B. (1995), "Six strategies of community change". *Community Development Journal*, vol 30. no 1. Oxford: Oxford University Press.

Christakopoulou, S., Dawson, J. and Gari, A. (2001). "The community well-being questionnaire: theoretical context and initial assessment of its reliability and validity". *Social Indicators Research*, 56: 321-51.

Connor, D. M. (1964). *Understanding Your Community*. Ottawa: Development Press.

Connor. D. M. (1966). *Diagnosing Community Problems*. Ottawa:

Development Press.

Conti, G. J. (1977). "Rebels with a Cause: Myles Horton and Paulo Freire". *Community College Review* 5: 36-43.

Darder, A. Baltodano, M and Torres, D (eds.). (2009). *The Critical Pedagogy Reader*. 2<sup>nd</sup> edition. New York: Routledge.

Dearing Report, *UK National Committee of Inquiry into Higher Education: Higher Education in the Learning Society*: Summary Report (London, HMSO 1997).

Dewey, J. (1927). *The Public and its Problems*. London: Allen and Unwin.

Derrida, J. (2001). "The Future of the Profession or the Unconditional University" in *Derrida Downunder*, Laurence Simmons and Heather Worth, eds. Auckland, NZ: Dunmore Press

Driscoll, M. P. (1994). *Psychology of Learning for Instruction*. Needham, Ma: Allyn & Bacon.

Erdal, D and A. Whiten (1996). "Egalitarian and Machiavellian intelligence in human evoltution", in P. Mellars and K. Gibson (eds), *Modeling the Early Human Mind*. Cambridge: McDonald Institute Monographs.

Fink, L. D. (2003). *Creating Significant Learning Experiences: an integrated approach to designing college courses*. San Francisco: Jossey-Bass.

Fisher, M. (2009). *Capitalist Realism. Is There No Alternative?* Winchester: Zero Books.

Fisher, R. and Ury, W. (1983). *Getting to Yes*. London: Hutchinson.

Flynn, T. R. (2006). *Existentialism: A Very Short Introduction*. Oxford: Oxford University Press.

Flyvbjerg, B. (1998). *Rationality and Power: democracy in practice*. Chicago: University of Chicago Press.

Foley, G. (1999). *Learning in Social Action: a Contribution to Understanding Informal Education*. Leicester: National Organization for Adult Learning.

Foley, M. (2010). *The Age of Absurdity. Why Modern Life makes it*

*Hard to be Happy*. London: Simon and Shuster.

Foucault, M. (1979). *Discipline and Punish: the Birth of the Prison*. Harmondsworth: Penguin.

Foucault, M. (1980). *Power/Knowledge: Selected Interviews and Other Writings, 1972-1977*. London: Harvester Wheatsheaf.

Freire, A and D. Macedo (Eds.), (2001). *The Paulo Freire Reader*. London: Continuum Books.

Freire, P. (1972a). *Cultural Action for Freedom*. Harmondsworth: Penguin.

Freire. P. (1972b). *The Pedagogy of the Oppressed*. Harmondsworth: Penguin.

Freire, P. (1987). *Pedagogy in Process: The Letters to Guinea-Bissau*. Continuum Publishing Group.

Fromm, E. (1941). *Escape from Freedom*. New York: Holt, Rinehart and Winston.

Gadamer, H-G. (1979). *Truth and Method*. (2nd edn). London: Sheed and Ward.

Galloti, K. (1995). "Reasoning about reasoning: a course project". *Teaching of Psychology*, vol.22, pp. 66-68.

Gandin, L. A and Apple, M. W. (2003). "Educating the state, democratizing knowledge: The Citizen School Project in Porto Alegre, Brasil". In M. W. Apple, *The state and the politics of knowledge* (pp. 193-219), New York: Routledge.

Gare, A. (1995). *Postmodernism and the Environmental Crisis*. London: Routledge.

Gargiulo, T. L. (2007). "Storytelling: Its Role in Experiential Learning" in *The Handbook of Experiential Learning* edited by Mel Silberman. San Francisco: John Wiley and Sons.

Gaventa, J. (1980). *Power and Powerlessness: Quiescence and Rebellion in an Appalachian Valley*. Oxford: the Clarendon Press.

Gee, J. P. (1989). "Literacy, discourse and linguistics: Introduction". *Journal of Education*, 171, 5-17.

Geerlings, T. (1994). "Students' thoughts during problem-based small-group discussions." *Instructional Science*, vol.22 (4). Pp.

267-278.

Geertz, C. (1973). "Thick description: toward an interpretative theory of culture". In Geertz, *The Interpretation of Cultures: Selected Essays*. London: Fontana.

Geertz, C. (1975). *Interpretation of Cultures*. London: Hutchinson.

Geertz, C. (1983). *Local Knowledge: Further Essays in Interpretative Anthropology*. New York: Basic Books.

Geertz, C. (1999). *A Life of Learning*. Charles Homer Hawkins Lecture. Occasional Paper no. 45. American Council of Learned Societies.

Gilbert, M. (2006). *A Theory of Political Obligation: Membership, Commitment and the Bonds of Society*, Oxford: Oxford University Press.

Giroux, H. (1988). *Schooling and the Struggle for Public Life*. Minneapolis: University of Minnesota Press.

Giroux, H and Giroux, S. S. (2004). *Take Back Higher Education*. New York: Palgrave Macmillan.

Gladwell, M. (2006). *Blink: The Power of Thinking Without Thinking*. London: Penguin.

Gleick, J. (1998). *Chaos: Making a New Science*. New York: Penguin.

Glen, J. M. (1988). *Highlander, No Ordinary School*. Lexington: University of Kentucky Press.

Godfrey, W. (1985). Down To Earth: Stories of Church Based Community Work. London: British Council of Churches.

Gramsci, A. (1971). *Selections from the Prison Notebooks* (Q. Hoare and G. N. Smith, eds.), London: Lawrence and Wishart.

Greeson, L. E. (1988). "College classroom interaction as a function of teacher and student-centered instruction". *Teacher and Teaching Education*, vol. 4(4), pp. 305-15.

Gutting, G. "Michel Foucault", *The Stanford Encyclopedia of Philosophy* (Summer 2010 Edition), Edward N. Zalta (ed.), URL

Habermas, J. (1984). *The Theory of Communicative Action*, vol. 1. Cambridge, England: Polity Press.

Habermas, J. (1975). *Legitimation Crisis*. Boston: Beacon Press.

Habermas, J. (1987). *The Theory of Communicative Action*, vol. 2. Cambridge, England: Polity Press.

Habermas, J. (1988). *On the Logic of the Social Sciences*. Cambridge: Polity Press.

Habermas, J. (1992a). *Autonomy and Solidarity: Interviews with Jurgen Habermas*, (rev.ed.) London: Verso.

Habermas, J. (1996). *Between Facts and Norms: Contributions to a Discourse Theory of Democracy*. Cambridge, MA: MIT Press.

Habermas, J. (2003). Truth and Justification. B.Fultner (trans), Cambridge, MA: MIT Press.

Habermas, J. (2005). "Religion in the public sphere". *European Journal of Philosophy*. 14: 1-25.

Hall, S. (1996). "The meaning of new times", in D. Morley and K.-H. Chan (eds), Critical dialogues in cultural studies, Routledge.

Harvey, D. (2005). *A Brief History of Neoliberalism*. Oxford: Oxford University Press.

Hausfather, S. J. (1996). "Vygotsky and Schooling: Creating a Social Context for Learning". *Action in Teacher Education*. (18) 1-10.

Heidegger, M. (1985). *Being and Time*. Oxford: Basil Blackwell.

Hey, A. and Walters, P. (2003). *The New Quantum Universe*. Cambridge: Cambridge University Press.

Hitchens, C. (1998). "Goodbye to All That: Why Americans Are Not Taught History". *Harper's Magazine*. Nov. pp. 37-47.

Hodes, A. (1972). *Encounter with Martin Buber*. London: Allen Lane/Penguin.

Hoggart, R. (1958). *The Uses of Literacy*. Harmondsworth: Penguin Books.

Hopkins, R. (1989). "Industrial Wales and the Enterprise Culture: the Community Development Aspect". *Community Development Journal*. Oxford: Oxford University Press.

Hopkins, R. (1992). *A Survey of Voluntary Activity in Cardiff*. London: Community Development Foundation.

Hopkins, R. (1995). "Community Economic Development: A Question of Scale". *Community Development Journal*. Oxford:

Oxford University Press.

Horton, M. (1990). *The Long Haul: An Autobiography*. New York: Doubleday.

Horton, M. and Freire, P. (1990). *We Make the Road by Walking: Conversations on Education and Social Change*. Philadelphia: Temple University Press.

Horton, M. (2003). *The Myles Horton Reader: Education for Social Change*. Knoxville, TN: University of Tennessee Press.

Husserl, E. (1995 Originally published 1950). *Cartesian Meditations: An introduction to Phenomenology*. The Hague: Kluwer Academic Publishers.

Illich, I. (1975a). *Tools for Conviviality*. London: Fontana.

Jacobs, J. (1992). *Systems of Survival: A Dialogue on the Moral Foundations of Commerce and Politics*. London: Hodder and Stoughton.

Jackson, K. (1970). "Adult Education and Community Development." *Studies in Adult Education*.

Jarvis, P. (1983). *Adult and Continuing Education: Theory and Practice*. London: Croom Helm.

Johnson, B, ed. (1982). *The Pedagogical Imperative: Teaching as a Literary Genre*. Yale French Studies 63.

Kanter, R. M. (1987). *The Change Masters*. New York: Simon and Shuster.

Keep, E and Rainbird, H. (2000). "Towards the Learning Organization?" In Bach, S and Sisson, K (eds), *Personnel Management in Britain*, 3rd edn, Oxford: Blackwell.

Keough, N. (1998). "Participatory development practice: Reflections of a western development worker". *Community Development Journal*, vol. 33. No.3. Oxford: oxford University Press.

Kellner, D. (1984). *Herbert Marcuse and the Crisis of Marxism*. London: Macmillan.

Kellner, D. (1989). *Critical Theory, Marxism and Modernity*. Baltimore: Johns Hopkins University Press.

Kelly, A. (2008). *People Centered Development: Development* Method. Centre for Social Response: Australia.

Klein, N. (2007). *The Shock Doctrine: the Rise of Disaster Capitalism*. London: Penguin Books.

Kizlik, R. (2001). "Teaching and Values". *Adprima*, www. adprima.com/values.htm Last update: January 6, 2008.

Kofman, F. and Senge, P. M. (1993). "Communities of Commitment: the heart of learning organizations". *Organizational Dynamics*. 22(2), 5-23.

Kolb, D.A. (1984). *Experiential Learning: experience as the source of learning and development*. New Jersey: Prentice-Hall.

Kuhn, T. (1962). *The Structure of Scientific Revolutions*. Chicago: University of Chicago Press.

Lederach, J. P. (2005). *The Moral Imagination: the Art and Soul of Building Peace*. Oxford: Oxford University Press.

Ledwith, M. (2001). "Community work as critical pedagogy: re-envisioning Freire and Gramsci". *Community Development Journal*, Oxford: Oxford University Press.

Lindeman, E. (1951). *The Meaning of Adult Education*. Norman: Oklahoma Research Centre for Continuing Professional and Higher Education. First published in 1926.

Linge, D. E. (1976). Editor's Introduction to H-G Gadamer. *Philosophical Hermeneutics* (trans. and ed. D. E. Linge). Berkeley: University of California Press.

Lipman, M. (1991). *Thinking in Education*. First Edition. Cambridge: Cambridge University Press.

Lukes, S. (1974). Power: A Radical View. London: Macmillan

MacDonald, J. D. (1970). *The Long Lavender Look*. Ballantine Books.

Marcuse, H. (1964). *One Dimensional Man: Studies in the Ideology of Advanced Industrial Society*. Boston: Beacon Press.

Marcuse, H. (1969). *An Essay on Liberation*. Boston: Beacon Press.

Marcuse, H. (1978a). *The Aesthetic Dimension: Toward a Critique of Marxist Aesthetics*. Boston: Beacon Press.

Makaryk, I. (ed.) (1993). *Encyclopaedia of Contemporary Literary*

*Theory*. Toronto: University of Toronto Press.

Massey, M. (1970). *The Massey Triad: 3 VHS Training Videos*. Gahanna, Ohio: TrainingABC.

Mayer, B. (1987). "The Dynamics of Power in Mediation and Negotiation". *Mediation Quarterly*, 16, 75-85.

McDaniel, M. A. (1986) "Encoding difficulty and memory: toward a unifying theory". *Journal of Memory and Language*, vol.25 (6), pp.645-656.

John McIlroy and Sallie Westwood (eds.). (1993*). Border Country: Raymond Williams in Adult Education*. Leicester: National Institute of Adult Continuing Education.

Mezirow, J. (1981). "A critical theory of adult learning and education". *Adult Education*, 32 (1).

Mezirow, J. (1991). *Transformative Dimensions of Adult Learning*. San Francisco, USA: Jossey-Bass.

Mills, C. Wright. (1959). *The Sociological Imagination*. New York: Oxford University Press.

Middlebrook, A. (2008). "Nurturing Critical Reflections and Perspectives through the Kiva". *Journal of Leadership Education*. Vol 7, Issue 1.

Morris, G. & Beckett, D. (2004). "Performing identities: the new focus on embodied adult learning", in Kell, P., Singh, M. & Shore, S. (eds.), *Adult education in the 21$^{st}$ century*, New York: Peter Lang: 121-134.

Morris, S. And Knol, N. (2007). "Retrospective insights on teaching: exploring teaching excellence through the eyes of the alumni". *Journal of Further and Higher Education*. Vol 31. No.2. May.

Nelson, J. (1992). *The Perfect Machine*. New York: New Society Publications.

Newman, M. (1994). *Defining the Enemy: Adult Education in Social Action*. Sydney: Stewart Victor.

Newman, M. (2006). *Teaching Defiance: Stories and Strategies for Activist Educators. San Francisco*: Jossey-Bass.

Noddings, N. (2003). *Happiness and Education*. New York: Cambridge University Press.

Noddings, N and Shore, P. (1984). *Awakening the Inner Eye: Intuition in Education*. New York: Teachers College Press.

Nonaka, I and Takeushi, H. (1995). *The Knowledge-Creating Company*. New York: Oxford University Press.

Oakeshott, R. (2000*). Jobs and Fairness: the logic and experience of employee ownership*. Norwich: Michael Russell.

Obama, B. (2007*). The Audacity of Hope: thoughts on reclaiming the American dream*. Edinburgh: Canongate Books.

Oldenburg, R. (1999). *The Great Good Place: Cafes, Coffee Shops, Community Centers, Beauty Parlous, General Stores, Hangouts and How They Get You Through the Day*. 3rd edition. New York: Marlowe and Co.

Orlik, T. (1986). *Psyching for sport: mental training for athletes*. Champaign, IL: Human Kinetics.

Orwell, G. (1949). *1984*. London: Secker and Warburg.

*"The Rights of Man"* in *The Thomas Paine Reader* (1987). London.

Packard, V. (1962). *The Hidden Persuaders*. Harmondsworth: Penguin Books.

Packard, V. (1963). *The Status Seekers*. Harmondsworth: Penguin Books.

Packard, V. (1967). *The Waste Makers*. Harmondsworth: Penguin Books).

Palmer, Parker, J. (1993). "Change: Community, Conflict and Ways of Knowing – ways to deepen our educational agenda". *Change Magazine*, no 6, pp. 8-13. Washington DC: Heldref Publications.

Palmer, Parker, J. (1993). *To Know as We are Known. Education as a spiritual journey*. San Francisco: Harper San Francisco.

Palmer, Parker, J. (1998). *The Courage to Teach. Exploring the inner landscape of a teacher's life*. San Francisco: Jossey-Bass.

Parks, R. (1992). *Rosa Parks: My Story*. New York: Dial Books.

Paulin, Chrita. (2007). The Importance of Critical Thinking. EzineArticles (April,16), http://ezinearticles.com/?The-

Importance-of-Critical-Thinking&id=529412 (accessed January 16 2008)

Pirsig, R. M. (1974). *Zen and the Art of Motorcycle Maintenance.* William Morrison & Company.

Polanyi, M. (1967). *The Tacit Dimension.* New York: Anchor Books.

Pope, R. (2005). *Creativity: Theory, History, Practice.* London: Routledge.

Prigogine, I. and Stengers, I. (1984). *Order Out of Chaos.* New York: Bantam Books.

Putnam, R. D. (2000). *Bowling Alone: the collapse and revival of American community.* New York: Simon and Schuster.

Revans, R. W. (1998). *ABC of action learning.* London: Lemos and Crane.

Richardson, R. (1991). *Daring to Teach.* Trentham Books.

Rogers, E. M. (1962). *Diffusion of Innovations.* Glencoe: Free Press.

Rohs, F. R. (1984). "Group Methods and Techniques". Cooperative Extension Service, Athens: University of Georgia.

Rorty, R. (1989). *Contingency, Irony and Solidarity.* Cambridge: Cambridge University Press.

Rose, J. (2001). *The Intellectual Life of the British Working Class.* Yale: Yale University Press.

Rothman, J. (1974). *Planning and Organizing for Social Change: Action Principles for Social Science Research.* New York: Columbia University Press.

Rothman, J. (1976). *Promoting Innovation and Change in Organizations and Communities: A Planning Manual.* New York: J. Wiley and Sons.

Royle, N. (2003). *The Uncanny.* Manchester: Manchester University Press.

Ryan, J. and Sackrey, C (1995). *Strangers in Paradise: Academics from the Working Class.* University Press of America.

Saeger, C. and Remer, B. (2001). *GURU: Reflective practice for experiential learning.* Presented at a conference of the North American Simulation and Gaming Association, Bloomington, Indiana.

Sahlins, M. (2003). *Stone Age Economics*. London: Routledge.

Said, E. W. (1985). *Orientalism*. Harmondsworth: Penguin.

Said, E. W. (2001). *Reflections on Exile and Other Essays*. Cambridge, Mass: Harvard University Press).

Saul, J. R. (1995) *The Unconscious Civilization*. Anansi/Penguin

Scott, I. (1985). *The Periphery is the Centre: a study of community development practice in the West of Ireland 1983/84*. Langholm: The Arkleton Trust.

Scott, J. C. (1990). *Domination and the Arts of Resistance*. Yale: Yale University Press.

Schoenfeld, A. H. (1989). "Ideas in the air: speculations on small group learning, environmental and cultural influences on cognition and epistemology". *International Journal of Education Research*.

Schon, D. A. (1973). *Beyond the Stable State: Public and private learning in a changing society*. Harmondsworth: Penguin.

Schon, D. A. (1983). *The Reflective Practitioner. How professionals think in action*. London: Temple Smith.

Schon, D. A. (1987). *Educating the Reflective Practitioner*. San Francisco: Jossey-Bass.

Searle, J. (1990). *Collective Intentions and Actions*, Cambridge: Cambridge University Press.

Senge, P. (1994). *The Fifth Discipline Fieldbook*. New York: Doubleday.

Shor, I. (1992). *Empowering Education: Critical Teaching for Social Change*. Chicago: University of Chicago Press.

Simmons, A. (2002). *The Story Factor: Inspiration, Influence and Persuasion through the Art of Storytelling* . Cambridge MA: Basic Books.

Smail, D. (1998). *Taking Care: An Alternative to Therapy*. London: Constable.

Smith, G. (1969). *Letters of Aldous Huxley*. London: Chatto and Windus.

Stacey, R. D. (2000). *Strategic Management and Organizational*

*Dynamics: The Challenge of Complexity*. London: Routledge.

Stefanovic, I. L. (2000). *Safeguarding Our Future: Rethinking Sustainable Development*. State University of New York Press.

Steiner, G. (1978). *Heidegger*. London: Fontana Books

Sternberg, R. J. (1989). *The Triarchic Mind: A new theory of human intelligence*. New York: Penguin.

Strathern, M. (1997). '"Improving ratings": audit in the British university system". *European Review*, vol 5, No. 3.

Sutton, R. I. (2002). *Weird Ideas: 111/2 practices for promoting, managing and sustaining innovation*. New York: The Free Press.

Tawney, R. H. Quoted in M. Mayo and J. Thompson (eds.). *Adult Learning, Critical Intelligence and Social Change*. Leicester: NIACE. (1995).

Tennesse Valley Authority, (1990). *Leadership Development in the South*. Knoxville: TVA.

Thomas, G. (1997). "What's the Use of Theory?" *Harvard Educational Review*, vol.67, no.1, pp. 75-105.

Thomas, G. (2002). "Theory's Spell - On Qualitative Inquiry and Educational Research", *British Educational Research Journal*, Vol.28, No.3, pp.419-434.

Tsoukas, H. (1998). "Introduction: Chaos, Complexity and Organization Theory". *Organization*, vol.5, no.3, pp 291-313.

Tuckman. B. W. (1965). "Developmental sequence in small groups". *Psychological Bulletin*, 63, pp 384-399.

Turner, D. A. (2004). *Theory of Education*. London: Continuum.

Uslaner, E. M. (2002). *The Moral Foundations of Trust*. Cambridge: Cambridge University Press.

Vandenberg, L. and Sandmann, L. R. (1995). "Community Action Leadership Development: A Conceptual Framework". *Challenging Boundaries in Leadership Education*. Colorado Springs: Association of Leadership Educators.

Vygotsky, L. (1962). *Thought and Language*. Cambridge: MIT Press.

Vygotsky, L. (1978). *Mind and Society: the development of higher mental processes*. Cambridge, MA: Harvard University Press.

Wainwright, H. (2003). *Reclaim the State: Experiments in Popular Democracy*. London: Verso.

Weber, M. (1967). "Science as a Vocation". *Max Weber: Essays in Sociology*. London: Routledge and Kegan Paul.

Weber, M. (1968). *On Charisma and Institution Building*. Chicago: University of Chicago Press.

Welton, M. R. (1993). "Social revolutionary learning: the new social movements as learning sites". *Adult Education Quarterly*, 43, 3: 152-64.

Welton, M. R. (2003). "Listening, Conflict and Citizenship: Towards a Pedagogy of Civil Society". *International Journal of Lifelong Education*, 21(3).

Werner, D and Bill Bower. (1982). *Helping Health Workers Learn: A Book of Methods, Aids, and Ideas for Instructors at the Village Level*. Palo Alto: The Hesperian Foundation.

West, C. (1991). *The Ethical Dimensions of Marxist Thought*. New York: Monthly Review Press.

Westoby, P. and Owen, J. (2010). "The sociality and geometry of community development practice". *Community Development Journal*. Vol. 54. No. 1. Oxford: Oxford University Press.

Wilkinson, R. and Pickett, K. (2009). *The Spirit Level: Why More Equal Societies Almost Always Do Better*. London: Allen Lane.

Williams, R. (1960). *Border Country*. London: Chatto and Windus.

Williams, R. (1961). *The Long Revolution*. London: Chatto and Windus.

Williams, R. (1966). *Communications*, rev. ed. New York: Barnes and Noble.

Williams, R. (1975). "You're a Marxist, Aren't You?" In B. Parekh (Ed), *The Concept of Socialism*. London: Croom Helm.

Williams, R. (1977). *Marxism and Literature*. Oxford: Oxford University Press.

Williams, R. (1983). *Towards 2000*. London: Chatto and Windus.

Willis, P. (2002). *Inviting Learning: an exhibition of risk and enrichment in adult education practice*. Leicester: National Institute of Adult

Continuing Education.

Wilson, C. (1984). "Neighborhood-Based Groups: A Key Ingredient in Reviving Distressed Areas". *The Entrepreneurial Economy*. American Enterprise Institute.

Yeats, W.B. (2004). *The Celtic Twilight*. Kessinger Publishing.

Yeaxlee, B. A. (1929). *Lifelong Education: a sketch of the range and significance of the adult education movement*. London: Chatto and Windus.

Young, I. M. (1997). "Asymmetrical reciprocity: on moral respect, wonder and enlarged thought". *Intersecting Voices: Dilemmas of gender, political philosophy and policy*. Princeton, NJ: Princeton University Press.

# Index

intuition, *28, 233, 234, 237*
intuitive thinking, *30, 32, 33, 327*
I-You mode, *49*

Jacobs J, *173, 174, 175, 176*
Jeffersonian ideal, *328*

Kanter R, *21, 26, 122*
Kiva exercise, *245, 246*
Klein Naomi, *13, 170*
knowledge as social product, *291*
Krugman H, *108*

leadership characteristics, *156*
Ledwith M, *289*
lifeworld, *106, 107, 178*
Lindeman E, *9, 133*
listening, *134, 229, 237, 243, 244, 245, 246, 255*
Listening skills, *209*
learning from experience, *197*
local development strategy, *313*
local power structures, *11, 255, 258, 273*
Lost On the Moon exercise, *221*
Lukes Stephen, *258, 259, 260*

MacDonald J, *109*
Mantel H, *287*
Marcuse H, *82, 116, 117, 118,*

*119, 120, 124, 125, 127*
Massey M, *276, 277, 278, 279, 280, 283*
Material Contributed for Discussion, *78*
Mayer B, *251, 253*
McMaster learning process, *54*
mega-stories, *90, 92*
Mezirow J, *82*
midwife method, *289*
Mills C W, *23, 135, 136, 284, 285, 286, 330*
magical thinking, *126*
managing conflict, *229*
Mondragon Co-operative, *294*
music, *233, 237, 238, 239, 240, 241, 269*
my pedagogy, *62*

*Naive consciousness, 126*
needs assessment survey, *201*
negative liberty, *119*
neo-liberal policies, *13*
networking, *317, 318*
*networks, 35, 93, 98, 177, 255, 280, 298, 312*
Newman M, *3, 45, 147, 193, 236, 251, 253*
Noddings Nel, *37, 237*
Nonaka, *234, 235, 248*

Obama Barack, *115, 307*
Oldenburg Ray, *94*
one dimensional

375

# BOOKS

O is a symbol of the world, of oneness and unity. In different cultures it also means the "eye," symbolizing knowledge and insight. We aim to publish books that are accessible, constructive and that challenge accepted opinion, both that of academia and the "moral majority."

Our books are available in all good English language bookstores worldwide. If you don't see the book on the shelves ask the bookstore to order it for you, quoting the ISBN number and title. Alternatively you can order online (all major online retail sites carry our titles) or contact the distributor in the relevant country, listed on the copyright page.

See our website **www.o-books.net** for a full list of over 500 titles, growing by 100 a year.

And tune in to myspiritradio.com for our book review radio show, hosted by June-Elleni Laine, where you can listen to the authors discussing their books.

MySpiritRadio